Why Resurrection?

Why Resurrection?

An Introduction to the Belief in the Afterlife in Judaism and Christianity

CARLOS BLANCO

☙PICKWICK *Publications* · Eugene, Oregon

WHY RESURRECTION?
An Introduction to the Belief in the Afterlife in Judaism and Christianity

Copyright © 2011 Carlos Blanco. All rights reserved. Except for brief quotations in critical publications or reviews, no part of this book may be reproduced in any manner without prior written permission from the publisher. Write: Permissions, Wipf and Stock Publishers, 199 W. 8th Ave., Suite 3, Eugene, OR 97401.

Scripture taken from the New King James Version®. Copyright © 1982 by Thomas Nelson, Inc. Used by permission. All rights reserved.

Pickwick Publications
An Imprint of Wipf and Stock Publishers
199 W. 8th Ave., Suite 3
Eugene, OR 97401

www.wipfandstock.com

ISBN 13: 978-1-60899-772-5

Cataloging-in-Publication data:

Blanco, Carlos.

    Why resurrection? : an introduction to the belief in the afterlife in Judaism and Christianity / Carlos Blanco.

    xii + 230 p. ; 23 cm. Including bibliographical references and index.

    ISBN 13: 978-1-60899-772-5

    1. Resurrection (Jewish Theology). 2. Resurrection—History of Doctrines—Early Church, ca. 30–600. I. Title.

BT872 .B66 2011

Manufactured in the U.S.A.

Contents

Acknowledgments • *vii*

List of Abbreviations • *viii*

Introduction • *ix*

1 Theodicy: Philosophy of Religion and the Problem of Evil • 1

2 History and Meaning • 45

3 The Apocalyptic Conception of History, Evil, and Eschatology • 76

4 Death • 137

5 The Kingdom of God • 182

Bibliography • 217

Index of Names • 227

Acknowledgments

This book would not have been possible without the help of many people from whose teaching and direct advice I have greatly profited.

I am particularly grateful to Michael Velchik, a Harvard University student and an extraordinary friend, for his assistance in editing the text.

Also, I want to express my gratitude to Gonzalo Aranda (Universidad de Navarra), Santiago Ausín (Universidad de Navarra), and Manuel Fraijó (Universidad Nacional de Educacción a Distancia), from whose scholarship in the fields of biblical studies and philosophy of religion as well as from whose valuable insights I have been able to learn many things, and Luis Girón-Negrón (Harvard University), who has been a true mentor and, moreover, a great friend to me, and whose wisdom in so many areas of knowledge has been a source of inspiration.

Abbreviations

HEBREW BIBLE/ OLD TESTAMENT

Gen	Judg	Neh	Song	Hos	Nah
Exod	Ruth	Esth	Isa	Joel	Hab
Lev	1–2 Sam	Job	Jer	Amos	Zeph
Num	1–2 Kgs	Ps	Lam	Obad	Hag
Deut	1–2 Chr	Prov	Ezek	Jonah	Zech
Josh	Ezra	Eccl(Qoh)	Dan	Mic	Mal

NEW TESTAMENT

Matt	Acts	Eph	1–2 Tim	Heb	John
Mark	Rom	Phil	Titus	Jas	Jude
Luke	1– Cor	Col	Phlm	1–2 Pet	Rev
John	Gal	1–2 Thess			

APOCRYPHAL/DEUTEROCANONICAL BOOKS

Tob	Wis	1–3 Esd	Sg Three	Add Esth	Bel
Jdt	Sir	Ep Jer	Sus	Pr Man	Bar
Lev	1–2 Sam	Job	Jer	Amos	Zeph

Introduction

THE BELIEF IN THE afterlife in Judaism and Christianity emerges as a response to a real challenge: the problem of evil. As the Swedish theologian Krister Stendahl wrote, "in its original setting the resurrection is an answer to the question of Judaism in the time of Jesus: the question of theodicy. Will justice win and the promises of God to the faithful be fulfilled?"[1]

The fundamental question is that of theodicy: What is the meaning of life and history in the midst of a world in which evil, injustice, and ultimately death persist and seem to achieve a constant triumph over the wish for life and endurance?

First, we shall examine the classical problem of theodicy, showing the gravity of the problem for a theistic perspective, and then we will extend its scope to consider the meaning of history as a whole (if there is one) and how we should interpret the dynamics of human history on the basis of some of the principal philosophical proposals of contemporary Western philosophy. Since the focus of this introduction is the Judeo-Christian tradition, we will not deal with these aspects in the context of Eastern religions and philosophies, which undoubtedly offer important illumination on the issues we are treating.

The next step will be the analysis of apocalypticism. Apocalypticism is, as Ernst Käsemann wrote, the "mother of Christian theology."[2] Jesus' life and message cannot be understood without the influence of apocalyptic intertestamental literature. In particular, its emphasis on eschatology, universal history, and afterlife generated an almost everlasting impact on the Western culture, which can be felt even in contemporary philosophical proposals.[3] It is therefore worthwhile to study the nature of the apocalyptic movement and of its principal theological contributions.

---

1. Stendahl, *Immortality and Resurrection*, 7.
2. "The Beginnings of Christian Theology," 17–46.
3. Jacob Taubes studied the so-called occidental eschatology in his classic work

After examining apocalypticism, we shall delve into the problem of death, the "radical non-utopia," to use Ernst Bloch's terms, and how it is interpreted in atheism, pantheism, and theism. The specific Judeo-Christian response to the challenge of death is the belief in the resurrection of the dead. But, when did this belief emerge? Why did it take so long for the Israelites to believe in it? We will then study the principal hypotheses on the origin of the idea of resurrection in Judaism.

The belief in resurrection, however, cannot be conceptualized as an isolated concept that suddenly appeared. Resurrection is not a goal in itself. The question refers to the aim of resurrection, and the answer involves taking into consideration the Kingdom of God. The Kingdom of God is the central part of Jesus' teachings. Resurrection is an instrument serving a broader, more encompassing reality: the Kingdom of God. Such a utopian Kingdom gathers the final response to the problem of theodicy and to the question of the meaning of history. The idea of the kingship of God was present in the Hebrew Bible, but the idea of a Kingdom of God which is over the kingdoms of this world takes us back to apocalypticism and to early Christianity. We shall analyze this concept in light of the Gospel of Matthew (in which it plays a very relevant role) and contemporary theologies, like the principal European tendencies and liberation theology in Latin America.

There is a thread from the problem of evil to the Kingdom of God. The Kingdom of God summarizes the Judeo-Christian interpretation of the individual and the collective human life. But in spite of its fundamental importance in Jesus' message, Jesus himself did not define the Kingdom of God in itself. He showed some of its features but not its ultimate nature.

Few questions exert such a great fascination on human conscience as those related with the meaning of life, history, and death. The interest in religions, which seem capable of providing a constant "utopia" for human beings, is ever increasing. It is true that secularization has diminished the relevance of religions in daily life in Western societies, but it is also true that all people, believers or not, feel always compelled by the questions that religions themselves pose and that religions themselves try to answer. Let us therefore assume the weight of those questions: as Heidegger wrote in *Die Frage nach der Technik*, "questioning is the piety of thought."[4]

Abendländische Eschatologie of 1947. For a detailed analysis of Taubes' views, cf. Faber et al., *Abendländische Eschatologie: ad Jacob Taubes*.

4. Cf. Heidegger, *Gesamtausgabe*, vol. 7.

There is some kind of mysticism in reality that invites everyone never to cease wondering about the world that surrounds us. The great Italian philosopher Antonio Gramsci taught that every person is a philosopher, because philosophy deals with the fundamental anxieties which concern us all. The principal problems of philosophy are not abstractions for select, elite academics: they affect us as human beings, and they influence how we conceive of ourselves and of history. Philosophy, in this sense, is an extremely political activity, which offers an interpretation of the world which necessarily determines how we manage social life.

As Jürgen Habermas has remarked, knowledge is always linked to a certain interest,[5] and the ultimate interest of knowledge must be the achievement of the highest possible state of both individual and collective freedom. Philosophy, as a both theoretical and practical activity, helps human reason to become more aware of its own dignity and of its responsibility in the edification of a more inclusive world.

---

5. Cf. Habermas, *Erkenntnis und Interesse*.

1

Theodicy

Philosophy of Religion and the Problem of Evil

THE PRESENCE OF EVIL IN THE WORLD

EVIL IS EVERYWHERE. WE can experience it in different ways, but it is certain that such a reality surrounds us. We see people suffering, and when we watch the news, we hear about wars, conflicts of various kinds, unending wills of power, constant violations of human rights, oppression, poverty, lack of freedom and equality, etc. Even in the developed countries, we perceive the huge social differences that build barriers between human beings, and within the most privileged groups of these affluent societies, evil is still present, taking the shape of illnesses that affect both the rich and the poor, learned and unlearned, and of deprivations of many other types. And, in ultimate terms, death puts an end to our projects and illusions.

Of course, it could be argued that evil is the result of a subjective perception. There is no evil in nature, but the fulfilment of immutable laws that may affect us in a favorable or in an unfavorable way for our interests. Within the human world, however, suffering is regarded as evil, and the existence of suffering that disables many people to live freely and happily is a fact. I cannot think that the 2010 catastrophe in Haiti—in which tens of thousands of people died and more than three million people were injured—is subjective. There is evil there. There is evil in the fact that nature, which we sometimes praise and exalt as the source of life and of beauty (*"On m'appelle nature, et je suis tout art,"* —"they call me nature, but I am all art"—as Voltaire wrote[1]), is also the source

---

1. "La Nature. — Mon pauvre enfant, veux-tu que je te dise la vérité? C'est qu'on m'a donné un nom qui ne me convient pas; on m'appelle nature, et je suis tout art." Voltaire,

of terrible ways of destruction that generally affect the poorest of the poor. Nature means the triumph of the fittest, of the strongest over the weakest. Nature means the consecration of the defeat of victims. This is the reason why I am quite sceptical about the idea of a natural law that might be applied in the human world. We know that we belong to nature, but we also know that our aspirations transcend nature.

Nature is not the only source of evil, and we can keep hope in the power of science and knowledge to gradually overcome its arbitrariness. The principal source of evil in our lives is humanity itself, because both nature and humanity are ambiguous realities, and we seem to be condemned to live with that contradiction.

According to the World Bank Development Indicators of 2008, at least 80 percent of humanity lives on less than ten dollars a day; the poorest 40 percent of the population accounts for 5 percent of the world's income, whereas the richest 20 percent accounts for 75 percent of the global income. The richest 20 percent of the population accounts for 76.6 percent of total private consumption. Some people live well because others live badly. There is a mechanism of dependency between nations and social groups, which has been brilliantly analyzed by Immanuel Wallerstein in his world-system theory.[2]

The world's 497 wealthiest people of 2005 accounted for over 7 percent of world GDP. In 2004, 0.13 percent of the population controlled 25 percent of the world's financial assets. According to UNICEF, twenty-five thousand children die everyday of severe hunger. In this precise moment, in this specific second, an average of seven children will be dying on account of poverty. In the developing world, about seventy-two million children who should be enrolled in primary schools do not take part in the education system. However, education is regarded as a universal right in the Declaration of the Rights of the Children, article 7, approved by the UN General Assembly in 1959. Nearly one billion people remain illiterate, incapable of enjoying the pleasure, which is also a human necessity (let us recall Aristotle in the beginning of his *Metaphysics*: "all men naturally want to know"), of learning some of the most valuable treasures that human wisdom has accumulated throughout the centu-

---

Questions sur l'Encyclopédie ("Dialogue entre le philosophe et la nature").

2. Cf. Wallerstein, *The Modern World-System*.

ries. This lack of proper education constitutes a severe obstacle to the exercise of our freedoms and capacities, as Amartya Sen has shown.[3]

In addition to these facts, it is even more discouraging to realize that less than 1 percent of the money spent in weapons every year all over the world might have sufficed to put every child into school in 2000. Regarding health, the panorama is devastating: about forty million people are infected with HIV, with three million deaths in 2004. Malaria affects between three hundred and fifty and five hundred million people a year, and 90 percent of the deaths due to it occur in the poorest continent, Africa. Some 1.1 billion people in the world have improper access to the most elementary condition of life, water, and some 1.8 million children die each year as a result of diarrhoea.[4] Rigid inequalities afflict women as well as racial, sexual, and religious minorities. Of course, this is not only a scandal, the result of a system, which is incapable of satisfying everyone's basic needs, and a clear injustice that should be avoided: it is also a loss of human resources. Let us think of how many of these children could help their countries become developed; let us think of how much human potential is wasted. But, beyond these pragmatic criteria, let us think of how much inhumanity is involved here.

In the world, there are approximately 2.1 billion Christians, 1.5 billion Muslims, and 14 million Jews, to mention only these three monotheistic religions.[5] This means that about 3.6 billion people believe, in one or another way, in a personal God who has created the world and who will grant eternal life. The question is legitimate: If such a God exists, why does He/She allow all of these horrible things to happen? Where is God in a world in which thousands of children die of hunger every day? Some people might pose the question in a different manner: Where is mankind to allow this? But we want to analyze the problem of evil in the world, the so-called *theodicy* (a term that means "the justice of God," coined by Leibniz in his *Essais de Théodicée sur la Bonté de Dieu, la Liberté de l'Homme et l'Origine du Mal*, published in 1710 as a response to Pierre Bayle's scepticism on the goodness of God and creation in his *Dictionnaire Historique et Critique*), from the perspective of monotheistic religions, and especially of Judaism and Christianity.

---

3. Cf. Sen, *Development as Freedom*.
4. For the data, cf. http://www.globalissues.org/article/26/poverty-facts-and-stats/.
5. Cf. http://www.adherents.com/Religions_By_Adherents.html.

Let us delve into the challenges that the problem of evil offers to theology and philosophy of religion. Theologians and philosophers of religion must feel still committed to dare to cope with evil. It is impossible to speak of God in the traditional terms, as an omnipotent and benevolent creator who wants the best for humanity, without first examining the reasons behind so much suffering and so much injustice, just as it is impossible to speak about God in the traditional terms after the critique of Feuerbach, Marx, Nietzsche, and Freud to the anthropomorphic image of God.

Evil has been a true rock for atheism. Atheism stems from three fundamental roots: scientific progress (which makes it unnecessary to believe in the supernatural), liberty (the existence of God challenges our freedom), and evil.

The French Jesuit theologian Henri de Lubac wrote a book titled *Le Drame de l'Humanisme Athée* (1944), in which he studied the atheistic philosophy of Feuerbach, Marx, Comte, and Nietzsche, and the Christian approach to life found in authors like Dostoyevski. One of the principal reasons for the so-called humanistic atheism is the search for freedom: a God who watches over men and women would put our freedom into danger. If God exists, we are not free. A little girl in Nietzsche's preface to *The Gay Science* asks her mother if it is true that God is everywhere. The mother answers yes, to which the little girl replies, "I think that's indecent!" Sartre insisted on this point: our freedom and dignity as human beings demand our full responsibility in our actions and our full capacity to build up a history without the interference of a deity. Dostoyevski said that without God, everything is permitted, but Albert Camus changed the sense of the sentence: without God, nothing is permitted, since the full responsibility belongs to us.

In any case, I believe that there is a deeper reason for atheism: the problem of evil. Even in a deistic conception that conceives of God as some sort of primeval watchmaker, as the universal architect of Voltaire, as the author of the pre-established harmony of Leibniz who has set everything in function, but who is alien to the problems of the world, so that the universe is a truly self-sufficient reality, it is sill possible to account for the coexistence of God and human freedom. But this God would be meaningless for many people. Many people believe in God because they need to believe in some entity that cares about them and that is immediately significant for their concrete existence. No one prays to a concept. Almost no one prays to the *Ipsum Esse Subsistens* [Subsistent Being Itself] of Scholasticism. Religion introduces a historical mediation in the access to the universal, omnipotent, eternal being, so that such a being may become significant to people. And the problem of evil directly challenges the pretension of a significant, meaningful God. For if he were significant to us and he really cared about our problems and our sufferings, how is it that He allows that there be so much suffering?

In a debate between Peter Singer and Dinesh D'Souza on the topic of the existence of God and its meaning for human beings,[6] Singer made the point that if an omnipotent, omniscient God really existed, He should know how much suffering there is in the world. He could have created a world that, if not totally good (to leave a margin of action to dialectics), at least might be less bad. Apologists have traditionally explained that God has granted us free will, but as Singer notices, this does not justify the fact that there is much suffering which does not come out of free will. Let us think of natural catastrophes, of the so-called physical evil by Leibniz (in opposition to the metaphysical and the moral evils). And Singer draws attention to an even more appealing consideration: animals suffer with no apparent guilt.

And regarding individual responsibility, how should we find it in a child who is born with Down syndrome? This takes us to a very important aspect in which we cannot delve into its proper terms, but which is extremely compelling for both theologians and philosophers: we have not chosen to exist. Existence has been given to us. It seems that we have been thrown into this world: according to Heidegger, we are a *Dasein*, a "being-there," thrown into the world. This element plays a central role in many of Samuel Beckett's plays: no one has asked us for permission to exist. No one asked you or me if we wanted to exist. The fact is that we are here, and that this *factum* certainly generates a responsibility for being, a responsibility that is shared by the whole of humanity, both the past generations and the future generations (to whom we shall not ask for permission on whether or not they want to come into existence). But apart from this *factum*, there is no *ius*, no "right" that may account for our existence: the fact is that we exist, but the fact is also that we do not know why we exist and that we do not have any responsibility in our having come into existence.

6. Cf. Singer, "The God of Suffering?"

DIFFERENT INTERPRETATIONS OF EVIL

One can identify four major solutions to the problem of theodicy.[7] Here, I am not referring to the explanations of how to reconcile divine goodness and divine omniscience with evil and human freedom (as in the traditional theses of Calvinism and Molinism), but to the justification of the fact of evil itself from a theistic point of view.

Relativization of Evil

Evil is not, after all, so important in comparison to the advantages of life. There is evil, there is negativity, but it does not constitute a true antithesis to the goodness of creation. Evil is *prope nihil* ("almost nothing"). Evil means nothing for the goodness of creation. The suffering of the world adds almost nothing to the beauty and wisdom of creation. As it is written in Wis 11:20: "You have disposed all things by measure and number and weight." Knowledge, love, beauty, pleasure, welfare . . . they mean more than evil and suffering.

This perspective also appears in traditional Christian theology: both St. Augustine and St. Thomas Aquinas define evil as *privatio boni debiti*, the "deprivation of the good which is owed." As the Bishop of Hippo explains:

> And in the universe, even that which is called evil, when it is regulated and put in its own place, only enhances our admiration of the good; for we enjoy and value the good more when we compare it with the evil. For the Almighty God, who, as even the heathen acknowledge, has supreme power over all things, being Himself supremely good, would never permit the existence of anything evil among His works, if He were not so omnipotent and good that He can bring good even out of evil. For what is that which we call evil but the absence of good? In the bodies of animals, disease, and wounds mean nothing but the absence of health; for when a cure is effected, that does not mean that the evils which were present—namely, the diseases and wounds—go away from the body and dwell elsewhere: they altogether cease to exist; for the wound or disease is not a substance, but a defect in the fleshly substance,—the flesh itself being a substance, and

---

7. I am very grateful to Prof. Manuel Fraijó for his suggestions. For a more detailed account of the different answers to the problem of theodicy, see Fraijó, *Dios, el Mal y Otros Ensayos*.

therefore something good, of which those evils—that is, privations of the good which we call health—are accidents. Just in the same way, what are called vices in the soul, are nothing but privations of natural good. And when they are cured, they are not transferred elsewhere: when they cease to exist in the healthy soul, they cannot exist anywhere else.[8]

In *Summa Theologica*, when addressing the question about the existence of God, Aquinas answers the following objection: "It seems that God does not exist; because if one of two contraries be infinite, the other would be altogether destroyed. But the word "God" means that He is infinite goodness. If, therefore, God existed, there would be no evil discoverable; but there is evil in the world. Therefore God does not exist."

His response goes as follows: "As Augustine says (*Enchiridion* xi): "Since God is the highest good, He would not allow any evil to exist in His works, unless His omnipotence and goodness were such as to bring good even out of evil." This is part of the infinite goodness of God, that He should allow evil to exist, and out of it produce good."[9]

The position of both St. Augustine and St. Thomas Aquinas may be well named "de-ontologization of evil." Evil turns to be in function of goodness. It is the denial of the substantiality of evil. Evil is not a substance, but an accident, something that, in Aristotelian categories, exists *in alio*, but not *in se*. It does not constitute an ontological reality, and hence, it cannot be put on the same level as goodness, which is indeed a reality in its full sense.

In a parallel relativization of the gravity of evil, for Hegel history itself is theodicy, because the fulfilment of the goals of the spirit, which are its self-realization as absolute spirit, demands suffering: "nothing in history was done without passion", as he writes in *Lectures on the Philosophy of History*. The achievement of the highest form of the spirit as absolute spirit needs the existence of a dialectical antagonism within history, within the temporal determination that the spirit assumes in order to gain a richer knowledge of itself. There is no reason to complain about the presence of evil because evil has to exist so that what is necessary may emerge, so that the spirit may recognize itself as absolute spirit.

---

8. Oates, *Basic Writings of St. Augustine* 1:662: "Malum est omnis et sola privatio boni debiti."

9. St. Thomas Aquinas, *Summa Theologica* part I, question 2, article 3.

Dualism

For many religious and philosophical traditions, reality is composed of two co-principles: good and evil. There is a constant fight between Good and Evil that either will be decided at the end of time or will endure for ever. Zoroastrianism, Manicheism (to which St. Augustine belonged in his youth), Gnosticism (with its differentiation of the bad God—the God of the Old Testament—and the good God, the God that teaches men and women how to achieve their salvation by their self-knowledge) are examples of a dualistic worldview. There is evil because, in the same way as there is a God, to whom all the goodness can be attributed, there is an evil principle with an equal degree of majesty and power, which is responsible for it.

This conception remains, although in a different sense, in the late Jewish and Christian idea of the devil as a personal being. However, Judeo-Christianity and Islam have repeatedly reminded us that the devil is not of divine nature, and that his power is severely limited. Also, the importance of the devil, at least in the context of Christian theology, has radically decreased in the last decades, especially after the historical-critical examination of biblical texts, the project of demythologization of Rudolf Bultmann (who considers the belief in demons to belong to ages past, when the scientific method for the inquiry of reality had not been born), and books like *Abschied vom Teufel*, by Herbert Haag, in which he analyzes the dramatic psychological consequences that the constant reiteration of the danger of the devil has caused to many people. The persistence and strength of evil, however, make many men and women believe that there must be some sort of demi-god, invested with sufficient power to challenge the will of God of goodness.

In dualism, there is a struggle between Good and Evil, between God and his radical antithesis (like Ohrmazd and Ahreman in Zoroastrianism), whose outcome has not been decided yet. In the scenario of this struggle, sometimes the good principle triumphs, and sometimes it is the evil principle that wins.

But there is, of course, a fundamental problem: we have two gods instead of one. Is it possible for two hypothetically absolute beings to coexist?

Substitution of Theodicy with Anthropodicy

Theodicy tries to justify God, but for many thinkers it is mankind, instead of God, that needs to be justified. This is so in Karl Barth's theology and in his *Offenbarungspositivismus* ["positivism of revelation"]. God needs no justification, for He is perfect. He is the absolute reality, the totally-Other [*Das ganz-Andere*] to the world. It is the world that needs to be justified. This brings to my mind Nietzsche's famous remark in *Thus Spoke Zarathustra* about how the person who has climbed the highest mountains laughs at the tragedies of life and drama. Depending on the position in which we stand, we look at reality in different ways. And if we make theology from God, from above, all the contradictions and contingencies of the world seem almost insignificant.

According to this perspective, mankind is to blame for evil. This is the case in the Augustinian doctrine of original sin, which, up to a point, results from a misreading of Rom 5:12 ("Therefore, just as through one man sin entered the world, and death through sin, and thus death spread to all men, because all sinned"). The Greek text goes: ἐφ' ᾧ πάντες ἥμαρτον, but is nonetheless read as *in quo, id est, in Adam, omnes peccaverunt* by St. Augustine: "in whom [referring to Adam] all sinned."[10] This reading is also in St. Jerome's *Vulgate*.

St. Augustine's doctrine of original sin (which may be drawn back to St. Irenaeus of Lyon in the second century CE) was accepted by the Second Council of Orange in 529 against the disciples of Pelagius, who denied original sin. For St. Augustine, original sin is transmitted from one generation to another, and is reflected in the presence of *concupiscentia* in the human spirit, that affects our intelligence and our will. Human creatures are therefore corrupted, and baptism is necessary so that divine grace may clean the original stain [*macula originalis*]. In a more radical way, Luther and Calvin taught that even after baptism the stain is so severe that it remains: human nature is radically corrupted. The Council of Trent, in its fifth decree, condemned the Lutheran absolute identification of original sin and concupiscence but maintained Augustine's doctrine of original sin transmitted through sexual intercourse. Even in the Enlightenment, Immanuel Kant's idea of radical evil, as expressed in his famous book *Die Religion innerhalb der Grenzen der blossen Vernunft*

---

10 .Augustine, *Contra Duas Epistolas Pelagianorum*, book 4 chapter 7, in Migne, *Patrologiae Cursus Completus*. 549ff.

[*Religion within the Boundaries of Mere Reason*], of 1793, seems to keep some relation with original sin.

Mankind is responsible for evil. No one has the right to blame God for evil, because it is a result of our free will, a consequence of our capacity to act. It is interesting to consider that such a perspective, which theoretically seeks to justify God, is actually taking God away from the discussion. In this point of view, God is, after all, meaningless: evil is human responsibility, so why do we have to speak about God? He is not a significant actor. His role is merely passive. As Feuerbach put it, God is eternally exonerated. God is always free from any responsibility. He has no guilt in what happens to us. The difference between this and an atheistic conception is not so big, after all. Why do I need to believe in a God that is absent from my worries, from my suffering, just because I am, as a human being, to blame for evil? What is the sense in keeping a hieratic God, eternally sitting in his divine throne as a *Pantokrator*, who is free from all possible accusation?

On the first of November of 1755 something terrible happened. A huge earthquake destroyed the beautiful city of Lisbon, with its romantic, melancholic buildings looking at the Atlantic Ocean, met by the Tagus, the longest river in the Iberian Peninsula, creating one of the most extraordinary views in Europe. It was the Feast of All Saints, and most people were attending Mass in the churches of Lisbon. The earthquake took place at about 9:40 a.m., and it is estimated that it reached 9 on the Richter scale. It was one of the most destructive natural phenomena of modern history. Some people think that about thirty thousand to forty thousand people died, in addition to ten thousand others in Spain and Morocco. Shocks from the earthquake were felt as far away as Finland.

José de Carvalho e Melo, the marquis of Pombal, the great figure of the Portuguese Enlightenment, decided to look forward: "Bury the dead and feed the living," even though, as the great Portuguese writer and Nobel laureate José Saramago recalls, these words were actually pronounced by an army official, deprived of his own creativity in favor of someone who was more powerful, as often happens in history.[11]

11. "Conta-se que à pergunta inevitável "E agora, que fazer?" o secretário de Estrangeiros Sebastião José de Carvalho e Melo, que mais tarde viria a ser nomeado primeiro-ministro, teria respondido "Enterrar os mortos e cuidar dos vivos." Estas palavras, que logo entraram na História, foram efectivamente pronunciadas, mas não por ele. Disse-as um oficial superior do exército, desta maneira espoliado do seu haver, como tantas vezes acontece, em favor de alguém mais poderoso" ("Quantos Haitis?" in

Pombal launched a plan for reconstructing Lisbon, and he undertook policies of modernization in the huge maritime empire. He also managed to limit the influence of the Jesuits, eventually expelling them from the Portuguese territories in 1759 (a measure that would be followed by France in 1762 and by Spain in 1767). He even named his brother Inquisitor General of Portugal, with the intention of condemning the renowned Jesuit preacher Gabriel Malagrida to death (as a priest, he could not be executed by a civil tribunal), as a sign of the fighting between "lights" and "obscurantism" (Malagrida had attributed the earthquake to the revenge of God). Malagrida was, in fact, the last victim of the Portuguese Inquisition.

The Lisbon earthquake inspired many great thinkers of the Enlightenment, like Voltaire, Rousseau, and Kant, to meditate about the problem of evil in the world. Voltaire's novel *Candide, ou L'Optimisme*, his famous satire of 1759, uses the catastrophe to ridicule Leibniz's theory that one world is "the best of all possible worlds." The metaphysical wisdom of Doctor Pangloss is useless at explaining the magnitude of evil. Voltaire challenges the Christian idea of God: such a God would have never allowed this to happen. People were in Mass in the Catholic city of Lisbon, but God did not care. He did nothing to avoid it, as He did nothing to avoid the tsunami of 2004 and hurricane Katrina in 2005. For Voltaire, to think that this had happened "for the greater good," following an unredeemable optimism, made no sense and was simply absurd. Alexander Pope, on the contrary, had written:

> Remember man, the universal cause,
> acts not by partial, but by general laws.
> And makes what happiness we justly call,
> Subsist not in the good of one, but all.[12]

According to Pope, "One truth is clear: whatever is, is right." The same person who had written of Newton, "Nature and its laws lay hid in night; God said 'Let Newton be' and all was light," admiring the progress in natural sciences, shared an equally invincible optimism regarding human life.

Outros Cadernos de Saramago: http://caderno.josesaramago.org/2010/02/08/quantos-haitis/).

12. Pope, *An Essay on Man*, epistle 4.

For Voltaire, however, things did not look so easy. The suffering in Lisbon was simply meaningless, escaping from all power of understanding. The catastrophe could not be attributed to human sinfulness and to the wrath of God. As Voltaire writes in 1755 in his *Poème sur le Désastre de Lisbonne*, a preparation for *Candide*:

> And can you then impute a sinful deed
> To babes who on their mothers' bosoms bleed?
> Was then more vice in fallen Lisbon found,
> Than Paris, where voluptuous joys abound?
> Was less debauchery to London known,
> Where opulence luxurious holds the throne?[13]

Voltaire was endorsing Pierre Bayle's scepticism, and he was directly attacking the idea of Providence, which had been central to many interpretations of history, for instance those of St. Augustine and Jacques-Bénigne Bossuet.[14]

Voltaire sent a copy of his poem to Rousseau, who replied in a letter on August 18th 1756.[15] For Rousseau, God is not to blame: humanity is to blame. Who asked people to build tall buildings that could easily fall under the effects of the earthquake? Who asked people to gather themselves in huge cities instead of remaining in the pleasant dispersion of the rural areas? Voltaire's text gives no consolation to a man, like Rousseau who, expressing the sentiment of so many others, is in a deep need of consolation:

> All my complaints are . . . against your poem on the Lisbon disaster, because I expected from it evidence more worthy of the humanity which apparently inspired you to write it. You reproach Alexander Pope and Leibnitz with belittling our misfortunes by affirming that all is well, but you so burden the list of our miseries

---

13. The translation is taken from Clive, *The Riches of Rhyme: Studies in French Verse*, 208.

14. St. Thomas Aquinas defined Providence as "Ratio ordinis rerum in finem in mente divina preexistens" (*Summa Theologica* prima pars, q. 22, art. 1). According to Aquinas, Providence establishes a link between causes and natural ends. The Dominican philosopher rationalizes Providence, which is not regarded as a manifestation of unpredictable grace but as the existing coordination between the world and its metaphysical end.

15. The letter can be found in Rousseau, *Oeuvres Complètes*, 4:1060. The English translation is taken from the following website: http://geophysics-old.tau.ac.il/personal/shmulik/LisbonEq-letters.htm/.

that you further disparage our condition. Instead of the consolations that I expected, you only vex me. It might be said that you fear that I do not feel my unhappiness enough, and that you are trying to soothe me by proving that all is bad. Do not be mistaken, Monsieur, it happens that everything is contrary to what you propose. This optimism which you find so cruel consoles me still in the same woes that you force on me as unbearable. Pope's poem alleviates my difficulties and inclines me to patience; yours makes my afflictions worse, prompts me to grumble, and, leading me beyond a shattered hope, reduces me to despair ... I do not see how one can search for the source of moral evil anywhere but in man ... Moreover ... the majority of our physical misfortunes are also our work. Without leaving your Lisbon subject, concede, for example, that it was hardly nature that there brought together twenty thousand houses of six or seven stores. If the residents of this large city had been more evenly dispersed and less densely housed, the losses would have been fewer or perhaps none at all.[16] Everyone would have fled at the first shock. But many obstinately remained ... to expose themselves to additional earth tremors because what they would have had to leave behind was worth more than what they could carry away. How many unfortunates perished in this disaster through the desire to fetch their clothing, papers, or money? ... I have suffered too much in this life not to look forward to another. No metaphysical subtleties cause me to doubt a time of immortality for the soul and a beneficent providence. I sense it, I believe it, I wish it, I hope for it, I will uphold it until my last gasp ... I am, with respect, Monsieur, Jean-Jacques Rousseau.

The literary genius of Rousseau shines with unmatched brightness in the last line: "I sense it, I believe it, I wish it, I hope for it, I will uphold it until my last gasp ..." It is the power of sentiments, whose fighting is meaningless. Rationality cannot eclipse the presence of God in the realm of human sentiments. God is, as St. Augustine said, "*intimior intimo meo et superior summo meo*," ("more intimate than the most intimate of mine, and higher than the highest of mine"). God "exists" there, and even the most compelling arguments regarding the impossibility of believing in

---

16. Society, and not nature, is to blame: this is a fundamental idea in Rousseau's philosophy, found in his celebrated *Discours sur les Sciences et les Arts* (1750), in which he denounces the evils generated by the development of human civilization.

an omnipotent God who leaves humanity alone in her struggle against evil lose their capacity of persuasion.[17]

Rather than about evil, in its generic expression, Rousseau speaks about "evils": the different evils that we experience. God is not to blame, because there is no evil, in its radical connotation, but evils whose causes may be rationally explained. These evils are necessary for the general good. Rousseau needs to believe in God, as dramatic as these evils may seem. This necessity that makes Rousseau keep his faith in a provident God in spite of the evidence of mankind's loneliness in a hostile world, is very much connected with Feuerbach's critique of religion in *Das Wesen des Christentum* [*The Essence of Christianity*] of 1841: God is a necessity (in German, *Bedürfnis*) for mankind, a necessity which emerges out of suffering and lack of meaning. We need to project our anxieties, our deepest wills, onto a divine being that satisfies all our needs. God is a necessity, the result of our finitude and earthly misery. Marx will basically accept Feuerbach's critique of religion ("*Die Religion . . . ist das Opium des Volkes*" ["Religion is the opium of the people."]) in his *Zur Kritik der Hegelschen Rechtsphilosophie* ["Critique of Hegel's Philosophy of Right"] of 1843:

> The struggle against religion is, therefore, indirectly the struggle against that world whose spiritual aroma is religion. Religious suffering is, at one and the same time, the expression of real suffering and a protest against real suffering. Religion is the sigh of the oppressed creature, the heart of a heartless world, and the soul of soulless conditions. It is the opium of the people. The abolition of religion as the illusory happiness of the people is the demand for their real happiness. To call on them to give up their illusions about their condition is to call on them to give up a condition that requires illusions. The criticism of religion is, therefore, in embryo, the criticism of that vale of tears of which religion is the halo.[18]

In the context of critical theory and the Frankfurt School, Max Horkheimer characterized religion as an expression of protest. According to him, religion possesses a critical function, as a relativization of the

---

17. For a deeper analysis of the intellectual exchange between Voltaire and Rousseau about the Lisbon earthquake, cf. Marques, "The Paths of Providence: Voltaire and Rousseau on the Lisbon Earthquake."

18. Marx, "A Contribution to the Critique of Hegel's Philosophy of Right. Introduction," 251.

present and as a sign of a wish for a new, better, more humane world. Religion assumes the inextinguishable impulse against reality, claiming for it to change and for justice to overcome the curse of its absence.[19] Religion is the "longing for the Totally-Other" [*Sehnsucht nach dem ganz-Anderen*], linked to praxis of resistance and of solidarity in history.

In fact, many people, like Rousseau, still feel that they need to believe in God. The greatest natural disasters, the most astonishing and inexplicable presence of the biggest evils in the world, are not enough to shade the power of the faith in a provident, omnipotent God: why do we have those illusions, those so high aspirations, which even in a classless society would still remain?

Omnibenevolentia *versus* Omnipotentia

Hans Jonas was a German philosopher of Jewish origin, who was born in Mönchengladbach in 1903 and died in New York in 1993. He was a prominent scholar of Gnosticism, the ethics of a technological civilization, bioethics, and the philosophy of biology (heavily influenced by Heidegger). His mother was killed in a gas chamber in Auschwitz.

In 1987 he published *Der Gottesbegriff nach Auschwitz: eine jüdische Stimme* [translated into French as *Le Concept de Dieu après Auschwitz: une Voix Juive*], in which he suggests a radical distinction between a God who is almighty and a God who wishes the best for his creation. Both of them are incompatible. The almighty God would have done something to avoid the horror of Auschwitz after which, as Theodor Adorno said, it is impossible to write poetry. But God did not: "*aber Gott schwieg*" ["but God was silent"]. Jonas prefers to choose a God who wishes the best and who sees everything, but who is not omnipotent, than a God who is omnipotent and does not see everything that is happening to humanity.

Jonas demonstrates that we need a humane God, a God who may be meaningful for humanity, and humanity asks for a meaning. In a postmodernist way, such a quest for meaning might be regarded as illusory and misleading: both Foucault and Derrida show that a genealogical survey and a deconstruction of the knowledge and the reality we experience take to no final point: there is no final point, no ultimate sense, no hidden meaning that unveils the absolute truth of history.[20] But many

19. Horkheimer, *Anhelo de Justicia: Teoría Crítica y Religión*, 226.

20. An example of this can be found in Michel Foucault's preface to *Les Mots et les Choses*: "Une étude qui s'efforce de retrouver à partir de quoi connaissances et théories

religions and philosophical traditions continue to pursue the quest for an ultimate meaning, to which the idea of God is so closely associated.

Jonas prefers a God who wishes the best and who sees everything that is happening on earth to the traditional almighty God who, in spite of his power, did not act in Auschwitz. The contradiction between omnipotence and omnibenevolence had been already stated by Epicurus. According to Lactantius, a fourth-century writer and philosopher, Epicurus offered a famous argument regarding the impossibility of reconciling the infinite goodness of God with his infinite power, for there are four options which show the incompatibility of certain divine attributes:

1. God is able and is willing to eradicate evil, but then, why doesn't he do it?
2. God is able but unwilling, therefore he is bad.
3. God is unable but willing, therefore he is not omnipotent.
4. God is unable and unwilling, therefore he is not omnipotent and he is bad.

For Jonas God was willing, but unable. God was not absent in Auschwitz: He was seeing everything, but He could not do anything to avoid it. The relevance of eschatology resides in its accounting for a final end of times in which God will reveal himself in his full power, and the victims of history will be finally vindicated. However, the danger of a Hegelian conception in which present suffering is the necessary path to

---

ont été possibles; selon quel espace d'ordre s'est constitué le savoir; sur fond de quel a priori historique et dans l'élement de quelle positivité des idées ont pu apparaître, des sciences se constituer, des expériences se réfléchir dans des philosophies, des rationalités se former, pour, peut-être, se dénouer et s'évanouir bientôt. Il ne sera donc pas question de connaissanes décrites dans leur progrès vers une objectivité dans laquelle notre science d'aujourd'hui pourrait enfin se reconnaître; ce qu'on voudrait mettre au jour, c'est le champ épistémologique, l'épistémé où les connaissances, envisagées hors de tout critère se référant à leur valeur rationnelle ou à leurs formes objectives, enfoncent leur positivité et manifestent ainsi une histoire qui n'est pas celle de leur perfection croissante, mais plutôt celle de leurs conditions de possibilité; en ce récit, ce qui doit apparaître, ce sont, dans l'espace du savoir, les configurations qui ont donné lieu aux formes diverses de la connaissance empirique. Plutôt que d'une histoire au sens traditionnel du mot, il s'agit d'une 'archéologie'" (Foucault, *Philosophie: Anthologie*, 230–31).

the accomplishment of the omnipotence of God is also latent in these considerations.[21]

For Jonas, God saw what happened in Auschwitz, but He did not do anything because He was unable to do so. In this point Jonas, who knew the Jewish Kabbalistic tradition very well (he was a good friend of Gershom Scholem), is adopting a very similar approach to the sixteenth-century Jewish thinker Isaac Luria's idea of *tzimtzum* ("contraction"): in order to create the world, God has been forced to give up some of his "space."

If, to express it in Spinoza's terms, there can be only one infinite, absolute substance, the creation of other beings necessarily involves that such an absolute substance must "renounce," so to speak, its infinity. God has to leave margin for the creatures to exist, otherwise everything would be "overwhelmed," eclipsed by the existence of God, and totality would encompass everything. According to Luria, when God decided to create the world, He "contracted" Himself in the very center of His light, so that there remained a hollow empty space in which the new beings might subsist.[22]

The reception of Luria's concept was important in the context of German philosophy, especially in the thought of Jacob Böhme (1575–1624) and in the idealistic system of Schelling (1775–1854). According to Schelling, the almighty God shows his omnipotence in the emergence of another, yet equally divine "god": an *alter deus*. By virtue of His omnipotence God can think of Himself as being the origin of another god. However, and as a consequence of this, God compromises His own fate. The risk assumed by God becomes real when the *alter deus* uses his freedom in a misguided and rebellious way, "falling" in history and making the primeval God fall with him.[23] Therefore, the destiny of God is related to the destiny of history and to the destiny of humanity, and His contraction gives birth to a construction (that of history and humanity).[24]

---

21. A similar approach (namely, that God is walking with us in history, fighting against evil together with us) appears in Levenson, *Creation and the Persistence of Evil*.

22. Cf. Vital, *Etz Chayyim*, Heichal A, K, anaf. 2. On Isaac Luria, see Fine, *Physician of the Soul, Healer of the Cosmos*; Scholem, *Die jüdische Mystik in ihren Hauptsströmungen*.

23. Schelling, *Werke*, 4:331.

24. Habermas, *Teoría y Praxis*, 175–85.

For both Luria and Schelling, the contraction of God does not consist of an occlusive turning into Himself, but of delivering His own destiny to someone else. Love is capable of overcoming divine selfishness, and God becomes a captive of love.

The only necessity that constrains God is His unlimited self-disposal. The only possible liberation from this necessity comes from the emergence of a being like Him. God demonstrates His absolute power over everything when He allows the emergence of another absolute entity, but there is a danger: that of rejection. The other god can freely decide to reject the primordial God. By doing so, an inversion of principles takes place, and a corrupted world arises with an inverted god: humanity.

The contraction of God gives rise to the "age of the world" [*Weltalter*]. God is not the author of evil but evil is the result of the wrong use of the absolute freedom which God granted to His *alter deus*, to His "counter-image." In opposition to dualism, in Schelling's philosophy evil is not an eternal co-principle but has a historical origin in the misuse of freedom, and because it has an origin it can also have an end.[25]

Humanity is the *alter deus*, which has rejected the love of God.[26] Humanity possesses a divine condition, manifested in its capacity to edify history, and it must finally respond to the offering of the love of God. However, can humanity save itself or was Heidegger right when he said "only a god can still save us"?[27]

An essential concern arises after learning about this interpretation of the problem of evil: it seems that God is no longer God. Has God actually died? Are we condemned to having no absolute being? Can God reject his own divinity? If God, in traditional metaphysics, is a necessity of the world (*Ens Necessarium*), how is it that there is no God any more?

---

25. As Habermas remarks, Schelling did not draw the materialistic consequences of his idea of an "age of the world." He preserved a conception in terms of "historical idealism" which was not inverted, just as in Marx, by "historical materialism." As Habermas indicates, in his analysis of the development of productive forces Marx is based on Hegel's "dialectics through objectification" rather than on Schelling's "dialectics through compression/contraction." On the relation between Schelling and Marx, see Habermas, *Teoría y Praxis*, 206–10. On the philosophical and historical effects of the idea of a "contraction of God," see Habermas, *Teoría y Praxis*, 185–92.

26. There is a connection between the notion of humanity as *alter deus* and Feuerbach's atheistic critique of religion as an anthropological projection, as noted by Habermas, *Teoría y Praxis*, 189.

27. "Nur noch ein Gott kann uns retten" ("only a god can still save us") is a famous statements made by Heidegger in an interview with *Der Spiegel* in May 1976.

Wasn't it a universal philosophical assumption the fact that if God exists, He is beyond space and time? The difficulties of making God too meaningful for mankind are obvious, and the suspicion of projection is completely legitimate.

The philosopher of religion may limit his analysis to the phenomenological account of the different approaches to the problem of evil in both religion and thought, and may even give his own interpretation of the gravity of evil and the human necessity to find a meaning for it. But the theologian faces a greater challenge, with which he or she has to cope to follow the imperative of 1 Pet 3:15: "Always be prepared to give an answer to everyone who asks you to give the reason for the hope that you have. But do this with gentleness and respect." Asking God about the meaning of evil is not a blasphemy or an offence but an act of piety. It is also the duty of the theologian.

We shall examine the treatment of the problem of evil in one of the principal contemporary Christian thinkers, the German theologian Wolfhart Pannenberg (1928–), as an example of the relevance that the topic preserves nowadays.

WOLFHART PANNENBERG'S PROPOSAL OF THEODICY

Wolfhart Pannenberg is one of the most outstanding Christian theological minds of our time. He has been in constant dialogue with the principal philosophical streams of the last century.[28]

The programmatic manifesto *Offenbarung als Geschichte* [*Revelation as History*], co-authored with Rolf Rendtorff, Ulrich Wilckens, and Trutz Rendtorff, constituted a turning point in twentieth-century Protestant theology. It represented the foundational act of a new theological approach which intended to challenge the prevailing "theology of the word" of Barth, Bultmann, and others. In opposition to the Barthian and Bultmannian accentuation of the word as the *locus theologicus* of the revealing act of God, this group of authors defended the centrality of history in the dynamics of divine revelation. The philosophical background was the Hegelian conception of history as the self-unfolding of the absolute, so that history itself, in its universal condition, unveils the divine being. Pannenberg was in charge of writing the chapter "Dogmatische

---

28. Braaten, "The Current Controversy in Revelation," 233–34.

Thesen zur Lehre von der Offenbarung" ["Dogmatic Theses on the Revelation"].

God reveals himself in history. This synthetic statement allows us to envision the advantages and the risks involved by Pannenberg's approach. Without analyzing the problem generated by the idea of a "universal history" through which, according to Pannenberg, God reveals himself to the creatures, we can immediately realize that one of the most compelling questions to be met by this approach is that of the meaning of history. The notion that God reveals himself in history implies an ultimate meaning of history as a whole.

The acceptance of a meaning in history has been a defining element of Christian theology. St. Augustine in *The City of God*, Bossuet in his *Discourse on Universal History*, and Hegel in *Lectures on the Philosophy of History*, assume this perspective. The theologian who thinks about the meaning of history is admitting the premise that history is driven by a plan, by an *economy*. However, Christian tradition has been aware of the deep contrast that exists between the theoretical construction represented by the theology of the sense of history, and the presence of an inexorable reality: evil. Who can understand the meaning of history, those who have won or those who have lost (the victims, all those who suffer in the different realms of human life: sociological, psychological, and physical)?

The *theologia gloriae* of meaning, beauty, and harmony in creation and in history is radically opposed by the *theologia crucis* of pain, evil, and suffering. What a great paradox, undoubtedly, but what a great Christian paradox, because Christianity is characterized by the simultaneous assumption of both realities: good and evil, meaning and lack of meaning, glory and cross. Luther wonderfully described this apparently contradictory state when depicting the human being as *simul iustus et peccator*, "just and sinner at the same time." Evil poses a challenge to Christianity, but this challenge belongs to the essence itself of the Christian message.

A Persistent Problem

Pannenberg has tried to provide a global understanding of the Christian faith and of its relation to a philosophy of a history. The problem of evil brings a very serious objection to the possibility of finding a meaning for the course of times.[29]

29. On Pannenberg's approach to the problem of evil, see also his articles "Der Gott der Geschichte: Der trinitarische Gott und die Wahrheit der Geschichte," in *Metaphysik*

According to him, the whole history of salvation points to the act of creation. The salvation of God starts with creation, in itself a convergence of divine creating will and of divine will of salvation. Hence the importance of faith in creation for Christianity: nothing in this religion can be understood without the idea of creation and without the conviction that the different beings are dependent upon their Creator. The beings of the world are "creatures," the result of the divine act of creation. So is mankind. In the same way, ethics of Christian inspiration is based on faith in creation: its fundamental orientation consists of stating that human being is a creature coming from God and going towards God. This notion shapes the means and ends which are present in the individual's actions. Human beings have an origin and a destiny: God, the creating God.

Heidegger's *An Introduction to Metaphysics* begins with the ultimate question of metaphysics, which is capable of encompassing every possible question: "why being instead of nothingness?" Leibniz had posed the same question centuries earlier. Heidegger acknowledges the fact that Christianity offers an answer to his question: the reason why there is something instead of nothing is the divine act of creation. An intelligence possessing a creating will has produced that "something." Such a creating intelligence must be eternal and omnipotent. Classical Christian theology has followed this argumentative direction. It seems clear that the idea of God in Christianity is deeply linked to the concept of creation, so that "when theology fails to take up this task the danger threatens that the word "God" will lose any credible meaning."[30]

Some texts from the Holy Scripture express the conviction that created things manifest the glory of God. Ps 19 raises a hymn of praise to the Creator: "The heavens declare the glory of God; and the firmament shows His handiwork. Day unto day utters speech, and night unto night reveals knowledge. There is no speech nor language where their voice is not heard. Their line has gone out through all the earth, and their words to the end of the world."[31]

St. Paul says that the invisible power of God has become visible through created things (Rom 1:20). Creation is contemplated as a sign

---

und Gottesgedanke, 112–28, and "Die christliche Deutung des Leidens," in *Beiträge zur systematischen Theologie*, 2:246–53.

30 Pannenberg, *Systematic Theology*, 2:162.

31. We will be using the New King James Version.

of the eternal, omnipotent, good, and merciful God. Creation is good because it is the work of the good God. This conscience prevailed in the faith of the people of Israel and in the Christian community since its earliest beginnings, and it is the same conscience underlying the attempts of a rational demonstration of the existence of God, whose paradigmatic instance is Aquinas' "five ways" [*quinque viae*].[32]

However, there are serious reasons to doubt that world and history are actually the result of the work of God. Just as theologians and philosophers have recurrently found legitimacy in elaborating cosmological and teleological proofs of the existence of God throughout the centuries, the inverse situation has taken place too: thinkers and scientists have found legitimacy in elaborating anti-cosmological and anti-teleological proofs. The issue resembles the so-called antinomies of pure reason in Kant's *Critique*: examples in which both the thesis and the antithesis have the same argumentative weight. Depending on the clues one values more, it will be possible to argue in either way.

Reality itself is contradictory: on the one hand, it stands as a transparent mirror of God and His glory for the person who believes; on the other hand, it exhibits the character of an autonomous entity which functions on its own, often hostile to humankind and whose imperfections are improper for a good, omnipotent, perfect God. The autonomy of the natural and historical world represents a verily complicated problem for all Christian theologians. The advancement in the field of scientific knowledge has gradually unfolded the structure of matter and the laws behind it. Is God an unnecessary hypothesis? Was Laplace right when telling Napoleon "*Je n'avais pas besoin de cette hypothése-la*" ("I had no need of that hypothesis")?[33] Human mind has been capable, itself alone, of unveiling—incompletely—the processes of nature. The world functions on its own, autonomously, and a peculiar combination of chance and necessity (following Lucretius and Jacques Monod) explains the

---

32. Aquinas' five ways are cosmological, in the sense that they try to prove the existence of God from the facticity of the world, in opposition to the ontological argument (which reasons from the idea of God itself). The five ways are the following: motion (there must be a primeval mover), efficient causes (there must be a first, non-caused cause), necessity (there are things that can either be or not be), the degrees of perfection, and the teleology or finalism which exists in nature. Cf. *Summa Theologica*, I pars, q. 2, art. 3.

33. Ferrater Mora, "Laplace," in *Diccionario de Filosofía*, vol. 3.

current state of things. Divine intervention is out of play, and the idea of a provident God seems superfluous.

As Pannenberg writes, echoing these considerations, "the independence of creaturely forms and processes . . . leave the impression that they need no divine Creator to explain them."[34] This autonomy emerges out of both the natural and the social processes. Experimental science grants us a rational vision of the universe out of purely material principles, with no reference to a transcendent Creator. Twentieth-century physics, with Quantum Mechanics and Relativity, gives us a description of the laws of nature, and nowadays it is directing its efforts to identifying the unifying principle of the four fundamental physical forces. Life sciences received a great impulse in the mid-nineteenth century, with Darwin and Wallace's theory of evolution of species, and in the twentieth century with the discoveries in the field of Genetics, the structure of DNA, and the human genome project. Natural reality, even in its most detailed aspects, finally finds a scientific explanation and a place within the great edifice of science.

Social sciences end up attributing all social change to the action of individuals and to the over-individual structures generated by those actions. Where is God? Rather than finding a place for God to dwell, a problem posed by the evolutionary biologist Ernst Haeckel (1834–1919), it is a matter of underscoring the theologian's commitment to admit the legitimacy of the question, how is it possible to "see" God in nature and in history? Both the natural and the social sciences promote what, following Max Weber, one could call the disenchantment of the world. There is no mystery in the world. Reason is ultimately capable of explaining how it functions. But, on the other hand, every scientific answer conceals a new question. There is still place for a *docta ignorantia* (Nicholas of Cusa), since we know that we will always be ignorant.

The autonomy of world and history and the presence of evil and suffering both offer an important challenge to the assumption that "the work of creation is good according to the creative will of God."[35] The scepticism about the goodness of creation is caused by reality itself. It is by no means an arbitrary speculation but a concern provoked by how reality manifests itself.

---

34. Pannenberg, *Systematic Theology*, 2:162.
35. Ibid., 163.

As a theologian, Pannenberg's way to cope with the question involves the reference to the sources of Christianity: the Holy Scriptures. Historical and critical methods identify two different traditions behind the two tales of creation in the book of Genesis: the Yahwistic (pre-exilic) and the priestly (essentially post-exilic) tales. The first verse of this biblical book, "In the beginning God created the heavens and the earth," belongs to the priestly tradition, written in the fifth century BCE. The priestly tale contains the phrase: "And God saw that it was good." The biblical hermeneutic of the act of creation is clear: creation is good, wanted by God, and human being is its culmination. Human being is, in fact, the key to the biblical understanding of the goodness of creation.

However, the Bible also leads us into the most flagrant and at the same time most realistic contradiction: God has created everything good, and everything is good because it has been created by God, but when the flood comes upon the Earth, we are told that all living beings were to blame for the state of corruption that had been reached: does this mean all the living beings, even those which are not acting freely? The biblical tale seems to suggest that creatures have corrupted a world which was initially good. Evil does not emerge out of the original configuration of the world, but its irruption occurs later. It is in fact alien to creation.

The priestly tale (P) also refers to the Law (Torah) and to its strict fulfilment as a way to return to the initial state of goodness and perfection which God wants for his creation. The priestly orientation, institutionalized in post-exilic Judaism by Ezra and Nehemiah, is still present in a late book like Ecclesiasticus: Jesus Ben Sira goes as far as to identify the pre-existing wisdom of God with the Torah. Torah is the most precious reality of creation. The fulfilment of the Torah brings creation back to its original splendour (cf. Eccl 24:23–29).

Christianity inherits a theological *corpus* which is closely connected with the idea of promise and with the late apocalyptic Jewish literature: consummation is not performed through the Torah, but it is an eminently eschatological reality. Christ is the eschatological manifestation of the new man (cf. 1 Cor 15:46), and the idea of a perfect, initial state, privileged by the priestly thought, becomes relativized by the effects of the eschatological projection.

Monotheism is reluctant to blame God for the presence of evil in the world. Judaism, Christianity, and Islam consider it an intolerable blasphemy, through which the human being pretends to judge God. God has no need to justify himself before the world. For Barth, the goal of theodicy is to justify creatures. Barth's radical theocentricism makes him reflect "from above," from God, the Creator. The creature, and not God, falls into a deep questioning, just as for certain streams of German idealism it was the world, rather than God, that was problematic.

Nevertheless, this lack of questioning the role of God regarding the presence of evil in the world contrasts with the firm support that unfair suffering has given, and still gives, to the phenomenon of unbelief, "for clearly there is an open denial of belief in God the Creator, and not without reason this unbelief appeals to the fact of evil in the world, recalling the innocent and disproportionate suffering especially of creatures whose lives could not develop at all. The pitiful suffering and death of children is the most cogent argument against belief in a Creator of the world who is both wise and good."[36] This pitiful suffering has been superbly depicted in literature by Fyodor Dostoyevsky and Albert Camus. The rebellion against injustice is more than a theoretical objection to the possibility of a good God: it is an objection based on experience.

And "if the objection is to be met, then it will be met only by a real overcoming of evil and suffering such as Christian eschatology hopes for in the resurrection of the dead," for "suffering, guilt, and tears cry out for a real overcoming of evil."[37] In this point, Pannenberg mentions one of the most relevant theological statements on the problem of evil: the relationship between theodicy and eschatology.[38] There is no answer to the problem of evil without its examination in light of the eschatological faith of Christianity. Pannenberg's theology, with its categorization of history as *locus revelationis*, recognizes the intrinsic opening of history to a future consumption. The future, what is about to come, defines how one should look at history. The perspective of the eschatological future becomes a core aspect of how Christianity meets the challenge of evil.

Understanding the deepest meaning of creation involves the assumption of the perspective of "eschatological redemption": created reality is essentially incomplete. Christianity contemplates creation

---

36. Ibid., 164.
37. Ibid.
38. According to Pannenberg, the eschatological salvation is the true horizon of life: "die vollständige Ganzheit des Lebens ist das Heil" (Pannenberg, *Beiträge zur systematischen Theologie*, 2:246).

not as a definitive entity, in a static sense, as if "what is given" could be absolutized or conceptualized as the only possible reality. The future order of reality is more important than the current state of things. Eschatology constitutes the ultimate scope of creation, as the world is a history *in fieri*.

According to Pannenberg, Judeo-Christianity represents a turning point in the development of a historic conscience. In contrast with ancient Eastern cultures, which tried to introduce the category of history within the cosmic order (an attempt finally frustrated by the intensity of historical changes), Israel provides a novel contribution: that of the lordship of God over history regarded as a total, unified reality. The idea of God is now dependent upon the historical rather than upon the cosmic sphere. In a situation comparable to that of Socratic philosophy, which marked a shift from cosmology to ethics as the new central interest of Greek philosophy, Israel's originality in the history of religions resides in its favoring a transition from a cosmocentric religiosity onto a religiosity fundamentally based upon the historical experience of the people of Israel over time.

By means of rooting the divine in history, Israel was able to imagine history as a reality in possession of a deep sense, with an origin and with a final goal. God has designed a plan, an "economy" for history, and even failures may be interpreted as the ways to perform those objectives. It is so that even the worst tragedies did not make Israel, and especially the prophets, doubt about the wisdom of God and power and about its superiority over human understanding, and for Job suffering was a divine test.[39]

Historical-critical methods have shown that many biblical tales were subject to a long process of elaboration, greatly influenced by events and tragic experiences that left a profound trace in Israelite religiosity. On account of this, the reference to the meaning of the category of history in the Israelite mind does not imply taking biblical tales as purely historic narrations. What matters is not the *de facto* but the *de iure* historicity of these texts: the fact that Israelite self-consciousness was modelled by a deep perception of the centrality of history.

Pannenberg thinks that Christianity dissolves human nature into history: Adam's (the mythological denotation of the first human being) creation is the initial but not the final point of human development. The

---

39. Cf. Pannenberg, *Beiträge zur systematischen Theologie*, 2:249.

first Adam points to the last Adam. Mankind is in its way towards the eschatological consummation. The natural and the historical dimensions do not simply overlap: the natural reality is integrated into the historical realm. The first Adam is inserted into the last Adam, and the "human" is built up by the historical dynamism. Human nature needs to be interpreted in light of future.

History as a totality transcends the horizon of the particular histories: every single subject encounters a series of connections of sense [*Sinnszusammenhänge*] that are not a result of his own activity. History goes beyond the sum of individual actions: every individual action assimilates some sort of "surplus" that affects the remaining individuals, and history must be therefore seen from a universalistic perspective, according to which individual and collective actions are mutually influential. Those individual experiences that are independent of rational, planned actions seem to reinforce this consideration.

Pannenberg speaks in terms of a priority of experience over action [*Priorität des Erlebens gegenüber dem Handeln*], which is to say, the necessity of analyzing not only the "active" happening of history, propitiated by every individual agent, but also what history generates beyond the results of particular actions. This intersection beyond the individual and the collective elements encourages looking at history as a totality. The experiential and social contexts overcome the particularity of the specific subject and set a universal history. The totality of history is also related with its unity: history is a substantial reality, overcoming the sphere of individual histories. Without comprehending history as a unified "all" which owns a substantial character, it is extremely difficult, but not impossible, to give an account of the formation of the individual's identity.[40] It is the experience of totality what allows the individual to edify his own identity.

The relevance of history affects certain metaphysical ideas that had been traditionally examined as supra-historical or even non-historical entities. Pannenberg explains that, in opposition to the Greek concept of *aletheia* ("truth"), the Hebrew *'emet* is not interpreted as a non-temporal but as a historically situated reality whose permanent nature is manifested through a history in which the future is always open.[41] Truth in its biblical understanding is not a development from a primeval point

40. Cf. Pannenberg, *Anthropologie in theologischer Perspektive*, 497–99.
41. Pannenberg, *Grundfragen systematischer Theologie: Gesammelte Aufsätze*, 202–22.

that we may know in advance, but it consists of an essentially historical reality, and since history is incomplete, our knowledge of the historic reality is provisional. Our understanding of truth needs the mediation of history, and it will not be final until history, in its dimension of totality, will achieve its completion in the eschatological consummation of times. There is therefore a deep link between truth and eschatology; there is even a "history of truth," alien to the Greek *Weltanschaaung*. This consideration will prove to be of fundamental importance in Pannenberg's theological approach to the problem of evil.

Because of the central role played by history in Pannenberg's thought, his approach to the problem of evil will involve the careful consideration of the nature of the historical process, moving towards a final consummation in which its true sense will be revealed. However, Pannenberg does not ignore the fact that some of the most ambitious and intellectually compelling attempts of providing a rational answer to the classical question of theodicy have undertaken a rather different path of reasoning. A paradigmatic instance of this point is Gottfried Wilhelm Leibniz (1646–1716). Against the temptation of over-simplification or even caricaturing of Leibniz's theodicy, Pannenberg acknowledges its value and courage. A man like Leibniz, whose scholarly position is extraordinary (having made fundamental contributions to philosophy, logic, and diplomacy, and the co-discoverer—together with Newton—of infinitesimal calculus, one of the greatest creations of mathematics), being one of the brightest minds in human history, could not remain untouched by the power of the hard problem that affects so many people: how is it possible to reconcile infinite divine goodness and the existence of evil?

Pannenberg thinks that the principal mistake of Leibniz's theodicy does not come from an excessive optimism about the effects of evil in the world, as if it were insignificant in comparison with the majesty of divine creation. Leibniz wanted to justify God *ab origine*: he tried to explain the presence of evil in the world and its compatibility with a good God, bringing his metaphysical analysis back to the origin, back to the initial moment of creation: "the most serious defect of the traditional treatment of the problem of theodicy, precisely in the classical form that Leibniz gave it, is that he has thought he could give a proof of the righteousness of God in his works exclusively from the standpoint of the origin of the world and its order in the creative work of God, instead of taking into consideration the history of God's saving action and the eschatological fulfilment that has dawned already in Jesus Christ."[42] Leibniz did not understand, in Pannenberg's view, the eschatological nature of history: the hope in a future, definitive consummation of the world is a constitutive element of Christianity. History unveils the being of God (as Pannenberg has underlined in many of his works), and it is therefore impossible to grasp the meaning of the present suffering without assuming an eschatological projection.

Pannenberg himself warns about the danger of using the reference to the eschatological future as a subterfuge to avoid the clear, direct answer that the gravity of evil demands: "even in the standpoint of reconciliation and eschatological consummation, of course, it is an open question why the Creator did not create a world in which there could be no pain or guilt."[43] The problem, as Pannenberg has just pointed out, goes beyond the existence of evil, pain, and suffering (particularly in their condition of unfair realities), involving the existence of guilt.

The idea of guilt is present in the Hebrew Bible, for instance in Deuteronomistic theology, dominated by the model of promise and fulfilment, and of sin and punishment, in its interpretation of the history of Israel. The misfortunes of the people of Israel would have been caused by its incapacity to fulfil the law of God. This *forma mentis* will experience a deep crisis with the advent of wisdom literature, as it can be seen in the book of Job. The notion of guilt, however, has been central to many Christian theological developments. It is so in Paul, in St. Augustine, and in Luther, who have insisted on human guilt before God as a result of sin and on the absolute necessity of divine grace in order to achieve justification. Modern psychology has compelled theologians to reflect on the dangers created by the concept of guilt, in addition to the phenomenon of self-guilt, which are responsible for serious psychiatric damage in many people. Today's theologian looks with suspicion and with critical qualifications at the traditional notion of guilt.

However, following Pannenberg's argument, it is not possible to find a radical separation between theodicy and creation *ab origine*, even though Christianity thinks of history as a process oriented towards an eschatological future, hoping that this final consummation will unfold the true meaning of the historical events.

---

42. Pannenberg, *Systematic Theology*, 2:164–65.
43. Ibid., 165.

The idea which attributes evil to human sin and responsibility plays an important role in the writings of Clement of Alexandria in the third century, and it goes back to the Deuteronomistic tradition and to Pauline theology. This conception is insufficient, both for the believer and for the non-believer. Not only the unfair human suffering but also the huge pre-human suffering, existing before the emergence of human species (known thanks to the advancements in zoology and in the scientific investigation of the nervous system of higher organisms), cannot be justified by Clement's conception. Nowadays, we should not deny the fact that many living beings, aside from mankind, experience real suffering, since they all possess nervous endings that transform certain feelings into painful impulses. These species have inhabited the world for much longer than mankind. How can we explain their suffering? Animals commit no sin.

The problem may lie in something that was already noticed by Freud: human beings are concerned by the meaning of their lives and imagine great goals for themselves, but they are not normally concerned by the meaning of the lives of animals and other living beings. The question about the meaning of life hides, according to Freud, an anthropocentric vanity,[44] an inexorable consequence of the way our mind works: we tend to understand the surrounding reality by means of our endo-psychic categories, projecting ourselves in our understanding the external world, following a process of gradual humanization of nature. Human beings ask the question on their own fate, but they do not ask the question on the fates of animals and plants. Human beings think of themselves as the image and likeness of God.

This anthropomorphization is not necessarily negative, and scientific progress owes much to it. Without conceiving of nature in coherence with a set of laws that we are able to depict in mathematical terms, as Galileo supposed, our understanding of the physical reality might not have advanced as much as it has done over the last centuries. The assumption that the questions we ask nature by means of experiments are actually "answered" by nature lies on the basis of the scientific method. The consideration of our capacity to understand the way nature functions is, in some sense, a result of anthropomorphization, of very positive effects for the progress of knowledge and for the scientific vision of the world.

---

44. Cf. Freud, *The Future of an Illusion*.

Theodicy

But the guilt complex involves a "negative" anthropomorphization, and it is incapable of offering a convincing explanation of how to conjugate the presence of evil with the goodness of God. God could have created the world in such a way that bad actions did not take place, preserving his creatures from sin and evil. Human freedom is never absolute. Christian theology has always defended the existence of a divine "concourse" on human action. The intense controversy known as *De Auxiliis*, which involved Dominican (like Domingo Báñez) and Jesuit (like Luis de Molina) theologians in sixteenth-century Spain, shows that none of the positions stood for an absolute statement of human freedom.[45] The problem resided in how to make compatible the existence of a true, but limited, freedom, with the action of God.

Few theologians dare to represent human freedom as an absolutely independent reality from God and from his gift (grace). Therefore, the use of human freedom to exonerate God is a rather poor way of reasoning. It cannot be denied, in addition to this, that human beings are never totally responsible for their choices of means and ends. Our freedom is severely conditioned by culture, the religious environment, the social and economic context, the education one has received, psychology, physiology, and so on. Even without excluding the possibility of an ultimate freedom (at least in a Kantian sense: thinking of this ultimate freedom as a postulate of practical reason in order to formulate a theory of ethical action, but out of the scope of a "scientific" demonstration, as in the natural and in the social sciences), independent of physical and social circumstances, this freedom could never be regarded as absolute. And, from a Christian perspective, this freedom could never be radically alienated from divine action.

Human freedom to choose does not exonerate God, since Christian theology has constantly remarked that the human being is a divine creature, whom God maintains in existence: the act of creation is a continuous, not a discrete event. Does freedom revoke the condition of creature?

---

45. According to Báñez, who followed Thomism, God brings, through *concursus previus* or *praemotio physica*, the created power from potency into act, and through *concursus simultaneus* He accompanies the activity of the creature through its whole duration. The preliminary movement is therefore initiated by God. Molina, on the contrary, thinks that the immediate physical cooperation of God depends upon the free will of the human beings. Molina only accepts the divine *concursus simultaneus*, emphasizing the freedom of will over the dependency of creatures (See Ferrater Mora, "Luis de Molina," in *Diccionario de Filosofía*, vol. 3).

If so, the risk run would be too high, and the representatives of the so-called atheism of freedom (Feuerbach, Nietzsche, Sartre . . .) would be right when denying the existence of God because of its incompatibility with human freedom and dignity. A radical split between human being and God as a way to safeguard the goodness of God, blaming humanity alone, constitutes an illegitimate absolutization of freedom. In Pannenberg's words, "concern to absolve the creator has been a mistake in Christian theodicy."[46] In the New Testament, God assumes his responsibility over creation. This is perhaps the deepest sense of the theology of the Cross: "responsibility for the coming of evil into creation unavoidably falls on the God who foresees and permits it, even though creaturely action is the immediate cause."[47]

The Cross, the symbol of Christianity, defines a second core element in the consideration of the problem of evil. Pannenberg has noticed that theodicy cannot be separated from eschatology. The approach to theodicy will have to assimilate the Cross as a central theological category. Theology cannot ignore the scandal of the Cross, although it cannot simply revive St. Anselm's theory of satisfaction. The return to the Cross is a *sine qua non* condition for Christian theology.

As Pannenberg highlights, the freedom and the autonomy of creatures, although not absolute, imply different risks. The traditional idea of Providence referred to God's running the risk of human sinfulness and evil in order to achieve the full communion between the Creator and the creator. Providence was meant to signify that God assumes the risks involved in human freedom with the intention of bringing everything to its ultimate goal. God does not want evil in itself: evil is the necessary condition for the realization of creatures. This argument, Pannenberg remarks, was present in Leibniz's theodicy. God can get good out of evil and, following Gregory of Nyssa and St. Augustine, God allows sin for the sake of Providence.

Can we therefore say that evil has a salvific purpose? Medieval theology inspired in Augustinianism went as far as to consider evil and condemnation to be integral parts of cosmic aesthetics: without evil, good cannot outlast. The exaltation of Adam's sin (which paradoxically contrasts with the simultaneous statement of the gravity of the evil generated by original sin and transmitted onto successive generations,

46. Pannenberg, *Systematic Theology*, 2:166.
47. Ibid., 169.

subordinating the sacrament of Baptism to the necessity of "cleaning" the *macula originalis* left by Adam), in line with the liturgical hymn *O felix culpa*, belong to the attempts of building "theological aesthetics." However, theological aesthetics, which justify evil as the necessary antithesis so that good may stand out, forgets, according to Pannenberg, that the goodness of creation is only an anticipation (and never an ultimate realization) of the eschatological consummation.

Christianity and Evil

In Christianity there is a clear instance to which all complaints about the presence of evil in the world should be addressed. Just as human beings implore divine *benevolentia*, there is a theological legitimacy in denouncing injustice, suffering, and the emptiness of many lives. This is not a blasphemy or a lack of piety, since Christian tradition has rarely considered petitions to be irreverent. In contrast with Kant, Christian tradition has not called a "religious illusion" all that, apart from the good behaviour in life, people think they can do in order to gain divine favour. The Protestant Reformation in the sixteenth century (and the theological reflection it inspired on justification) has generated a gradually deeper conscience about the fundamental conviction that the heart of Christianity does not lie in what mankind can do before God but in the free gift of God, in his self-communication in history. But not even the concept of justification excludes the appeal of humans to God through prayer. And, as a consequence, this acceptance of a theological foundation of the value of prayer (in spite of our awareness that many things we ask for would constitute a flagrant violation of the laws of nature and of the course of history, the necessity of praying to God seems to persist in the minds of so many people) means that it is equally admissible to accept the right of denouncing the presence of evil in the world and of directing this complaint to God.

Pannenberg remarks that the theology of the Cross, a scandal for Jews and a foolishness for Gentiles (cf. 1 Cor 1:23), represents the assumption of God of his own responsibility. The Cross is no excuse to demand a mere admission of facts (evil, pain, and suffering) as they are. There is probably nothing in Christianity that may encourage so much reflection as the Cross. The Cross is never an immunizing *theologoumenon* against the problem of evil. It is, on the contrary, the constant question to be posed. The God who reveals himself in Christ has consented Christ's unfair, cruel death. Why? Wasn't there any other way to perform redemption, which is in no way a simple rescue from sinfulness and from human offence to God but, in an integral perspective—that of salvation—it involves a deep liberation from all ties that deprive human being from a full life? The Cross exemplifies the responsibility of God as creator. In the Cross, God does not leave the world behind.

The question, however, remains: why so much pain, so much suffering, so much injustice? It reproduces the fundamental problem of theodicy: God creates the world in order to communicate himself freely to creatures, but why has it been created in this way? Why has the world been created with so much pain, so much suffering, so much injustice? The theology of the Cross is a questioning theology, capable of encompassing the whole theodicy. Rather than a response to theodicy and to the intriguing problems emerging out of it, the Cross is the Christian expression of theodicy itself.

The Cross situates Christianity in the horizon of the deepest questioning. It does not avoid reflection; instead, it acknowledges the impossibility of understanding what has taken place. The Cross is the perennial symbol of the necessity of asking, and at the same time, it is the real and effective performance of an unfair, cruel suffering, a mirror of what happens in the world. Christianity cannot be accused of hiding the problem of evil, of taking refuge in the theology of the Cross. What kind of refuge does the Cross offer against evil, if the Cross is the most direct, horrendous expression of the evil that led Jesus of Nazareth to death? The Cross is no refuge, but a permanent challenge and, moreover, a scandal.

Nevertheless, Christianity does not end with the Cross. First Corinthians 15, probably one of the oldest strata of the New Testament, states "For I delivered to you first of all that which I also received: that Christ died for our sins according to the Scriptures, and that He was buried, and that He rose again the third day according to the Scriptures, and that He was seen by Cephas, then by the twelve. After that He was seen by over five hundred brethren at once, of whom the greater part remain to the present, but some have fallen asleep. After that He was seen by James, then by all the apostles" (1 Cor 15:3–7). The Cross, its deep and radically humane question, cannot be understood without the attempt of answer that Christianity offers through resurrection. There is a promise of a new life, extended to creation as a whole, which expects the final liberation from death. This is the Christian hope, and as St. Paul writes: "For we know that the whole creation groans and labors with birth pangs together until now" (Rom 8:22).[48]

As Pannenberg says, Christian theology seems to be subject to a dialectics whose terms are easily recognizable. We find, on the one hand, a thesis: the will of God of creation. But, on the other hand, we must cope with its antithesis: the negativity of evil in creation. What synthesis does Christianity suggest? That of reconciliation and of eschatological consummation of creation, whose anticipation or *prolepsis* is the resurrection of Jesus Christ. The answer to the question posed by the Cross comes from the resurrection of the dead, a doctrine which, according to Pannenberg, expresses the dignity of the finite beings, as it offers the possibility of communion with the eternal God while respecting individuality, instead of subsuming it into the absolute.[49]

The fact that Jesus, dead in the Cross, was resurrected by the Father, is seen by Pannenberg as a *prolepsis* or anticipation of the final, eschatological consummation that will take place at the end of times. We shall all rise again. The answer offered by Jesus' resurrection is therefore an anticipation of the total, full answer that is to come. Theodicy needs a reference to the eschatological consummation of creation in the future time.

Theodicy, the meditation on the antithetical character of the good of God in creation, demands a synthesis, which Christianity associates with the faith in the eschatological consummation of history at the end of times. But not even this faith can completely numb the spirit emanating from the fundamental question of theodicy: why evil? It seems that such an eschatological consummation could be performed without so much sacrifice, so much suffering, so much injustice, so much coexistence of victims and executioners, of oppressed and oppressors.

---

48. The idea that the radical transformation that will take place at the end of times is going to affect not only humanity but the entire creation is present in Rom 8:22, in apocalypticism, and, according to Pannenberg, in Trito-Isaiah (Isa 65:17; 66:22). On the apocalyptic background of this Pauline verse, see Hahne, *The Corruption and Redemption of Creation*. Pannenberg highlights the importance of the Christian hope in the universal scope of the redemptive action of God in his essay "Die christliche Deutung des Leidens": the belief in a final overcoming [*Überwindung*] of suffering is a defining element of Christianity (Pannenberg, *Beiträge zur systematischen Theologie*, 2:246).

49. Cf. Pannenberg, *Metaphysik und Gottesgedanke*, 49.

Evil and Finitude

According to Pannenberg, there is an inseparable connection between theodicy and eschatology. This is one of the principal conclusions which have been drawn so far by the German theologian. However, every step forward seems to conceal a potential step backward, to the point of departure, and there is no visible way out from the initial situation: the question about the meaning of evil is still present.

The being of a creature involves mutability,[50] and mutability constitutes an expression of an ontological weakness. Movement implies a lack of something; otherwise, no movement would be necessary. This reasoning is typical of classical Metaphysics, both in Aristotle and in Thomas Aquinas. The Christian idea of creature, of a created entity wanted by God, assumes the concept of mutability in order to state the difference between the immutable creator and the mutable creature. We are approaching one of Leibniz's most famous theses: evil is the result of the original imperfection that exists in all creatures, the so-called metaphysical evil. Without such an intrinsic imperfection, creatures would resemble God, but there is only one possible God. In order to be creatures and so that an effective otherness with God may exist (instead of thinking of creatures as mere "emanations" from divine essence or simple parts within a divine whole) it is compulsory to affirm the mutability of creatures. Hence, a contrast with divine immutability can be established.

For Leibniz, the plurality of creatures is a manifestation of the plurality of possible modes of limitation within the order of finitude. Mutability is consubstantial to finitude. In its ultimate sense, Leibniz's argument is purely analytical. It is based upon the identification of creature with limitation, deducing its metaphysical consequences, and assuming that the only barrier to divine omnipotence is the impossibility of performing what is essentially contradictory. God can do nothing contradictory, and since a non-finite (non-mutable and therefore alien to the effects of evil) creature would be contradictory, God is unable, on account of a logical-analytical imperative, to exclude evil from creation.

As we can see, Leibniz's philosophical system is far away from Voltaire's depiction in his famous novel *Candide, ou l'Optimisme*. There is not much optimism in Leibniz's theodicy. There is, on the contrary, a

---

50. Cf. Pannenberg, *Systematic Theology*, 2:169.

deep fatalism: logic is the supreme God, and logic compels all creatures to be finite and therefore to be able to do and to suffer evil. God, or at least the God Christianity praises to achieve his favor, can do nothing to avoid evil, because his freedom and omnipotence are limited by the unsurpassable power of logic. Our world is the "relatively better" one that can be found within that necessary, congenital imperfection. The question that comes out at this point is whether it would have been better that God had created no world at all, knowing as He did that every possible world would be inevitably subject to imperfection and evil. Mephistopheles offers a supreme expression of this shadow of nihilism in Goethe's *Faust*:

> *Ich bin der Gest, der stets verneint!*
> *Und das mit Recht; denn alles, was entsteht,*
> *Ist wert, dass es zugrunde geht;*
> *Drum besser wär's, dass nichts entstünde.*[51]

In effect: the spirit that always denies is right in doing so, since everything that begins moves towards destruction. Then, it seems that it would have been better that nothing began at all.

Leibniz, on behalf, again, of logical-analytical impositions (and we should not forget that Leibniz is one of the greatest logicians in history, and a true pioneer in modern mathematical logic), makes God choose the best. God must necessarily choose the best, because his perfect knowledge leads him to the best possible choice. God, just as creatures, cannot escape from logical necessity. The supremacy of logic is absolute in Leibniz's thought. However, and as Pannenberg points out, imposing the best choice on God forgets that, before an infinite range of possibilities, divine will founds the goodness of the being of creatures. It is the will of God what makes creation good. God has not made creatures on account of logical demands but on account of his good will. Leibniz's strict logic contrasts with the biblical idea of creation, and it seems closer to the fatalism of philosophers like Aristotle, Avicenna, and Averroes.

There is a great power of persuasion in Leibniz's argument. Every attempt of dialogue between faith and reason seems to involve a compromise. If faith wants to become *foi pensée*, an enlightened faith which is subject to the scrutiny of reason, capable of satisfying the demands of the wise (and the demands of all human beings), as the pastoral consti-

---

51. Goethe, *Faust*, part 1.

tution *Gaudium et Spes* of the Second Vatican Council once indicated, it must open itself to a critical examination. In this way, and even though it might be unpleasant for faith to admit that divine action had to cope with a certain degree of necessity imposed by logic (a logic which is discovered by reason itself, frequently contradicting the apparent "logic of faith"), it is important to acknowledge the legitimacy of Leibniz's approach. Leibniz cannot be regarded as a naïve optimist, but as a thinker who felt the deepest appeal from the problem of evil, trying to assume the demands of reason in his analysis of the question: "there is some truth in the tracing back of evil, including the moral evil of sin, to the conditions of existence bound up with creatureliness."[52]

It is possible to admit that, following Leibniz, evil constitutes some sort of void, but it is also true that evil is not only a void. Otherwise, the essence of a creature would be, itself, a failure and a mistake: an evil. God would have created new evil with every creature He made. Creatures would have no substantial reality, being mere expressions of an inner negativity. Christian metaphysical tradition has found no inconvenience in attributing the condition of substances to creatures (in opposition to Spinoza's philosophy and his idea of an only substance). Creatures are substances, subjects of action and passion, at least according to the great medieval Scholastic and humanistic theologians (Aquinas, Bonaventure, Duns Scotus, Francisco Suárez). The reference to the primary identification between evil and void as a means of justifying the problem of evil constitutes no convincing solution. In fact, "we are to seek the root of evil, rather, in revolt against the limit of finitude."[53]

Evil does not belong to the essence of what has been created; it rather belongs to its "anti-essence." In the Christian perspective, evil is the pathology of creation rather than one of its attributes. The biblical reflection is clear on this point: God saw that everything he made was good. What right do we have to grant logic in its abstract sense a supremacy that goes beyond the supremacy of God? Should we believe in God or in logic? This disjunctive may seem rather extreme. God does not act against logic, but logic cannot limit or even exhaust the possibilities of God. It would be patently contradictory that the infinite and absolute God, whose scope of action is virtually infinite, had his possibilities "finitized" by logic. No logic can compel God to create a bad

52. Pannenberg, *Systematic Theology*, 2:171.
53. Ibid.

world simply because it necessarily had to be a bad world. Being other than God does not mean anything bad: the otherness with respect to God is no evil at all. This otherness makes us imperfect, but imperfection is no synonym of evil. Void is not evil. There are good voids. God lacks finite attributes, and this is good.

Hence, "not limitation, but the independence for which creatures were made forms the basis of the possibility of evil."[54] The limitation that is inherent to the metaphysical condition of creature is not necessarily bad. It may be good to be limited; otherwise, every distinct being from God would be bad, and the only possible philosophical interpretation of Christianity would be pantheism. It is autonomy, the capacity to be ruled by oneself, what gives place to the presence of evil in creatures and in the created world. Evil can come out of autonomy but, again, autonomy is not evil. Such autonomy is the "perfection" of the creature, since autonomy is related with self-possession, with the status of a subject, capable of disposing of its own existence. The fact that Christianity has often considered creatures to be autonomous, subjects acting on their own, projecting worlds from themselves, has a deep theological, philosophical, and human relevance. We are not simple gears within the mechanism of the universe, but autonomous beings, whose autonomy is wanted by God. However, autonomy poses the risk of "apostasy from the Creator."[55]

Anyway, and as if we were before a phantasmagoric question in constant stalking, the problem reappears: what about the unfair suffering? One could concede (and it is too much to concede) that a fundamental part of the evil which exists in the world may come out of the wrong use of the autonomy creatures possess. It is too much to concede in the argument because God could have made it possible for autonomy and goodness to be in permanent reconciliation, as complicated and unimaginable as it may seem. Nevertheless, the problem of unfair suffering still persists. Unfair suffering does not emerge from our free, conscious actions. The evil suffered by the victim is different from the evil suffered by the executioner. Natural disasters, such as earthquakes, congenital syndromes, random metastasis in cancer . . . Unfortunately,

---

54. Ibid.

55. Ibid., 172. In "Bewusstsein und Geist" Pannenberg endorses the idea that the possibility of evil resides in the "Selbstzentrierheit" [self-centredness] of each creature. Cf. Pannenberg, *Beiträge zur systematischen Theologie*, 2:140.

there is too much evil in the world, and this evil is too serious as to make all the potential victories of reason and theology seem to be rather premature. We can explain certain types of evil, but there is so much evil in the world that the theologian and the philosopher find themselves completely overwhelmed.

Leibniz called "physical evil" the natural evils that creatures suffer as a result of living in a world that is subject to physical laws and phenomena independent of their will. This evil affects people, animals, plants ... It belongs to the dynamics of life. Big natural disasters, like the huge meteorite that, according to many scientists, generated the extinction of dinosaurs sixty-five million years ago, propitiated the emergence of mammals too. It meant a shift to which life finally managed to become adapted. Many living beings suffered and died, but many others survived, paving the path for the birth of new species.

There is no apparent justice in nature. Things follow blind physical laws and chance: they are never motivated by the performance of justice. Every single dinosaur that died sixty-five million years ago as a consequence of a terrible natural disaster was subject neither to justice nor to injustice: it simply perished in the context of a general struggle for life. Human being is the only living being that, as far as we know, poses the problem of the demands of justice. Human beings imagine a world ruled by justice: laws, institutions ... Human beings project justice and try to make justice, but they face the fatality of natural behaviour. Nature is not just or unjust with the child affected by Down syndrome: it is simply as it is, moved by biological laws and by pure chance, in which genetic mutations stand behind this genetic malformation.

Evil and Eschatology

Christianity echoes the aspirations for justice (with no apparent biological sense, and whose significance belongs to the realm of the quest for a deep human, social, and cultural meaning) and promises eternal, definitive justice. However, isn't this promise too utopian and illusory, designed at making worldly existence easier to cope with?

Pannenberg considers that physical evil cannot be attributed to human freedom. For the German theologian, physical evil is a result of the second law of thermodynamics. This law states that natural processes always lead to an increase in a variable known as "entropy," the degree of disorder of a system. There is a fundamental asymmetry in

Theodicy

41

nature: heat is always transmitted from the hotter to the colder body, and never the other way around, an asymmetry due to the second law of thermodynamics. The metaphysical implications of the second law of thermodynamics allow Pannenberg to underscore the importance of the future, of the openness of creation to new realities and to a potential self-improvement.

Theologians must be aware of the dangers involved by the use of scientific concepts, paradigms, and facts in their reflection. Science is an ambiguous instrument for theology. The same science that in the sixteenth century discovered the laws of thermodynamics has discovered in the twentieth century that, thanks to the advancements in the field of chaos theory and in the study of complexity, disorder may be a significant source of order. The great Russian-born Belgian scientist Ilya Prigogine (1917–2003), winner of the Nobel Prize for Chemistry in 1977, made outstanding contributions to the study of this phenomenon.[56] Disorder gives rise to new, self-organizing structures. Pure order would be equivalent to death, to inaction, to inertia. Cosmic and vital evolution has consisted of the gradual emergence of order out of disorder. This is the essence of complex systems: by means of interactions amongst its constituents, they are able to generate new structures and systems. Therefore, Pannenberg's association of physical evil with entropy (or natural tendency to disorder) runs the risk of forgetting that the same disorder which, in his view, lies behind the existence of physical evil, is also the cause of relevant physical goods, such as the birth of new structures and of new levels of reality.

In addition to this, the danger of confusing evil (an ethical idea) with entropy (a concept coming from experimental sciences, which is susceptible of quantification and empirical contrast) exists. Nature knows no evil: it only knows the factuality of the development of a series of processes, many of them irreversible. Pannenberg's argument might ultimately lead to the contradiction of accepting that it would be better not to be a creature and not to see oneself compelled to reach some sort of substantial autonomy, on account of the cruel destiny imposed by the second law of thermodynamics.

---

56. Cf. Prigogine and Stengers, *La Nouvelle Alliance*; and Prigogine and Stengers, *Order out of Chaos*.

Concerning "the interdependence of creatures,"[57] there is a problem in Pannenberg's way of reasoning, since he understands suffering and evil as consequences of the finitude of the forms of life, that "by making themselves independent . . . fall victim to entropy."[58] But, who has given creatures the option of becoming independent or not? Isn't this the result of a curious combination of chance and necessity rather than the effect of a voluntary decision?

Pannenberg's considerations seem to constitute a theological and philosophical extrapolation of a strictly scientific issue, because they go on to analyze human sin as the highest expression of a tendency towards independence, which is incipient in less developed creatures. In any case, and since the independence of the less developed creatures can be eventually explained through purely biological causes, is it legitimate to obtain such a deep, far-reaching theological conclusion? Again, the risk of interpreting scientific facts with theological and philosophical bias is present. The question is sufficiently transparent: can living beings subsist without searching for survival and pleasure? The results in the fields of life sciences, psychology, and sociology in the last decades show the effects of the impulse of libido and its role in shaping both individual and social action. The success of civilization resides, to a certain extent, in its capacity of joining the interest of the different individuals in the quest for a common progress, but a selfish goal remains, oriented towards a higher state of independence: the higher individual and social welfare.

Pannenberg seems resigned to admitting that the divine plan of making finite, autonomous creatures involves the possibility of evil, because without this contradiction, without this contrast generated by the *positivitas* of creatures and the *negativitas* of their existence, it would be impossible for them to recognize themselves and to freely undertake the path of progress. The resonances of Hegel's philosophy are undeniable.

Pannenberg's intellectual commitment to offering a reasoned exposition of the Christian hope in a world so seriously affected by evil and suffering is verily laudable, and it is part of a great tradition of quest for a sincere, honest dialogue between faith and reason that has existed throughout the history of Christianity (the debate between Jürgen Habermas and Joseph Ratzinger in 2004 is a good example of

---

57. Pannenberg, *Systematic Theology*, 2:172.
58. Ibid., 171.

this).⁵⁹ The German theologian has tried to carefully justify each of his argumentative steps, underlying the potential antitheses and assuming the legitimacy of the suspicion about the meaningless condition of world and history. And, in spite of the attempts to provide a rational, both philosophically and theologically, explanation of the presence of evil in creation, Pannenberg ends up acknowledging the place of piety: "praising God for making this world presupposes dissatisfaction with the present state."⁶⁰ The core idea of Pannenberg's treatment of the classical problem of theodicy brings us back to his initial considerations: there is no theodicy without eschatology.⁶¹

The belief in creation involves the belief in the eschatological overcoming of evil. Thinking of this world as a created reality belongs to the order of faith. And this is the same faith that stands in the hope in an eschatological consummation, capable of overcoming what must be overcome: evil, pain, and suffering. Here, there is a total intersection of faith and hope, extended also to the realm of love: faith in creation founds the hope in the eschatological consummation and edifies the *praxis* within history aimed at transforming present reality. Hegel was not so misguided, after all, when he saw human beings as actors in a play which goes far beyond their particular *hic et nunc*, "here and now." Those who believe in the God of love see themselves forced to admit their own finitude as a manifestation of their dependence upon the Creator. This assumption, proper of faith, encourages praising God in spite of an existence in which evil and disgrace are constant realities: "Praise the Lord, all you Gentiles! Laud Him, all you peoples!" (Ps 117:1).

After all, and as Boethius wrote, "*Si quidem Deus est, unde mala; bona vero unde, si non est?*" ("For if God exists, where do evils come from? If God does not exist, where do goods come from?").⁶² Theism faces an apparently unsolvable problem, but atheism is not capable of offering a solution either. Or is atheism a solution?

Personally, I believe that we must admit that we live in a situation of philosophical indigence. Theism does not offer a unified, satisfactory explanation of the problem of evil, but atheism offers no solution either,

---

59. Cf. Ratzinger and Habermas, *Dialectics of Secularization*.

60. Pannenberg, *Systematic Theology*, 2:173.

61. The technical use of the term *eschatology* was introduced by the German systematic theologian K. G. Bretschneider in 1804. It is a modern concept.

62. Boethius, *De Consolatione Philosophiae*, I, 105.

because it means the recognition of our condition of natural beings with antagonistic interests, in which evil emerges both from nature and from humanity, in the same way as nature and humanity can be sources of good things, too. Is this an explanation? What about the victims of nature and history?

Monotheistic religions dare to offer a solution, even if it seems to be a utopian narrative: the final retribution after death. God will vindicate those who have suffered. But this means that history, after all, has a meaning, that it has been worth living, and that the miseries of our present existence, just as its joys, have a sense. However, does history have a meaning?

2

History and Meaning

Heidegger, Bloch, Hegel, and Pannenberg

HEIDEGGER, BLOCH, CONDORCET, KANT, HEGEL, AND PANNENBERG

THE PROBLEM OF EVIL is closely related with the question about the meaning of history. Some people could argue that the idea of a meaning in history is not clear at all: why is it necessary that there be a meaning, a sense for the historical events? Isn't history an abstraction, the generalization of particular experiences that the individuals have in their own lives, and that we project onto a universal scenario which encompasses the whole of humanity?

As we can see, there are many interesting, convenient, and legitimate questions to pose regarding the nature of history. The doubts that emerge when considering the meaning of history are quite analogous to those that emerge when considering the meaning of evil. It could be said that neither evil nor history has a meaning: they are facts that take place in the world, and mankind feels the intemperate necessity to interpret them in accordance with its rationality. But the quest for a meaning might be an illusion, a definitely appealing one which has inspired numerous philosophies and religions throughout the centuries. According to the French philosopher Louis Althusser (1918–1990), history is a process without subject and goals:[1] it is a blind dynamism. For many, the idea of a "meaning" in history hides a theological presupposition.[2]

---

1. Cf. Althusser, "Remarque sur une categorie: Procès sans Sujet ni Fin(s)." In *Réponse á John Lewis*, 91–98.

2. In his book *Weltgeschichte und Heilsgeschehen* the German philosopher Karl Löwith studied the understanding of history found in authors like Burckhardt, Marx,

In this way, it can be said that if there is a meaning for history there may be a meaning for the problem of evil. If history is significant, and a sense can be extracted out of its complexity, evil has an answer. Evil happens within history and it is always referred to a history, individual or collective, because all human experiences are historically conditioned. The manner in which we view natural catastrophes, a form of "physical evil," to adopt Leibniz's terminology, varies with history, and our perceptions are always historically conditioned. A time may eventually arrive in which they will not be seen as evil but merely as natural events that follow the invariable laws of the universe. For centuries, many natural phenomena have been regarded as manifestations of evil, and their causes have been attributed to elements as different as supernatural entities and human guilt. Some voices interpreted the Lisbon earthquake as a result of the anger of God. In some regions of the world, physical handicaps are still seen as divine punishments, whereas in advanced, scientific societies they are understood as the effects of genetic mutations against which there is little to do.

According to Heidegger, the question about meaning cannot be separated from the understanding of *Dasein*, and *Dasein* is understood from its own existence, from the possibility of being itself or not being itself. There is, in fact, no understanding of being without an understanding of *Dasein*. *Dasein* faces the task of asking about the sense of being. Every question about being must first consist of a question about *Dasein* (the so-called existential analytics in *Sein und Zeit*), and for Heidegger the understanding of *Dasein* is inextricably associated with temporality: *Dasein* is temporal and it has to be understood as temporal.

Hegel, Proudhon, Comte, Condorcet, Turgot, Voltaire, Vico, Bossuet, Joachim of Fiore, and St. Augustine, developing the idea that the philosophy of history is based upon theological presuppositions [*Voraussetzungen*], and that it is in fact impossible without these presuppositions. Modern philosophical approaches to history inspired by the conviction that the course of time has a meaning—through the notion of progress (Voltaire), through self-display of the spirit (Hegel), through the path toward the kingdom of freedom (Marx) consist, according to Löwith, in a secularization of the Judeo-Christian theology of history oriented to an *eschaton*, to a final fulfilment: "Die moderne Geschichtsphilosophie dem biblischen Glauben an eine Erfüllung entspringt und dass sie mit der Säkularisierung ihres eschatologischen Vorbildes endet" (Löwith, *Weltgeschichte und Heilsgeschehen*, 11–12). Against the view that modernity is essentially the result of a process of gradual secularization from its Christian substrate Hans Blumenberg, in *Die Legitimität der Neuzeit*, defended the autonomy of modernity from its hypothetical debt to Christianity.

For some thinkers, the question about the meaning of history might sound rather pretentious. There is no possibility of understanding history, because history is not an autonomous entity, but the result of the individual historical experience that one has. In Heidegger's philosophy, "historicity" [*Geschichtlichkeit*] comes before "history" [*Geschichte*]. History is dissolved into the historicity of the individual existence of *Dasein*. There meaning of history is therefore determined by the meaning of *Dasein*, which is related with its temporal condition. There is no substantial character to be attributed to history: history is subordinated to the historicity of *Dasein*, and it is therefore a possibility of *Dasein*. It seems that there is no legitimacy in asking about the meaning of history as a whole without having understood the meaning of the individual existence of *Dasein*. If *Dasein* bears an unauthentic existence, history will lose its capacity of becoming meaningful, because it is absolutely dependent upon how it is experienced in the context of the individual existence of *Dasein*. The only possible foundation for a universal history is, according to Heidegger, historicity, the happening of the *Dasein*, without which there is no participation in a universal history. History is the possibility that *Dasein* has of becoming historical:

> But in so far as *Dasein's* Being is historical—that is to say, in so far as by reason of its ecstatico-horizontal temporality, it is open in its character of "having-being," the way is in general prepared for such thematizing of the 'past' as can be accomplished in existence. And because *Dasein*, and only *Dasein*, is primordially historical, that which historiological thematizing presents as a possible object for research must have the kind of *Dasein* which has-been-there. Along with any factical *Dasein* as Being-in-the-world, there is also, in each case, world-history."[3]

The primacy of the existential perspective of *Dasein* reaches such a high degree in Heidegger's thought that the historical knowledge [*Historie*] is only possible as a mode of being of *Dasein* that is posing the question. It is, again, dependent about the knowledge we can have of the existence of *Dasein*. History seems a projection of the individual existence. It is in no way a substantial reality in Heidegger. This view has been very influential not only in philosophy, but also in Christian theology, principally in the work of Rudolf Bultmann, himself a Heideggerian and a proponent of "existentialist theology": what matters is not the

---

3. Heidegger, *Being and Time*, 445.

historical facts surrounding Jesus, of which very little can be known, but how the spiritual encounter with the message of Jesus affects my own existence, and what kind of existential decision I undertake.

However, if history appears as the result of a question that *Dasein* poses about itself, and the question concerning history is not but a question concerning the meaning of *Dasein*, there is a danger, for Heidegger, of hiding the question about being behind the question about the meaning of history. As it is known, Heidegger called for a "destruction" of the Western metaphysical tradition, which had forgotten being [*Seinsvergessenheit*] and had eclipsed the truly authentic question: the question about being. In his *Brief über den Humanismus* ["Letter on Humanism"], a letter sent to the French philosopher Jean Beaufret in 1947 and a controversial writing because of his involvement with Nazism when he was rector of the University of Freiburg between 1933 and 1934, Heidegger asks for a humanism that is capable of thinking of the humanity of man from the proximity of being, and he accuses metaphysics of having ignored the basic fact that the essence of man is only present inasmuch as man is challenged by the question about being.

For Heidegger, the reduction of history into historicity makes it pointless to ask about a meaning of history as a whole, as universal history. There is no place for the proposal of a big project that can illuminate history. In this sense, postmodernism inherits much from Heidegger. In the Hegelian tradition, however, in which Marxism participates, history possesses substantiality, and it is therefore legitimate to speak in terms of an orientation of history towards an end, which for Marx is freedom (the true goal of history), achieved through human action (historical materialism). This goal goes beyond the historicity of the individual existence. In a Hegelian frame of understanding, history has its own direction, and individual existences serve such an end. There is a project, a meaning that clarifies individual existences and individual historical facts.

Marx thinks that history is the history of class struggle: "The history of all hitherto existing society is the history of class struggles," as it is written in the first chapter of *The Communist Manifesto* (1848), and the sense of history is the gradual development of productive forces, which will lead to the final emancipation of all individuals in a classless society. What is important to notice here is, beyond the specific way in which Marx understands the concrete evolution of history, the fact that he, like Hegel, is accepting that history has a consistency beyond the individual experience of history (historicity). *Geschichte* comes before *Geschichtlichkeit*. There is a point in conceiving of a utopia for history, since it is an objective reality which can be improved. From this perspective Walter Benjamin, generally associated with critical theory, and who committed suicide in 1940 after crossing the Pyrenees into Spain when fleeing from the Nazis, conceived of utopia as the motor of history. But the possibility of a utopia for history demands the intellectual acceptance of, first, a unity in universal history and second, a meaning in universal history which overcomes the meaning (or absence of meaning) of individual existence.

A distinguished exponent of the Marxist tradition is Ernst Bloch (1885–1977). Bloch was the author of books like *Geist der Utopie* (1918) and *Das Prinzip Hoffnung* (1938–1947), and one of the most relevant figures within the so-called utopian thought of the twentieth century.

Das Prinzip Hoffnung [*The Principle of Hope*] is Bloch's most celebrated work. The book constitutes a true encyclopaedia of the human quest for a better future. In the analysis of the "anticipatory conscience," Bloch examines the impulses that exist within human beings and which claim to be satisfied. The first of these impulses is the impulse towards self-conservation. But there is another impulse, associated with broadening forward the realm of human life: Bloch calls this the "active waiting," which can be seen in the human inclination to dreaming in order to satisfy wishes. There is a constant wish in every human being to improve his life, and this wish is translated into the collective human will for a better future. This consideration is found in Kant, too, who in *Der Streit der Fakultätten*, of 1798, supports the idea that the human race has always sought progress towards the better and that progress will continue in the future.

All of this marks a radical difference with Heidegger's view of history, because there is a "substantial constant" within history: the quest for something better, for a future better dawn. No one can ever free himself from having wishes, according to Bloch. Individuals, the same as humanity as a whole, have always dreamed with a better future.

The human tendency towards fantasy expresses, for Bloch, a human tendency to dreaming with something better. In this point, Bloch recalls Freud, for whom the best productions of fantasy are the "daydreams," in opposition to the "night-dreams." In daydreams, the *ego* is not as weak as in night dreams. Also, daydreams are broader than night dreams. This broader scope is reflected in the fact that the subject of daydreams may even represent other subjects. The person who dreams awake is capable of dreaming in the place of other people. Night dreams, on the contrary, are always individualistic, gravitating around the *ego* of the dreamer. Daydreams are open to an improvement of the world, whereas night dreams are essentially egocentric, and they only pay attention to individual experiences and to individual wishes. Night dream is regressive and archaic, motivated by childhood traumas (to follow Freud's interpretation). However, anticipations referred to people, social utopias, and beauty, are only present in daydreams. For Bloch, daydreams are essentially open to the future: if the content of night dreams is hidden and deformed, the content of day fantasy is open and anticipatory and always looks forward.

In night dreams the subject does not come out of himself, and there is no projection towards the dimension of a better future. Such a dream remains in the past and in the subject's unconscious. This dream is incapable of transforming the world, and it therefore lacks a utopian project. The content of day fantasy, in opposition to this, is the result of the broadening of both the subject and the world, and it represents a will towards the better, the wish of knowing more. Daydreams have a goal and they move forward.

Bloch's analysis of day fantasy is intended to show that human life itself is projected onto the future and, moreover, onto the accomplishment of a better future. Daydreams stay in what Bloch calls "affections of the act of waiting," like anguish, fear, lack of hope, hope, and confidence. All of them point forward, being the future the temporality of their content. They underscore the projective dimension of the human being, oriented towards a future. They can be negative or positive, but they all indicate the future.

There is a conscience in human beings directed to the future. Such a conscience cannot be identified with the conscience of "what is already conscious" (conscience *stricto sensu*), nor with the unconscious (the already-not-conscious): it is the "not-yet-conscious" [*noch-nicht-bewusst*]. This "not-yet-conscious" appears in day dreams, in their fantasy projected to the future. It is the pre-conscious of what is to come, and for Bloch, it constitutes the psychic place of the birth of new realities. Hope is expressed in the not-yet-conscious as a utopian function, oriented towards a better being and towards a different being. It is "*docta spes*," whose expectations are, rather than anything, a better future and a present different from the current one: it is the positive utopian function. It is a realistic hope because genuine realism realizes that reality has a horizon, and that there is a natural tendency within reality: reality is incomplete without a real possibility, which Bloch names "concrete utopia" [konkrete Utopie], and which is latent in the horizon of all reality.

The fourth part of Das Prinzip Hoffnung deals with the study of the projections of a better world that appear in human life: the impulse towards what is now absent never ceases. In fact, this void causes pain and suffering, and it therefore has to be eliminated. There is an inveterate wish of a better life and of the overcoming of a bad situation. As Fichte remarked, every human being wants to live in a way as pleasant as it may be possible, and since this is a common demand, shared by all people, everyone has the same right to satisfy it.

There is a projection of a better world in aspects as different as bodily exercise, the struggle for health, and the great social utopias. They all participate in a fundamental will: the will for something better. Social utopias, to which Bloch pays more attention, began as individual dreams which only displayed internally. However, they gradually became social utopias, like the utopias of Greece (e.g. Plato's and the Stoic utopia of the unity of human genus), the Bible (the utopia of the Kingdom of God, governed by love and liberation from all earthly chains), St. Augustine, Joachim de Fiore, Thomas More, Campanella, Owen, Fourier, Cabet, St.-Simon, anarchism and the individualistic utopias of the nineteenth century (Stirner, Proudhon, Bakunin . . .), the feminist utopias, the Zionist utopia, and Marxism as the concrete utopia.

The projection of the different spheres of human life towards a better future brings the category of *novum* into a central position. History is capable of offering a new scenario. In opposition to a cyclic vision of time, and even to Nietzsche's eternal recurrence, there is something really new in history. The *novum* is the "not-yet-come-into-being," analogous to the "not-yet-conscious" that emerges within the human spirit. *Novum* is a synonym of the incompleteness of reality and history.

The question is: what do these projections of a better world actually mean? Do they simply highlight the fact that in humanity, in the world, and in history there is always a horizon of novelty in the future that allows to conquer what is now absent and to achieve a better life? For Bloch, the projections of a better world can only mean that humanity is gradually becoming more humane and reaching a higher degree of solidarity amongst its members, since all of them are bounded by a common destiny: "*homo homini homo*," this is Bloch's key principle. Man is not a *lupus* for man, as in Hobbes, but a human being, and the challenge of history is to achieve a moment in which this sentence may be pronounced with the greatest intensity and pride: "man is a man for man." Regarding society, the projections of a better world mean that every man has to become a man for the other men: a humane humanity. Again, let us recall that for Bloch, unlike for Heidegger and for existentialism in general, there is a goal in history: that of a more humane history. This goal links humanity as a whole. It is the common goal of every individual.

The fifth part of Bloch's monumental work examines morality, music, the images of death, and religion. They all belong to what the German philosopher calls "desiderative imagines of the fulfilled instant." The treatment of religion as a manifestation of the presence of hope in human history is far from representing a concession of an atheistic thinker to the theistic perspective, as if the theological weight on the notion of "hope" eclipsed the humanistic and atheistic approach to this idea. Atheism is meant to affirm mankind and its possibilities. What we can be lies within us and within our own scope and reach.

Human beings, according to Bloch, are in constant disposition to gain independence and liberty. This is the root of all utopias. But human beings face the greatest possible non-utopia: death. The fear of death has been oppressive to mankind since its earliest stages. The utopian illusion of humanity pointing towards a better world, whose practical translation appears in the great accomplishments of technique and fantasy, has to cope with the fate of death as non-utopia, as the negation of the very idea of utopia itself, since it denies life. Death is certainly more serious and compelling than it was for Lucretius, who in *De Rerum Natura* wrote: "Now you lie in death's quiet sleep . . . removed from all distressing pains."[4]

Death could be seen as a final reward after a life of suffering: the resting relaxation that follows after an exhausting life, thanks to which all worries, all anxieties, all fights come to an end. But death also represents the end of a vital project and the annihilation of an identity. It brings a desperate concern about the meaning of our existence: why did we have

---

4. Lucretius, *De Rerum Natura III*, 904–5. See Quainton, *Ronsard's Ordered Chaos*, 137.

to live, why did we have to die? Why did we have to enjoy the pleasures of life, if these pleasures had to come to an end? Again, the risk of nihilism, as in Goethe's Mephistopheles, is legitimately present.

Death occupies a privileged position in the message of the great religious traditions, carefully analyzed by Bloch, including Egypt and Greece, the biblical resurrection in the context of Jewish and Christian apocalypticism, the concept of *nirvana* in Buddhism, and even the reflection on death in Western philosophical nihilism and the disappearance of the "lethal nothingness" in the socialist conscience by means of the idea of solidarity over time. The final stages of Bloch's study are atheism and the utopia of the Kingdom of God.

Religion, for Bloch, does not finish with its offering a solution to the problem of death: religion emerges as the most unconditional utopia that can be imagined. The high utopian ideas present in religion are an expression of the "frontier-content" of human mind. In other words: the history of the conscience of God in humanity is not the history of the conscience that God has of himself (as it could be thought in a Hegelian perspective: the absolute spirit is trying to know himself through human conscience), but the history of the conscience that mankind has of its own nature and of its own possibilities.

The trace of Feuerbach is clear. Religions show the highest possible utopian content that mankind is capable of hosting in its conscience, and all religions drink from the fountains of the intensity of their radical anxiety, seeking to anticipate an *ens perfectissimum* which constitutes the final content of that wish. Religion is therefore a utopia, specifically the unconditional utopia, because it is the utopia that comes out the most radical will that humanity possesses. The desiderative dimension of religion is an undeniable fact for Bloch who, along with the anthropological critique of religion of Feuerbach and Freud, thinks that a projection takes place of a human desire on a being other than the human being. However, Bloch does not consider this desiderative projection as an illusion, in the negative sense that it adopts in Freud's famous essay *Die Zukunft einer Illusion* ["The Future of an Illusion"], of 1927, for this illusion is not in vain: it represents an attempt, a rehearsal of a true utopia. It is, in fact, an illusion that stems from the constitution itself of human nature.

The horizon opened by utopia cannot stop in religion. Religion places God as the final goal of the utopian path. Atheism, which Bloch accepts, cannot accept what he calls the "God-hypostasis," the personification of the utopian will in a divine being. However, atheism cannot simply reject the utopian content of the idea of God. Atheism is forced to appropriate the unconditional and total content of hope that lies hidden under the label of "God." This keeps a close relation, in some sense, with the proposal of contemporary philosophers who, like Jürgen Habermas, have asked for a secular translation of religious contents: what in religions adopts the linguistic form of dogma and even myth may have a valid teaching for the secular world. According to Bloch, the utopian hope represented by the different religious traditions must be assumed by a secular rationality. If, to follow Goethe, we must win back what we have been given, it is our duty to extract the positive, utopian content of religions in our quest for a better world. "God" is, for Bloch, the hypostasis of the utopian hope.

Atheism sets that hypostasis away, but it inherits its content: the radical utopian longing, which in the great religious traditions lies hidden as a "longing for the totally-other" (Horkheimer), for the divine being. There is no personal God different from the human conscience, but the content expressed by the idea of such a personal God may be assumed by a humanistic, atheistic philosophy. Atheism, according to Bloch, is capable of liberating the utopian content from the numinous representation, rescuing the hope that it hosts. The point is not to "assassinate" the human creative fantasy which is present in religions but, in a similar way to the task undertaken by Hegel, to look for a specific philosophical concept to grasp the ultimate intentional content of that fantasy. Hegel wanted to find the concept beyond the representation, philosophy beyond religion; Bloch wants to find the utopian will hidden under the religious discourse. In both authors, religion has to be overcome by philosophy, and the religious representation associated to the human fantasy and invested with a huge utopian power must be overcome by the philosophical concept in order to reach its true value and its true meaning.

The religious impulse points above, to the heights, and it is an impulse forward: the utopian content of religions, now deprived from its continent (the God-hypostasis), becomes a hope thrown to the future. For Bloch, all religions have been gigantic attempts to interpret the deepest human secret, which is the utopian will, and no anthropological critique of religion will be capable of erasing such a utopian will. This critique can perhaps separate the utopian will from the God-hypostasis and the duplication of human conscience generated by the belief in God. God is no longer a being distinct from mankind but the utopian entelechy of the human soul. Atheism recovers the most genuine content of the idea of God, its *raison d'être* as an expression of the utopian hope of humanity.

This capital aspect of religious faith has been subject to a bright analysis by the great thinker of the Frankfurt School, Max Horkheimer. According to Horkheimer, there is a fundamental wish of justice to be fulfilled, of justice to be established. In spite of his rejection of a return to the times of theism, since injustice and suffering in history make it impossible, he admits that religion offers a critical value: religion is the expression of protest (as Marx already saw); it is a utopia that relativizes and challenge the present, and it constitutes an inextinguishable impulse that goes against reality, claiming that reality must change and justice must come. Religion seeks the totally-Other, but this wish is connected with praxis of resistance and solidarity in history.[5]

In any case, it seems clear that the end of the God-hypostasis leaves an apparently insurmountable abyss. This is the reason why many people will still believe in God in spite of the power of the atheistic critique since Feuerbach. What are we supposed to do with the emptiness that comes out of the denial of the existence of God as a personal being? For Bloch, the answer to this question resides in taking into consideration the fact that such emptiness is rather relative. Atheism has rejected the continent but not the content. Atheism abandons God as a being different from mankind, but it does not abandon the concept of God, which has a practical meaning in the realm of action. God disappears, but mankind and nature remain, both of them oriented towards the future. The essence of mankind is not complete: it is an unfinished reality, a "not-yet." It is a real-objective hope.

When asked about how he could summarize his philosophy, Bloch said: "S is not P yet,"[6] where P, the predicate, refers to a future that has not come yet [*ungewordene Zukunft*]. Marxism was, for Bloch, the universal inheritor of the hopes of the past found in daydreams, in the arts, in the utopias, and in the great religions.

---

5. Cf. Horkheimer, *Anhelo de Justicia*, 226.
6. Cf. Gibellini, *La Teología del siglo XX*, 309.

Bloch's thought poses a big challenge to religion and in particular to Christian theology. From an atheistic perspective, Bloch has shown that there is still place for a utopian hope, traditionally bounded to the theological idea of a Kingdom of God. Utopia is in the structure of reality itself, and the hope in a new world is free from any theistic connotation. Atheism, the death of the God-hypostasis, is seen as the condition of possibility of recovering the most radical utopian content. Hope takes root in the anthropological constitution of mankind and has no need of a being that transcends both mankind and history. Is theism dead? Is God a superfluous postulate, no longer necessary to conceive of a hope in a better future?

Let us remember that modern atheism is an eminently intra-Christian phenomenon. Atheism was born as a critique of Christianity. Feuerbach's study is a detailed exegesis of the fundamental contents of Christian theology. The infinite being is no longer God but the human being as genus: humanity is the infinite being for Feuerbach. Feuerbach's critique constitutes in some sense the most powerful attack on Christianity and religion ever made, much deeper in philosophical terms that the so-called new atheism (Richard Dawkins, Sam Harris, Daniel Dennett). What had been predicated on God is now predicated on men in their opening themselves towards a future that belongs to them. Is atheism the necessary product of Christianity and of its humanistic ideal? Bloch's answer is "yes." In his book *Atheismus im Christentum* ["Atheism in Christianity"], published in 1968, he offers a categorical aphorism, completed by Jürgen Moltmann: "only a good Christian can be a good atheist, and only a good atheist can be a good Christian," because the exhortation to "be like gods," which is present in both the Old and the New Testament, expresses an ideal of humanization and of elevation of human nature which makes the existence of God dispensable. Religious Messianism acted as a catalyst of the unity between the human and the divine, promoting an elevation of the human by itself, and leading to forgetting God. For Bloch, the atheistic critique of religion marks the culmination of Christianity, liberating mankind from the religious heteronomy and keeping the utopia of the Kingdom of God, which is the shape of the deepest, psychological wills of human beings. The humanistic and atheistic recovery of the utopian content is a task for philosophy.

History and Meaning

In Bloch, we find a consistent example of a philosophical position in which history has a meaning, but a meaning totally disconnected from a theistic conception of God. The meaning of history lies in the edification of a more humane world in which the utopian wills that exist in our nature may be fulfilled. History has, therefore, a substantial character: it is not the mere individual experience of history, the "historicity," that defines its meaning, but a deeper structure, which goes beyond the realm of individuals and does in fact bind all individuals: the utopian will and the project of a more humane world in which "*homo homini homo*" may become the ruling social principle. History has a horizon, and humanity has a task: what a different perspective from Heidegger, in which history, in itself, has no goal.

Of course, the fundamental conviction that history has a meaning is not an original contribution of Marxism. It can be found in St. Augustine's *De Civitate Dei* and in Jacques-Bénigne Bossuet *Discours sur l'Histoire Universelle* (1681), in which he tries to show that history is ruled by Providence, and that this same Providence is manifested in the reigning of Louis XIV, *Le Roi Soleil*.

The confidence in the action of Providence was transformed, with the emergence of the Enlightenment, into a confidence in the action of reason. Thus, Condorcet believed that human nature can reach an unlimited degree of perfection.[7] Condorcet wrote his *Esquisse d'un Tableau Historique des Progrès de l'Esprit Humaine* in 1793, when he was being persecuted by the revolutionaries and had to hide himself, putting down the whole manuscript by heart. How admirable indeed it is that Condorcet, in spite of the terrible circumstances he was experiencing at that time, could still keep an extraordinary degree of optimism regarding the future of mankind!

Condorcet identifies ten stages in the history of humanity:

1. The gathering of men and women into larger communities, with the birth of the first ideas of political authority and justice.
2. The transition into agricultural societies and sedentary life, with the birth of trade.

---

7. "La nature n'a marqué acun terme au perfectionnement des facultés humaines; que la perfection de l'homme est réellement indéfinie"(Condorcet, *Esquisse d'un Tableau Historique des Progrès de l'Esprit Humain*, 77).

3. The progression of sedentary peoples until the invention of alphabetic writing, with a gradual division of social labour.
4. The progress of the human spirit in Greece, until the time of the division of sciences around the age of Alexander the Great.
5. The progress of the sciences from their division until their decay, in which Alexandria was the metropolis of the sciences.
6. The decay of *les lumières* until their restoration by the time of the Crusades, which for him was a disastrous period in which the human spirit lost much of what it had previously gained.
7. The restoration of the sciences in the West until the invention of printing.
8. From the invention of printing until the time in which the sciences and philosophy triumph over the judgment of authority.
9. From Descartes to the formation of the French Republic.
10. The future progresses of the human spirit.

Condorcet, as we can see, pays much attention to progress in the realm of the sciences as a proof that our capacity to advance is practically unlimited. He thinks that just as we can predict phenomena by knowing their laws, we will be able to foresee the future of the human spirit by looking at history. Of course for Condorcet, like for many other rationalists, there is no place for chaos and unpredictability. Even Habermas accepted, until his rejection of this thesis in 1971, that history is the result of the self-constitution of mankind through labor. History could be entirely attributed to human actions. However, we frequently see how difficult it is to predict the direction of history. There are many factors that escape from our power of understanding. There is much complexity, which cannot be reduced to a linear addition of individual actions.

It is, nonetheless, surprising, when reading Condorcet, to be able to admire the astonishing degree of confidence in human nature that he shows, in spite of the terror that he had experienced during the French Revolution.[8]

---

8. "Nos espérances sur les destinées futures de l'espèce humaine peuvent se réduire à ces trois questions: la destruction de l'inégalité entre les nations; les progress de l'égalité dans un même people; enfin le perfectionnement réel de l'homme" (Condorcet, *Esquisse d'un Tableau Historique des Progrès de l'Esprit Humain*, 253).

The key is his belief in mankind's capacity of self-perfection, principally through education and science. The greatest progress in the realm of the human spirit is the destruction of prejudices and dogmatism. He finds consolation in history, by looking at what mankind has already achieved, which constitutes something eternal, permanent, some sort of unfolding of an eternal truth. This statement lies in the antipodes of Jean-Jacques Rousseau's *Discours sur les Sciences et les Arts* (1750), who argues that the sciences have corrupted human morality. The growth of civilization is no progression at all, for Rousseau, since it separates us from our condition of naturally good beings. What is surprising is that Rousseau's writing won the prize of the Academy of Dijon (the topic to compete for the prize was: "do the sciences and the arts contribute to the corrupting or to improving morals?"), when the Englightenment and the deification of human progress in civilization were at their height.

In a rather similar way, Immanuel Kant has confidence in the future of mankind. The Enlightenment fosters mankind's maturity: "Enlightenment is man's emergence [*Ausgang*] from his self-imposed immaturity. Immaturity is the inability to use one's own understanding without guidance from another. This immaturity is self-imposed when its cause lies not in lack of understanding but in lack of resolve and courage to use it without guidance from another. *Sapere Aude*! ['Dare to know,' which is found in Horace], 'Have courage to use your own understanding!'—that is the motto of enlightenment."[9]

The immaturity of humanity is self-imposed. We are to blame, since we have not had the courage to make use of our freedom. Freedom is a historical task, a historical responsibility for humanity.

In his writing *Idea for a Universal History from a Cosmopolitan Point of View* (1784) he admits that "in the end, one does not know what to think of the human race," since we experience the prevalence of many elements of irrationality, vanity, and lack of meaning. However, this legitimate indignation has to be followed by a rational inquiry into the principles that govern history, which Kant enunciates in nine theses:

1. "All natural capacities of a creature are destined to evolve completely to their natural end" (assumption of a natural teleology).

---

9. Cf. Kant, *On History*, 1.

2. "In man (as the only rational creature on earth) those natural capacities which are directed to the use of his reason are to be fully developed only in the race, not in the individual.

3. "Nature has willed that man should, by himself, produce everything that goes beyond the mechanical ordering of his animal existence, and that he should partake of no other happiness or perfection than that which he himself, independent of instinct, has created by his own reason." For Kant, "nature does nothing in vain" (this consideration is also present in Leonardo da Vinci's *Notebooks*, for whom there is nothing superfluous in nature). For Kant, if we possess the gifts of reason and liberty, it is because nature was designing us so that we were not lead by instinct. Nature seemed to have a goal: the self-growth of mankind, his self-constitution through his own actions.

4. "The means employed by nature to bring about the development of all the capacities of men is their antagonism in society, so far as this is, in the end, the cause of a lawful order among men." Antagonism is viewed as a means of progression, since it generates incentives to search for new forms of social organizations. In a completely peaceful, harmonic society, such a progression would not be necessary.

5. "The greatest problem for the human race, to the solution of which nature drives man, is the achievement of a universal civil society which administers law among men." This civil society is meant to unfold all human capacities, since human capacities can only be fully realized in the society with the greatest level of freedom. Nature seems therefore to have posed a challenge for us, humans: the achievement of a perfectly just civic constitution.

6. "This problem is the most difficult and the last to be solved." It is interesting to notice that, for Kant, the principal problem mankind has to solve is not the discovery of the laws of nature, or of our ultimate origin, but the discovery of our ultimate future as humanity: how we must live together in order to edify the best possible society. Rather than "what can I know?" or "what can I expect?" the principal question is: "what can *we* do?" In this sense, philosophy is principally concerned with mankind.

This tradition goes back to Socrates, who moved the focus of attention from *kosmos* to *anthropos* in the context of Greek philosophy.

7. "The problem of establishing a perfect civic constitution is dependent upon the problem of a lawful external relation among states and cannot be solved without a solution of the latter problem," a topic that Kant addresses in his famous essay, *Perpetual Peace* (1795). There is no utopian society if it is not universal. Here, like in Hegel's thought, truth is the whole. Otherwise, reality turns to be inherently contradictory, since one nation prevails at the expense of another nation, or one social class at the expense of another social class.

8. "The history of mankind can be seen, in the large, as the realization of nature's secret plan to bring forth a perfectly constituted state as the only condition in which the capacities of mankind can be fully developed, and also bring forth the external relation among states which is perfectly adequate to this end." The question is the following: is there such a secret plan, or are we imposing, *a priori*, the conviction that history is the display of our capacities instead of the scenario of chance and arbitrariness?

9. "A philosophical attempt to work out a universal history according to a natural plan directed to achieving the civic union of the human race must be regarded as possible and, indeed, as contributing to this end of nature." For Kant, the philosopher of history has a task, and reflection is never in vain: it has a goal. This is, in my view, a similar consideration to Habermas' famous division of knowledge into three categories (empirical-analytical sciences, historical-hermeneutical sciences, critical science), assigning to the critical science (philosophy) the task of contributing to the emancipation of human reason and to the achievement of a dialogue free of domain. History, for Kant, shows construction and destruction, but "seeds" of Enlightenment gradually appear, and history can offer the consolation that in the future these seeds planted by nature shall shine, and our destiny as human race shall be fulfilled on earth.

The conviction that our existence on earth must have some sort of meaning is very powerful indeed. Even Darwin, whose theory of natural selection might seem to open the gate for interpreting human existence as the result of chance (like, for instance, in the case of the French biologist and Nobel laureate Jacques Monod, author of *Le Hasard et la Nécessité*, of 1970), did not want to see evolutionary and human progress as meaningless. He admits that life on Earth will be, in the future, impossible, but since he believes that mankind will become a much more perfect creature, it is intolerable to think that both the human race and all the other beings on Earth are condemned to a complete annihilation after such a slow, hard, and continued progression.[10]

The most radical attempt to provide a meaning and a full rational explanation for history is, however, that of Hegel's philosophy. The key thesis of Hegel's philosophy of history is that reason rules the world and the course of times. The spirit, the substantial, permanent, and true reality, is displayed in history. The spirit seeks to acquire the highest conscience of its own freedom, and for that it needs to alienate itself in time. History is the history of the spirit's increasing conscience of freedom.

This statement is by no means esoteric, understandable only within the boundaries of the philosophical province of German idealism. Many people, still today, believe that in spite of all the tragedies of our time, we have achieved a higher conscience of our freedom, of our dignity, of our rights: we are the spirit that gains a deeper appreciation for itself. It is true that human rights are frequently violated, but it is also true that we are more aware of those violations than in times past. Centuries of philosophy, science, ethics, art, and politics gather an accumulated collective wisdom which it is impossible to obliterate. In Noam Chomsky's words, "Over the course of modern history, there have been significant gains in human rights and democratic control of some sectors of life. These have rarely been the gift of enlightened leaders. They have typically been imposed on states and other power centers by popular struggle. An optimist might hold, perhaps realistically, that history reveals a deepening appreciation for human rights, as well as a broadening of their range—not without sharp reversals, but the general tendency seems real."[11]

In Hegel's philosophy the reference to history does not take place in the realm of the particular histories of each people, but in the sphere

---

10. The citation can be found in Michio Kaku, *Parallel Worlds*.
11. Chomsky, *Hegemony or Survival*, 236.

of universal history. The spirit is displayed in universal history, and the philosopher sees himself compelled to think of history not as a rhapsody of actions which apparently have no sense: chance must be excluded in order to open philosophical reflection to the consideration of reason as the guide of history. Against a purely descriptive representation of the historical events, philosophy allows to regard universal history as the scenario of the necessary display of the spirit that looks for its own freedom. This is a fundamental philosophical principle behind Hegel's *Lectures on the Philosophy of World History*.

For Hegel, the spirits of the peoples have not emerged in a chaotic and disorganized way, but their ultimate cause is the activity of reason that, in its supreme freedom, grants itself different determinations. Philosophy in its thinking of history ends up admitting that there is a soul directing events which lies beyond all apparent contingencies.

There are, according to the great German philosopher, three fundamental categories that reflect how every change recalls the substantial, permanent truth of the spirit:

1. Variation: the changes in history are a response to the necessity the spirit has of denying itself in order to be born again, like the phoenix from its own ashes, but in a new shape. History is, according to Hegel, the hard and infinite struggle of the spirit against itself, negated in time. In *Sein und Zeit*, Heidegger has studied the firm relationship of spirit and time in Hegel's thought, and how the spirit actualizes itself in history. The progress of the spirit in history is not quantitative, but qualitative, since there is a liberating triumph in its historical path.

2. Rejuvenation: the spirit becomes younger again with every new determination that it acquires over the course of history.

3. Ultimate end: it consists of the absolute freedom of the spirit, which by overcoming all the former determinations has been capable of achieving the highest conscience of its dignity and magnificence.

History in its universality, rather than in its particularity (as history of each people), accounts for the display of the spirit and can be therefore regarded as a spiritual reality. Meaning belongs to the realm of universal history since it is there that what is permanent appears.

The question is clear: what is the spirit? As Pannenberg puts it in *Anthropologie in theologischer Perspektive*, the spirit is the presence of the true and definitive in the midst of the processes of history. Pannenberg, like Hegel, conceives of the spirit as the substantial reality underlying the contingency of historical changes (we can speak in terms of "the spirit of an age" or "the spirit of a people"). For Hegel, the idea of "spirit" is principally connected with conscience, whereas for Pannenberg, the theologian, it is principally linked with the biblical notion of life.

If universal history is, after all, the scenario of the display of the spirit, it must be ruled by the same rationality that runs the activities of the spirit. Such an absolute reason that guides history is identified with the religious concept of Providence [*Vorsehung*]. Universal history manifests the Providence of God in time. When the philosopher intends to understand the meaning of history, he is trying to understand the will of God and how it has been revealed in the historic course.

The peoples, like the ages, serve the spirit and are subordinated to its needs. They help express the concept of freedom that the spirit gains over the various stages it undergoes and which, for Hegel, can be summarized in three principal moments: that of the Eastern peoples, whose idea of freedom was extremely partial (only one individual, the despot, is free); that of the Greek peoples, who realized that some individuals, instead of only one, are free; and finally that of the Germanic peoples, whose religion is Christianity (the religion of freedom for Hegel), for whom every individual is free. The moment of the Germanic peoples, especially after the Reformation and the Enlightenment, is the maturity of the spirit. Universal history is the progress in the conscience of freedom. It is hard to find a more Eurocentric view of history, in which other continents and cultures are virtually forgotten or disregarded as "meaningless" for the understanding of the development of the universal spirit.

But beyond the limitations of Hegel's image of history and, in particular, of his radical Eurocentrism, we can see how current the fundamental focus of his thesis is: we admit that history shows many human failures and that progress is by no means uniform and universal. However, we also realize that now we have a greater conscience of our freedom, of our possibilities, of our rights, and we tend to judge other peoples, other religions, and other countries by virtue of the highest concept of freedom that we have reached. It seems as if it were impossible to go back to a "narrower" idea of freedom. This might be interpreted as a regression to the past. Progress as the advancement in our conscience of freedom may be under suspicion and criticism, but it works as some sort of subconscious principle in the modern mind. Otherwise, we would never propose ideals of freedom, justice, and equality.

In this sense, there was a very interesting debate between Michel Foucault and Noam Chomsky on Dutch television in the 1970s, in which Foucault interprets the idea of justice as a product of a Western, class-based civilization, whose ultimate concern is the expression of power (a claim of the oppressed classes and a justification of the oppressing classes), whereas Chomsky keeps a more universalistic, enlightened approach to the idea of justice (found in Habermas, too, with his idea of the Enlightenment as an "unfinished project"): there are universal criteria to judge something as just or unjust. This is impossible in Foucault's thought.

Hegel's systematization of the philosophy of history is an attempt to explain historic changes: why do some peoples decay while others, at that precise time, achieve leadership? Why does universal history appear as a continuous succession of peoples, kingdoms, and empires? Is there anything left, anything permanent in the middle of so much intense change? For Hegel there is no doubt: history serves the interests of the spirit. Peoples, in their particular spirits, allow the universal spirit to develop a higher conscience of its own freedom, but once that concept has been already expressed, and it has lost its interest, their activity ceases. These peoples vanish in the shade of history and are substituted by others. There is no reason to mourn: we must feel no sadness, because the decay of certain peoples and the emergence of others is a necessary step in the progress of the spirit towards its ultimate goal. The spirit is freedom, pure spontaneity, and it is not dependent upon any external reference to itself. The spirit denies itself because it wants to know itself to a better degree. It denies itself in history and it becomes determined in the succeeding stages of history, in order to achieve its self knowledge.

The spirit uses different means in order to achieve its goal, its self-knowledge: individuality is one of these means. The passions that govern the lives of the individuals, and which generate so many conflicts, serve the "astuteness of reason" [*List der Vernunft*]. Individuals transform history, but in Hegel's philosophy the ultimate cause of this transformation is not the individual will, but the will of the spirit that utilizes individual interests for its own sake. The spirit also uses different materials in which the gradual realization of the idea it has of itself is specified and concreted: the State, which represents the objectification of freedom, the *Rechtsstaat* ["state of law"], the spheres of life of a people (amongst which religion plays a central role), and the constitution of a country.

The goal of history is the ultimate goal of the spirit; the supreme concept of the spirit is the thought that thinks of itself (the Aristotelian idea of *noeses noeseos*), the absolute conscience of the spirit and of its absolute freedom once it has overcome all possible determination and has achieved its final synthesis.

What does Hegel understand, after all, by universal history? The basic content of his *Vorlesungen* is that universal history is the realization of the spirit, and therefore the evolution of the concept of freedom. The state is the temporal realization of freedom. History itself is theodicy: the justification of God demands the careful understanding of how He acts in history, of how history is actually the expression of his Providence. The examination of history is the justification of God: evil in history is necessary as the antithesis, the negation that makes the spirit adopt a further state, a further elevation [*Aufhebung*] in its way towards the absolute idea of its own freedom. Peoples and individuals serve the goals of the spirit, and the tragedies of life can be understood within the context of the progression of the spirit towards its ultimate goal. There is no reason to lament or even to dream of a history in which evil were absent: destruction is necessary as a prolegomenon to construction, within the dialectical path that rules history (quite similar to Joseph Schumpeter's idea of "creative destruction" in capitalism). Universal history, inasmuch as it is universal and transcends the realm of the particular histories of each people, expresses the gradual display of an eternal, substantial, and true reality, that of the spirit, that runs it in a rational way in its path towards its absolute conscience.

Within contemporary Christian theology the Hegelian conception of history has been highly influential in the thought of Wolfhart Pannenberg. In order to understand Pannenberg's idea of history, it is first necessary to take into consideration his approach to the method of knowledge. Pannenberg's epistemology is closely connected with the role he attributes to philosophy in the universe of the sciences. Philosophy poses the question about the ultimate meaning of events and in this point Hegel's trace is clear. Whereas the so-called nomothetic sciences look for causal explanations, philosophy seeks to grasp connections of sense, whose question refers to the "totality of reality," as Pannenberg writes in his work *Wissenschaftstheorie und Theologie* ["Theology and the Philosophy of Science"]. Neither events nor phenomena can be taken for isolated realities. The primacy of totality can be interpreted as an influence from Hegel: truth is found in the realm of totality, since what is partial demands the horizon of totality in order to be understood. Nevertheless, this experience of totality is always incomplete, because we never apprehend reality as a whole. It is necessary, for Pannenberg, to qualify Hegel's idea of totality through a concept which has been developed in Dilthey's and Heidegger's philosophies: that of anticipation (the Greek *prolepsis*).

The importance of the *Geisteswissenschaften* ["the sciences of the spirit"] resides, according to Pannenberg, in the fact that their methodology tries to place the meaning of the singular in relation to the whole in which it participates: the experience demands, as a condition of understanding, the idea of totality of reality. But such a totality is never given *stricto sensu*, though it can be anticipated as totality of meaning.[12]

The task of philosophy is the thematization of the totality of meaning, by examining the semantic relationships that are implicit in the different sciences, providing with a synthesis that is capable of transcending the analysis that each science performs in its level of research. Pannenberg is strongly committed to the Hegelian idea of totality as the condition of understanding of every singular reality, but, at the same time, he has also assimilated a more existentialist approach, manifested in the idea of anticipation.

The notion of "anticipation" allows Pannenberg to conjugate the defence of a total meaning of history with the statement of the unique value of singular events and, in particular, of the Christ-event. Let us remember that one of the principal objections to Christianity in the Enlightenment was expressed by Gotthold Ephraim Lessing (1729–1781): how can a contingent event stand as a universal truth?

---

12. This idea plays a very important role in Wilhelm Dilthey's thought: in opposition to the realm of nature, in the sphere of the spirit the "context" [*Zusammenhang*] is "lived," "experienced" [*erlebt*]. The context is "alive" [*lebending*] for us, instead of remaining abstract. (Cf. Dilthey *Der Aufbau der geschichtlichen Welt in den Geisteswissenschaften*, 142). For a detailed account of the different methodologies found in the sciences of nature and in the sciences of the spirit, cf. Dilthey's *Einleitung in die Geisteswissenschaften*, of 1883.

For Heidegger, *Dasein* has a basic void that makes him a "not-yet," demanding death as the mean of realization of its integrity, although at the cost of losing its condition of being-in-the-world. Anticipation is an expression of the essential lack of completeness of *Dasein*. Anticipation is, moreover, a task for *Dasein*, which is manifested in care [*Sorge*], since through anticipation *Dasein* disposes of its own existence, projecting it in accordance with its inner possibilities.

Pannenberg takes the idea of anticipation (which is also in the Epicurean philosophy, but in a more epistemological sense), but interpreting it through the mediation of Dilthey, who connects it with the unity of history.

Anticipation makes the conscience of identity possible, even in a history that has not ended yet. Every historic present can anticipate the final sense of history. But such a capacity of anticipation would be impossible if history did not constitute a unity. Anticipation, however, grants present peoples and individuals some sort of uniqueness that they lacked in a Hegelian perspective.

Unlike Heidegger, Pannenberg thinks that history is (following Dilthey) a net of meanings [*Bedeutungszusammenhänge*][13] in which all events are interconnected and recall a totality of meaning that transcends their particularity. Pannenberg criticizes Heidegger and Bultmann's reduction of history into historicity, into the concrete possibility of *Dasein*. The human being is essentially ex-centric, taking distance from its existential and historic position, and opening himself to a broader horizon. From the beginning, human beings have found a series of nets of meanings that they have not established. The individual sense of a particular event can be understood only in light of the final meaning of history. As Pannenberg writes in the second dogmatic thesis on revelation in *Offenbarung als Geschichte* ["Revelation as History"], revelation takes place not in the beginning but in the end of the revealing history. The understanding of history needs the consummation of history, the so-called eschatology. The proximity to apocalypticism is clear indeed.

The unity of history emerges from the connections of meaning that link all events amongst themselves, and the identity of every single subject is the result of the reception of a series of vital and social contexts: there is a focal point. By anticipating the end of history, it is possible to build up an identity. For Pannenberg, the conviction that history will

---

13. Cf. Pannenberg, *Anthropologie in theologischer Perspektive*, 499.

have a final consummation offers unity: the future end encompasses the multiplicity of both the past and the present events, integrating them into a unitary frame of understanding: that of history as a substantive, universal reality. An infinite, constantly unfinished history would make the quest for a unitary meaning of all historical events impossible. The presence of a focal point, although in the future, helps refer all events in history to a same objective frame of reference.

Every particular history recalls the future history, according to Pannenberg. This happens in the realm of life, too: life is ex-tatic, going out of itself. The life of the individual transcends itself in the community, and there is no individual without community. The spirit is the reality that transcends every individual and links every individual. Every community expresses a spirit: permanence and sense. The spirit anticipates in the present the unity that will be reached only in the eschatological realm.

Truth does not belong to any particular event but to the total process of history. However, truth is not, for Pannenberg, a static reality. The historical transformation belongs to the essence of truth, against a Greek conception of *aletheia* as an eternal, non-temporal reality (just as in Plato). The danger is, of course, the dilution of the individual within the historical process, and even the dilution of truth. The idea of anticipation plays a key role at this point: for Pannenberg, in the event of Christ an anticipation of the goal of the entire humanity and of every human being has taken place. History is open, against the Hegelian determinism, but history will not remain uncertain forever, since its final meaning has been anticipated in the fate of Jesus of Nazareth.

Pannenberg's future is an eschatological future, referred to the final consummation of history, which has been anticipated in the resurrection of Jesus of Nazareth. Unlike Hegel, past, present, and future history do not constitute, themselves, a theodicy: it is eschatology that accounts for theodicy, history regarded from the perspective of *eschaton*, of the ultimate consummated reality.

However, there is a fundamental philosophical problem with this conception. Pannenberg is speaking about the future, but not about any kind of future: he is referring to the eschatological future. Future could be open for ever. Is it legitimate, or even possible, to conceive of a definitive, final consummation of history? Like Kant says in his essay "Der Ende aller Dingen" ["The End of All Things"], of 1794, the idea of a final end of history goes beyond the power of human imagination. And, as a Christian, Pannenberg does not forget that there is mediation between history and its consummation: the final judgement. Between the temporal and the eternal there is a judgement. The theologian takes over the philosopher, because to believe or not that in Jesus Christ there is an anticipation of the eschatological future of history is an act of faith, although it could make sense.

According to Pannenberg, history is the revelation of God, just as for Hegel history is the revelation of the unfolding of the spirit in time in its quest for its ultimate conscience. However, such a revelation takes place only in history as a whole, as a universal reality, as the universal sense of particular events, and its final end has been anticipated in the fate of Jesus of Nazareth, the fate that we shall all share. Pannenberg goes as far as to state that history becomes universal history [*Universalgeschichte*] only after the eschatological event of Christ (his resurrection), since it is there that the future has been unveiled, and there is no unity and no universality without a focal point of history in the future.

Pannenberg's confidence in history as a reality which possesses meaning and orientation allows him to formulate a series of dogmatic theses on revelation[14] which try to show that God reveals himself through universal history, and that his final revelation will happen at the end of history:

1. The self-revelation of God does not take place in a direct way, through theophanies, but in an indirect way, through his works in history.[15] The Israelite religion might have evolved, in fact, from a more primitive understanding of God as manifesting itself through miracles and through specific interventions in history to a more spiritualized and transcendental view of the Deity, who reveals itself in history as a whole.

2. Revelation takes place at the end, not at the beginning of the revealing history.[16] The futurity of the historical process is, in fact, a guarantee of its having a meaning.

14. Cf. Pannenberg et al. *Offenbarung als Geschichte*.

15. "Die Selbsoffenbarung Gottes hat sich nach den biblischen Zeugnissen nicht direkt, etwa in der Weise einer Teophanie, sondern indirekt, durch Gottes Geschichtstaten, vollzogen."

16. "Die Offenbarung findet nicht am Anfang, sondern am Ende der offenbarenden Geschichte statt."

History and Meaning

3. History is open to all who have eyes to see it. It is universal, in opposition to certain particular interventions which only some people can, theoretically, contemplate, and *versus* all kinds of fundamentalism, fideism, and supernaturalism.[17]

4. The universal revelation of the divinity of God did happen in the history of Israel, but only in the fate of Jesus of Nazareth, inasmuch as in his fate the goal of all historic events was anticipated.[18] For Pannenberg, Christ actualizes the eschatological future. However, several theologians (e.g. Andrés Torres Queiruga[19]) have criticized Pannenberg, since the danger this thesis hides is that of ignoring the value of the religious experience of Israel prior to Jesus.

5. Christ's event[20] does not reveal the divinity of the God of Israel as an isolated event, but inasmuch as Christ is a member of the history of God with Israel.[21] In opposition to Hegel, for Pannenberg it is not the Incarnation, but his fate (his death and resurrection) which constitutes the most important reality of Christ's event. In fact, he accuses Hegel of monophysitism, of absorbing the historic reality of Jesus into the idea of Incarnation.[22]

---

17. "Im Unterschied zu besonderen Erscheinungen der Gottheit ist die Geschichtsoffenbarung jedem, der Augen hat zu sehen. Sie hat universalen Charakter."

18. "Die universale Offenbarung der Gottheit Gottes noch nicht in der Geschichte Israels, sondern erst im Geschichte Jesu von Nazareth verwirklicht, insofern darin das Ende aller Geschehens vorweg ereignet ist."

19. Cf. Torres Queiruga, *Repensar la Revelación*.

20. The expression "Christ event" also appears in authors like Bultmann (cf. *Essays Philosophical and Theological*, 286). According to John Hick, this idea is one of the possible answers to the problem of the absence of an exegetical and historical foundation of Jesus' divine self-awareness, and it is an alternative to a direct reference to the individual Jesus of Nazareth (now replaced by a reference to the effects of Christ in the existence of the Christian communities and in the ecclesiastical conscience). The "Christ event" designates not a concrete person but a reality that the primitive Christian communities experienced as present and actualized in their own lives. Cf. Hick, *The Metaphor of God Incarnate*.

21. "Das Christusgeschehen offenbart nicht als isoliertes Ereignis die Gottheit des Gottes Israels, sondern nur, sofern es Glied der Geschichte mit Israel ist."

22. Monophysitism underlined that Christ's human nature was absorbed by his divine nature. However, the sociological critique of the history of Christianity shows that in spite of its formal condemnation in the council of Calcedonia in 451 many elements of monophysitism remained in popular religiosity. Looking at the *Pantochrators* in the Romanesque churches in the West and in the Byzantine art in the East it is possible to see the enduring imprint of monophysitism in the Christian conscience.

6. The formation of extra-Jewish conceptions of the revelation in the Christian and in the pagan churches is an expression of the universality of the eschatological self-revelation of God in the destiny of Jesus of Nazareth.[23] Pannenberg interprets the assimilation of Greek philosophical categories by Christian theology (which had been strongly criticized by many prominent authors, including Adolf von Harnack, as a result of a process of "Hellenization" of Christianity, a betrayal of its Hebrew rooting) in a rather positive way, as a manifestation that the Judeo-Christian idea of God was universal enough as to being susceptible of adopting formulations that went beyond its original cultural substrate. A similar positive approach to Greek philosophy can be found in Pope Benedict XVI's speech at Regensburg in 2006, which goes beyond Pannenberg in saying that the assimilation of Greek philosophy was a necessity. The question is: does Christianity have to pass through Athens, or it can go directly from Jerusalem to other civilizations and to other symbolic universes? Is Christianity a fixed essence or a mutable narrative which becomes articulated under different cultural expressions?

7. The relationship between the word of God and his revelation is found in preaching, precept, and report.[24] The word of God as promise does not take place in the formulation of the promise itself but in its historical fulfilment; the recognition of the word of God in the Law and in the commandments is not in the text itself but in their showing the divine authority; and the word of God as Kerygma is associated, for Pannenberg, with the apostolic preaching ["*das Wort der apostolischen Verkündigung*"], driven by the experience of the resurrected Jesus.

Pannenberg's intentions with these theses on revelation are clear: he wants to go beyond supernaturalism and fideism, which concentrate the self-disclosure of God in the sacred words written down in the form of

---

23. "In der Ausbildung ausserjüdischer Offenbarungsvorstellungen in den heidenchristlichen Kirchen kommt die Universalität des eschatologischen Selbsterweises Gottes im Geschick Jesu zum Ausdruck."

24. "Das Wort bezieht sich auf Offenbarung als Vorhersage, als Weisung und als Bericht."

sacred books. Revelation must be a universal reality, opened to all, it it is really divine, against a rather self-centred approach, like the "theology of the word" of Barth (and particularly against his "theology from above") and Bultmann. However, in later years Pannenberg himself has moderated his theses, and in the first volume of his *Systematische Theologie*, of 1988, he speaks in terms of "revelation as history and as word of God," and not only as history, principally for two reasons: first, because the different biblical traditions about the word of God are, themselves, an integral part of the self-revelation of God through history, and second, because the expression "word of God" can be considered as a recapitulating feature of the revelation.

The fundamental problem involved in Pannenberg's approach stems from the question about the meaning of history itself. How should we interpret the meaning of history? History is not an objective reality, even if (*ex hypothesi*) we postulate, in theological terms, a disclosure of the divine reality over the course of times. In fact, Pannenberg is finally compelled to re-introduce the word (which he had rejected as the principal *locus theologicus*) into the historical fact through his idea of *Überlieferungsgeschichte* ["the history of traditions"], in order to be able to interpret a fact which, at first glance, offers no clear meaning.

MEANING IN HISTORY

The analysis of the four interpretations of history we have principally considered, namely those of Heidegger, Bloch, Hegel, and Pannenberg, shows that the question about who we are is inseparable from the reflection about our position in both space (world) and time (history). For Heidegger, the individual and his possibilities define history. For Bloch, history is ahead of mankind, and it is an expression of the constitutive openness of human nature to an eventual improvement. For Hegel, the individual serves a higher reality, that of reason, that guides history for the sake of the self-knowledge of the spirit. For Pannenberg, God reveals himself through history, but the final revelation will take place at the eschatological consummation of time. However, such an end has been anticipated in the destiny of Jesus of Nazareth.

Authors like Hegel and Kant, in spite of their deep differences, have tried to identify a transcendental foundation as the condition of possibility of a meaning in history: the logic of the absolute subject and the realization of the ideal of reason. Marx, on the contrary, limited the aspirations of the philosophy of history: meaning has to be produced as *praxis* instead of being deduced from a transcendental logic. Meaning is drawn from a historical and social situation, and it needs to be interpreted at each specific time. Philosophy cannot pretend to reach its self-foundation and its self-fulfilment: philosophy can only perform a critical task. As Habermas has remarked, such a critical task implies that the ultimate question is not, as it was for Leibniz and Heidegger, "why is there something rather than nothing?" but "why are things the way they are?" The critical function of philosophy is aimed at challenging history in its present constitution and not at intending to provide an absolute foundation for reality.[25]

However, can humanity renounce the possibility of a meaning capable of transcending the historical and social particularities, or are we condemned to accepting the inextricable force of the specificity of the historic moment, of the historic age, without any possibility of universality?

The dream of a universal meaning is certainly a great utopia, but it is possible to conceive of a transcendental foundation through the theoretical and practical ideal of a history that may be meaningful to everyone. If we were able to edify history in such a way that every individual and every society at any given time might find it meaningful and might recognize themselves in it, then we would have found, and also produced, the sense that we seek.

It is difficult to find a meaning for history, but it is hard to entirely refuse it. History is the scenario of ambiguity, and in some sense we must learn to live with this contradiction. But a legitimate quest emerges for a deeper understanding of a reality that seems to be incomprehensible, escaping our control, in which empires grow and fall and individuals live and die.

Moreover, it is more complicated to speak in terms of a "meaning of history" in a world in which many people have existed without enjoying any kind of recognition and happiness, and some of them are known only by their sufferings and disgraces. It is easy to keep in mind Aristotle, Galileo, and Einstein. They are all immortal in their works, in their extraordinary intellectual legacies that still today illuminate the present generations and create an ever growing admiration. But the majority of the human population will not have their names written in the history

---

25. Cf. Habermas, *Teoría y Praxis*, 408.

books, and they will be out of any kind of collective memory, although they live, of course, in the "spirit" of their age.

I confess that I find myself incapable of understanding the meaning of their lives. Some of our fellow human beings have only experienced misfortune and suffering. This shows the limitations of our reason. However, we still need to attribute a sense to life. Why? Some people need a meaning in their lives as the only way to dream with a future in which those stories of disgrace, loneliness, and pain will not recur. There is a shared wish that all men and women who have lived on Earth may be remembered and that their household may be the memory of the present and of the future generations, so that no one feels orphan in the only motherland, which is humanity. It is a rather utopian longing, but many people preserve it. It might be possible to accept an explanation of the world and of the human life that consists of defending that there is no meaning after all, but an eternal and blind process that leads to the emergence of life and consciousness. Meaning is given by humans. It is, so to speak, our contribution to the dynamics of the universe.

But again, this explanation seems to be insufficient for many people, as if there were some basic instinct that in spite of all adversities pointed towards a meaning. The reason may lie in compassion, in the longing for a vindication of the victims: we do not want to leave so many people who have enjoyed no happiness and no triumph without any possible hope of recognition. It could be enough to think that we are all parts of a reality that transcends us, be it the world or history and that we are elements of the great structures that build up nature. This idea of transcendence, of viewing ourselves as parts of a project that goes beyond us as individuals, includes those who had no fortune in life, too. Even if no one remembers them, even if their names will not be written in the books that summarize the collective memory and the collective aspirations of humanity, they will be present in the world and in history, because without them things would have been different. It seems that both world and history need us as their integrating parts in their progression towards a goal that we do not know.

Many people will find consolation in seeing themselves as part of a reality that transcends them. Religions identify such a reality with God. Be it God, the world, or history, it brings hope: maybe the sense of life is to build something that transcends us, to edify a world and a history and, moreover, to edify a humanity.

3

The Apocalyptic Conception of History, Evil, and Eschatology

THE GOAL OF THE sociological analysis of religious ideas is to help clarify the nature of the context in which they emerged, paying special attention to the motivations of the actors involved (individuals and groups with affinities and common interests). This is the way to reach a better understanding of the impact of the conceptions of some social groups and of why these ideas became hegemonic in a certain cultural space.

These considerations can be projected onto two fundamental axes: the one that links Hellenism and apocalypticism, and the one which connects apocalypticism and Judaism. We aim to study, on the one hand, the influence of the Hellenistic worldview in the origin of certain key concepts of apocalypticism, both in a positive (as acceptance) and in a negative (as rejection) way. And, on the other hand, we want to apply a similar analysis to the relationship between apocalypticism and Judaism: which aspects from traditional Judaism are assumed by apocalypticism, and which ones mark a distance (because of the assimilation of elements from a different worldview, endogenous or exogenous)?

HISTORICAL REMARKS

Society, Economy, and Culture in Palestine under Hellenism

In studying the connection between the multiple factors surrounding the irruption of Hellenism in Palestine and Ancient Near East since Alexander the Great (from 333 BCE to 31 BCE, date of the Battle of Actium),[1] Martin Hengel's work *Judaism and Hellenism* still constitutes a primary reference.

1. Cf. Sacchi, *Historia del Judaísmo en la Época del II Templo*, 219.

The Apocalyptic Conception of History, Evil, and Eschatology

The historical context drawn by Martin Hengel shows that Palestine never remained an isolated region in the ancient world. We find evidences of commercial exchanges as early as the second millennium BCE involving Palestine, Cyprus, and the Aegean isles. The presence of Greek mercenaries goes back to at least the seventh century BCE. In fact, Greek coins of the sixth century BCE have been found in a suburb of the Phoenician city of Tyre, aside from inscriptions of offerings to the god Apollo. According to Hengel, this means that the Phoenicians were the mediators between Greek culture and Palestine in the pre-Hellenistic period. The Phoenicians, a people characterized by their extraordinary commercial expansion throughout the Mediterranean Sea, favoured contacts between Greece and Palestine, although these contacts were limited to economical ones and they did not have a significant cultural influence.

What did the Macedonian conquest and the beginning of the cultural movement known as Hellenization of Palestine really add? Hengel believes that more than a radical irruption of totally novel cultural forms in Syria and Palestine, the Macedonian conquest might have intensified previous Greek influences in different ways.[2] And, even more relevant, the Macedonian conquest transformed Greek into the *lingua franca* of Eastern Mediterranean. Greek patterns in measures and weights were also adopted. It also allowed for an internationalization of trade and for the creation of a cosmopolitan culture in which an assimilation of Greek ideals and canons happened, in spite of the cultural variety of this geographical area.

After the death of Alexander the Great and the wars among his generals for the division of his huge empire, the Ptolemies from Egypt assumed power in Palestine. The rivalry with the Seleucids was constant, and it was a matter of fact that the Syrian empire was stronger in the military realm. However, the Ptolemies possessed great wealth generated by Egyptian wheat, which provided resources for financing their wars against the Seleucids. The Ptolemies adopted the ideal of an almost omnipotent sovereign, which was in radical opposition to the Hellenistic mentality. The king of Egypt enjoyed an almost absolute monopoly on products as different as oils and metals, and the monopoly in coining money. Egypt became a synonym of fabulous wealth. The domain of Caravan routes through the Palestinian and Jordanian deserts gave the

2. Cf. Hengel, *Judaism and Hellenism*, 32.

Ptolemies the chance to control the Nabataean kingdom, though only for a short time. But again, it consisted of an economically-centered domination.

This exclusive focus on economy could have had a positive effect for Israel, since the Ptolemies did not intend to export their cultural canons and their religiosity to neighbouring cultures: because their principal concern was the economic supremacy and the increase of their wealth (which would eventually allow them to beat the Seleucids and to establish their domain over the whole Middle East), they did not plan a religious or cultural unification.

The lack of a Hellenistic political perspective in the Ptolemaic dynasty meant the absence of an attempt to submit non-Hellenistic canons to Hellenistic standards. However, tensions did exist, especially in conflicts involving Egyptian lower classes and Greek upper classes, although they are class conflicts rather than cultural and religious confrontations. As Hengel shows, Hellenization became an alternative between poverty and wealth, rather than a cultural and religious option. The assumption of the Hellenistic culture represented the achievement of a new social and economic status, and keeping native cultural forms could have been seen as an expression of appertaining to less favoured groups.

Hellenization began as an economic phenomenon and later became a cultural and religious movement. Its changes initially shaped the class dynamics in the countries that fell under its impact, but they gradually experienced a cultural transformation. It is therefore more appropriate to speak in terms of the advent of the modes of economic production and of social organization imported from Greece and Macedonia,[3] which then became cultural modes. The understanding of the social and economic substrate of Greek cosmopolitanism is a fundamental step to comprehend Palestine in the last centuries BCE. The radicalization of the opposition of Judaism against Hellenism will only arise once Hellenism crosses the boundary of social and economic influence to interfere in religion and culture. The absence of significant conflicts between Jews and Greeks before the revolt against Antiochus IV supports this statement.[4]

Paolo Sacchi has also remarked the relatively high degree of religious tolerance that existed under the Ptolemaic rule, at least initially.

---

3. On the forms of social and economic organization under Hellenism, cf. Erskine, *A Companion to the Hellenistic World*, 331–54.

4. Cf. Hengel, *Judaism and Hellenism*, 38.

Furthermore, the interaction between the Greek and the Eastern world promoted by Hellenism since Alexander the Great had its first impact on the Greeks themselves. The Greeks tried to adopt Eastern manners, and they were subject to an intense influence coming from Eastern religious cults. Alexander assumed the imperial ideology of the East,[5] a sign of the fascination exerted by the Oriental world. The Greeks had a higher conscience of their freedom and of their individuality. Tolerance, even if not an ideal, was indeed a social reality in the Hellenistic world.

Hellenism favoured a progressive broadening of the concept of "Greek": classical philosophy (Plato, Aristotle) regarded Greeks and Barbarians as enemies, without a real chance for intercultural dialogue.[6] The Greeks were essentially defined by their membership to an ethnic group. The advent of Hellenism meant that the opposition between the Greek and the Barbarian turned from the ethnic into the cultural sphere: Greek is he who knows Greek language and customs (the so-called *pepaideumenos*), even if he does not belong to Greek race. Hellenistic cosmopolitanism and universalism, which recognized as Greeks not only those ethnically belonging to the Greek race but also those professing Greek cultural forms, left an important trace in Judaism. Certain voices, especially in the biblical books of Ruth and Jonah, had protested against the strict ethnocentrism of the Zadokite period, which discriminated the foreigner against the Jew, advocating for a different perspective, and in later times, a stream within apocalypticism made a decisive appeal to the adoption of universalism.

The impact of Greek culture was particularly strong in Diaspora Judaism, principally in Alexandria. Writings like the Letter of Aristeas show the tension between the inclination to accept Greek culture and the necessity of faithfulness to Jewish traditions. There was an inferiority complex before the evidence of Greek superiority in science, philosophy, technique, and army, leading many important people to adopt Greek names and to assimilate the logic of power of the surrounding world. The extraordinary cultural, social, and economic vitality introduced by Hellenism contributed to spreading the conviction of the existence of a *politeia*, a Greek citizenship capable of joining men beyond their ethnic origin. With the Greeks there was an astonishing expansion of knowl-

---

5. Cf. Sacchi, *Historia del Judaísmo en la Época del II Templo*, 224.

6. Aristotle goes so far as to suggest that the Barbarians have a more servile nature than the Greeks. Cf. *Politics* 1.2–7; 3.14.

edge by means of books; libraries were built and a deep anthropological examination of the nature of the individual took place not only through philosophy but also through the predominance of mystery religions, which integrated Eastern elements (such as the idea of salvation) and Hellenistic ideas.[7]

Hengel highlights the commercial boom in Palestine during the third century BCE: the production of asphalt grew near the Dead Sea, and artificial irrigation might have been introduced. In general terms, it can be said that agricultural and commercial production radically increased. Incomes and taxation grew, and so did the population.[8]

Again, Hellenism was at first an economic and social phenomenon. The Greek ideals of cosmopolitanism, rationality, and inclination to dialogue and to cultural exchange cannot be understood without the background of economic prosperity. The analysis of the evolution of religious ideas should not be separated from the awareness of this fact: not everybody was equally capable of taking part in the intercultural exchange, and the large majority of the population, living under deprivation, remained away from this process.

The economic development associated to the expansion of Hellenism was related to a particular way of communitarian organization: the primacy of cities over the rural environment. Hellenism was an eminently urban culture. Cities made it possible to establish important international commercial centres which concentrated a majority a large part of the trade with other parts of the Mediterranean. The Ptolemies promoted cities like Alexandria, whereas the Egyptian countryside was a mere supplier of agricultural resources. The idea of the Greek *polis* was present in the predominance of cities over rural areas under Hellenism. The general population (which in Egypt was concentrated in the country side) did not really take advantage of the prosperity of urban nuclei.[9]

---

7. Cf. Hengel, *Judaism and Hellenism*, 225.

8. Cf., on this topic, Albertz, *A History of Israelite Religion in the Old Testament Period*, 2:563–97.

9. This fact, regarded by Hengel as an "exploitation" of Egyptian peasantry by the Ptolemies and the Hellenistic aristocracy, together with the increase in the recruitment of enslaved labor, might have generated various social tensions. However, some natives felt tempted to compromise with Hellenism as a way of social climbing, intensifying the conflicts between the lower and the upper classes (cf. Hengel, *Judaism and Hellenism*, 50; Sacchi, *Historia del Judaísmo en la Época del II Templo*, 220), which gradually became a cultural and religious opposition. Concerning the importance of the "urban element"

The Apocalyptic Conception of History, Evil, and Eschatology

The latter situation was also experienced by Jewish theology. Priestly theology was quite ambiguous concerning wealth (perhaps because those in charge of formulating it assumed the ideas of the privileged classes), alternating praise and condemnation of money. Hasidic tradition, on the contrary, clearly opposed Hellenism, condemned the wealthy and sympathized with the poor. More traditional Jews, concerned with the increasing influence of Hellenism and with its potential effects on Jewish identity, condemned the accumulation of wealth. After the Maccabees, the tension might have been so strong as to restrict trade with foreigners, advocating for economic protectionism.

Goldstein has questioned the existence of a deep antagonism between Judaism and Hellenism, at least in the terms used by Hengel.[10] According to Goldstein, the condemnation or rejection of certain Greek cultural practices does not imply a rejection of Hellenism as such which, in his view, possesses six principal features: the presence of Greek individuals, the knowledge and usage of the Greek language, the influence of rational philosophies, the literary impact, the development of athletic education, and a characteristic architecture. None of these aspects was explicitly forbidden or rejected by the Hebrew Bible. Goldstein thinks that Ben Sira does not oppose Hellenism,[11] since he never uses this term (however, rejection might be implicit).[12]

Goldstein insists on the high degree of tolerance enjoyed by Judaism under Hellenism. The confrontation between Judaism and Hellenism would have crystallize only under the "critical period,"[13] between 175 and 163 BCE, after the reforms towards Hellenization issued by the usurper of the high priesthood, Jason. The creation of a gym in Jerusalem was not, according to Goldstein, the result of Antiochus' opposition to Judaism, but of his wish to create spaces for public meetings

---

in Hellenism, cf. Green, *Alexander to Actium: The Historical Evolution of the Hellenistic Age*, section "The New Urban Culture: Alexandria, Antioch, Pergamon."

10. Cf. Goldstein, "Jewish Acceptance and Rejection of Hellenism," 65.

11. Cf. Hengel, *Judaism and Hellenism*, 73.

12. Cf. Sir 2:12; 3:20–23; 41:8; his rejection of the dualism between the body and the soul contrasts with the more conciliatory attitude shown by the author of the book of Wisdom. Cf. Sicre, *Introducción al Antiguo Testamento*, 265–66.

13. Cf. Goldstein, "Jewish Acceptance and Rejection of Hellenism," 76.

of citizens, in imitation of Rome. Goldstein recalls that the Torah did not forbid entering gyms. Jason's reforms did not violate the Law.[14]

The problem with Goldstein's argument is clear: gyms posed no concern when the Torah was written, at least in its earliest stages, since a significant penetration of Hellenism had not taken place by that time. The controversy was focused on the interaction with the Canaanite culture.[15]

If Hellenism had not meant a first-order challenge for Judaism, we could hardly find stories of martyrs and a theological movement of the far-reaching implications of apocalypticism, which constitutes a cultural alternative to the Greek *logos*, even though it was heavily influenced by some of its ideas (and especially by its cosmopolitanism in the view of universal history). Goldstein bases his analysis on the undeniable fact of the acquiescence of many Jews to Hellenism, visible in the adoption of Greek names and manners, but he does not examine the sociological ground for this: which sectors of the population were favourable to Hellenization and which ones (the majority, in fact) had been excluded from the process.

Hengel's approach seems to be more convincing because it examines the polarization in terms of social groups and classes which stemmed from the process of Hellenization, centred upon the most privileged communities living in Jerusalem. Rural areas remained alien to the potential advantages of Hellenism. Had the matter been so peaceful, it would be difficult to understand the broad support that the Maccabees received in their revolt against Antiochus IV.[16]

The blossoming middle classes of Jerusalem, with small merchants and qualified workers, together with peasantry, distrusted the Judeo-Hellenistic aristocracy. The Maccabees came from the low Levitical clergy, and they personified the resentment against Hellenism, first

---

14. Cf. Hengel, *Judaism and Hellenism*, 81.

15. On the history of the Pentateuch, cf. Coogan, *The Old Testament*, section "The Formation of the Pentateuch."

16. It cannot be denied, however, that Hellenization had its own limits, since before Antiochus IV's reforms the linguistic, theological, and religious patterns that had been inherited from the traditions of Israel were preserved (cf. Collins and Sterling, *Hellenism in the Land of Israel*). These limits were associated, as Hengel has pointed out, with a strict distinction between the center and the periphery: Hellenization affected the upper social strata of Jerusalem.

social and economic and later religious and cultural.[17] The increasing importance of economy[18] and the power associated with money are denounced by certain wisdom texts: "A feast is made for laughter, and wine makes merry; but money [*ha-kesef*] answers everything" (Qoh 10: 19).

In the theological realm, Hellenism turned attention to problems that had not formerly played a relevant role in Judaism, such as the question about the scope of human knowledge (present both in Qoheleth and apocalypticism, not without the existence of contradictions between the two approaches). Sacchi thinks that a tendency grew characterized by its inclination to bring everything to its ultimate consequences, following the interest of Greek philosophy on questions concerning the world and human being.[19] The emphasis on the role of the individual and on the quest for personal salvation may be seen in the spreading of mystery cults all over the Hellenistic world, in an atmosphere of intense religious syncretism.[20] The increasing individualization of the different strata of the social life can be observed, for instance, in the Maccabean funerary practices: affluent families begin to build commemorative tombs for their members.[21]

Jewish theology adopted a universalistic orientation, especially under the form of apocalypticism, with its importance in the emergence of a vision of history as a universal reality. This gave birth to a universal eschatology, too. A change in the *Zeitgeist* took place, as difficult as it may be to thematize. As Sacchi points out, it is very interesting to notice how Hellenism involved the uprising of irrational and pathetic elements in Greek culture, while in the case of Judaism, its contact with the Greek culture led to an increasing quest for rationality and systematization.[22] There was a reciprocal influence.

17. Cf. Hengel, *Judaism and Hellenism*, 54.

18. Money promoted the relaxation in manners and the estrangement from traditional religious practices. This cultural materialism intensified the social differences between the upper and the lower classes. The impact of Greek culture was felt in all social realms: military, technical, economic, philosophical . . . The excessive attention to economy and money increased social tensions and prepared the way for apocalypticism and for the eschatological speculation on the cosmic wars (cf. Hengel, *Judaism and Hellenism*, 56).

19. Cf. Sacchi, *Historia del Judaísmo en la Época del II Templo*, 226.

20. Cf. Woschitz, *Parabiblica*, 37–41, on religious individualism under Hellenism.

21. Cf. Schaper, *Eschatology in the Greek Psalter*, 153.

22. Cf. Sacchi, *Historia del Judaísmo en la Época del II Templo*, 227.

Political and Religious History

The peaceful relationship between Hellenism and Judaism, which nonetheless had experienced increasing social tensions, came to an end under the rule of Antiochus IV Epiphanes. The Seleucids had controlled Palestine since their victory over the Ptolemies in the battle of Panion, 200 BCE. Then, Antiochus III (232–187 BCE) of Syria defeated Ptolemy V (205–180) of Egypt. This victory, however, did not represent a sudden assumption of political power by the Seleucids. Rather, it consisted of a gradual transition over a series of decades which also envisioned a deep evolution of Jewish mentality, and resistance to the Hellenistic cultural penetration and to its project of *oikumene*, which threatened to drown native traditions, was not exclusive of one time or region.[23]

The problem we face when attempting to learn about this period is the lack of historical sources. We must rely upon Josephus' book XII of *Antiquitates Judaicae*, but a large number of critics question its veracity, because it is closer, at some points, to a novel than to the historic genre. Meyer thinks that Josephus based his writings on three principal sources: a novel by Alexander, the Letter of Aristeas, and the novel of the Tobiads.[24] According to Josephus, Cleopatra, daughter of Antiochus III of Syria, married king Ptolomeus V of Egypt in 193 BCE, as the result of an agreement signed after the battle of Panion, leaving Phoenicia, Syria, and Palestine as an inheritance.[25]

Antiochus III could have allowed the priestly class (with Onias II as supreme priest) not to pay taxes, as a special privilege that contrasted with the general situation of the people. This exception caused serious social conflicts. The arrival of the Seleucids to Palestine favored a rather sudden irruption of Hellenism in Jerusalem. Under the Ptolemies, old measures against pagan influence had been effective in the preservation of the traditional Jewish culture. Now a superficial adoption of Greek manners prevailed in many realms of social life, in particular in the tendency towards religious syncretism and in the emphasis on individualism.

---

23. Cf. Eddy, *The King Is Dead*.
24. Cf. Sacchi, *Historia del Judaísmo en la Época del II Templo*, 232.
25. Cf. *Judean Antiquities* 12.154. This fact is also recorded by the Greek historian Polybius. On the discussion concerning the relationship between Josephus and Polybius, cf. Cohen, "Josephus, Jeremiah, and Polybius"; Eckstein, "Josephus and Polybius: A Reconsideration."

However, Antiochus III's victory resulted in bestowing different privileges upon Jews, as a response to their support against the Ptolemies. Fiscal exemptions were established, but they did not affect popular classes, because the agreement signed after the battle of Panion contained a clause under whose terms the Ptolemies could continue getting taxes from Coele-Syria, Phoenicia, Samaria, and Judea, with only few and unclear exceptions.[26] As aforementioned, priesthood was one of the only institutions that remained free from taxes. This fact must be added to the religious and political confusion that existed in the organization of Judea. It seems that Onias II, the high priest, gathered in his own person both the religious [*time arjieratiké*] and the civil [*prostasía toû laoû*] powers. Alarmed by the popular rebellions arising from the injustice of fiscal exemptions and the heavy charges imposed upon less favoured social sectors, Onias II asked his nephew, Joseph the Tobiad, to travel to Alexandria in order to negotiate a lowering of taxes. An agreement finally came, and a significant lowering of taxes took place. Under Joseph the Tobiad as the principal tax collector, Jerusalem reached a notable degree of economic and social development.

Wealth was everywhere present in Jerusalem, and the Temple kept important deposits which would be claimed later by Antiochus IV, but power was escaping from the hands of the high priest. Joseph was replaced by his son Hyrcanus in the task of collecting taxes. Hyrcanus was pro-Egyptian, while his brothers were pro-Syrian. One of his uncles, a son of Onias II, became the new high priest. His name was Simon II and politically, he was pro-Syrian. The first symptoms of internal disintegration within the Jerusalem community became manifest under the reign of Seleucus IV of Syria (187–175 BCE). The principal division was now between pro-Egyptians and pro-Syrians, and the high priest was no longer capable of managing these internal divisions.[27]

In 175 BCE Antiochus IV Epiphanes assumed the throne. Onias III, the current high priest, was favorable to the pro-Egyptian faction, expelling the Tobiad brothers from Jerusalem. His strategy was, nonetheless, fruitless, because his brother Yashua, who changed his name to Jason,[28] took over the position of supreme priest with the support of

---

26. Cf. *Judean Antiquities* 12.155.

27. Cf. Sacchi, *Historia del Judaísmo en la Época del II Templo*, 239. 2 Macc 3:4–8 gives an account of these increasing tensions.

28. Cf. *Judean Antiquities* 12.239.

the Seleucids, the promise of a greater effort in Hellenization, and the payment of a considerable amount of money. The high priesthood of Jerusalem had now passed into foreign hands, and simonist practices seemed to be the necessary key to access it.

Jason's commitment to Hellenization was behind the foundation of a gym in Jerusalem.[29] This gym was principally used by the wealthy classes, most of them coming from priestly lineage, and as Sacchi points out, the admiration for Greek culture was a synonym of the contempt for Jewish traditions.[30]

The situation worsened when Jason sent money to Antiochus IV with the intention of offering a sacrifice to Hercules. It was clear that a severe reaction would come sooner or later. As Sacchi suggests, the problem was not the assimilation of a Hellenistic *forma mentis* or the setting of cultural exchanges between both civilizations in themselves but the rather superficial and syncretistic assumption of Hellenistic practices without previously undergoing a true assimilation of ideas. Greek manners were adopted, but the ideological substrate of Jewish culture had not experienced substantial modifications, at least among popular classes and in such a short period. The deep values of Greek culture, principally cosmopolitan toleration, were confused with superficial syncretism, and hence the perception of Hellenism among normal people became negatively shaped.

In addition to this, the corruption within the institution of the high priesthood had reached such a worrying degree that a pretender called Menelaus tried to obtain the position from Antiochus IV via the payment of a considerable amount of money. Antiochus IV saw an opportunity to solve the financial difficulties he was living with because of his troubles with the emergent Rome.[31] Menelaus conspired to get Onias III murdered, but Antiochus IV's economic problems encouraged him to invade Jerusalem. Jason, who believed that Antiochus had died, tried to kill Menelaus as a revenge for his assault on the institution of the high priesthood but Antiochus, who was indeed alive, helped his protégé Menelaus and took advantage to plunder the treasures of the Temple.

---

29. Cf. ibid., 241; 2 Macc 4:9; 1 Macc 1:14. The fact that both 1 Macc and 2 Macc agree on this point, in spite of their frequent differences, seems to indicate the deep affront to the Jewish people caused by the construction of a gym in Jerusalem.

30. Cf. Sacchi, *Historia del Judaísmo en la Época del II Templo*, 242.

31. Cf. *Judean Antiquities* 12.246.

He set up a process of forced Hellenization and forbade the fulfilment of Law and circumcision.

The most absolute abomination, the so-called abomination of desolation (Dan 9:27; 11:31; 12:11), happened on the fifteenth of December of 167 BCE, when a pagan altar was built inside the Temple of Jerusalem: "And forces shall be mustered by him, and they shall defile the sanctuary fortress; then they shall take away the daily sacrifices, and place there the abomination of desolation" (Dan 11:31).

Sacchi suspects that the writer of the second book of the Maccabees is exaggerating when he claims that Jews suffered an intense and general persecution, for this would have gone against Antiochus' most immediate interests. Antiochus IV could not advocate a radical confrontation with traditional Judaism but only ensure his domain in Judea as a buffer against his enemies (the Ptolemies and the Romans). Many Jews were ashamed at certain practices like circumcision, and we should not forget that Antiochus, unlike Nebuchadnezzar II and later Titus, did not destroy the Temple. He probably intended to end with the Zadokite Judaism and not with Judaism itself. Traditional priestly Judaism rejected Hellenism, and this was viewed as a danger to the enhancement of Seleucid control over the region. At any rate, as Sacchi is quick to indicate, it would be too simplistic to reduce Judaism in that age to a dialectical opposition between traditional or Zadokite Judaism and modern or pro-Hellenistic Judaism. The question is much more complex.[32]

A twofold reaction happened: a political one and a religious one. The political rebellion against Antiochus IV sought to fight against Syrian power in Palestine, while the religious reaction confronted Hellenism and looked for the survival of traditional Judaism.[33] The Maccabees became the leaders of the revolt,[34] although some authors like Sacchi have serious reasons to suspect that their use of the Law had more to do with political rather than with truly religious reasons. Sacchi goes so far as to state that those groups which remained in Jerusalem and the surrounding areas developed a theology in continuation with the idea of

---

32. Cf. Sacchi, *Historia del Judaísmo en la Época del II Templo*, 245.

33. Onias IV, the son of Onias III and the legitimate inheritor of the Zadokite priesthood, went into exile to Egypt and built a temple in Leontopolis.

34. Mattatiah, the leader of the revolt against Menelaus and Antiochus IV, was not of Zadokite ascendancy but he belonged to a priestly family, the so-called *Yehoyarib*, who are mentioned in 1 Chr 24:7.

the covenant. On the contrary, groups fleeing from Jerusalem developed a theology under the light of promise. However, the theology of promise can be found in earlier biblical texts, too (for instance, in the promise of Davidic offspring in the second book of Samuel), although the birth of apocalypticism emphasized the eschatological projection of the promise of God to his people.

The merit of the Maccabees consisted of their capacity to capitalize on the opposition to the pro-Syrian movement led by Menelaus, under two principal flags: that of political freedom against the Seleucid Empire and that of religious purity against Antiochus's decrees. The revolt turned to be a true liberation movement against a foreign power.

Mattatiah died in 166 BCE and his son Judas assumed the leadership of the revolt. Judas reached an agreement with Menelaus, by which the latter would preserve the title of high priest, while admitting the political victory against the Seleucids. The triumph of the Maccabees had its visible result in the celebration of Hanukkah or new dedication of the Temple on the 26th of December of 164 BCE.[35] The ascent of Demetrius I (162–150), who was a nephew of Antiochus IV[36] and a son of Seleucus IV, to the throne of Syria, generated new problems in Judea. Demetrius wanted Alcimus to be named high priest, following the agreement reached by Judas and Menelaus that recognized the existence of two parallel powers: civil and religious. Demetrius' influence shows that the victory won by the Maccabees had not been as final as it might be imagined in principle: the Hellenistic party was still strong.

Judas the Maccabee was substituted by his brother Jonathan. In the Hellenistic side, the high priest Alcimus suddenly died in 159 BCE (153rd year of the Seleucid era, which began in 312 BCE). Jonathan was keen enough to become an ally of the Seleucid pretender, Alexander Balas,[37] a decision that would finally promote him to the high priesthood. The Hasmoneans achieved both the civil and the religious powers, aside from a relative independence from the Syrian rule. Jonathan died in 143 BCE and was succeeded by his brother Simon, who was elected

---

35. Cf. *Judean Antiquities* 12.321.

36. Antiochus' death is subject to different interpretations: whereas Polybius (*The Histories* 31:9) thinks that it was the result of plundering the Temple of Artemis in Elimais (Persia), Josephus regards it as a divine punishment for his actions in the Temple of Jerusalem (*Judean Antiquities* 12.9).

37. Cf. Sacchi, *Historia del Judaísmo en la Época del II Templo*, 265.

to the position of high priest by the people instead of being named by a foreign ruler. The Hasmonean dynasty had started.

The Hasidim and the Birth of a New Religious Imagery

Palestine was not alien to the deep sociological, economic, and political changes that resulted from the penetration of Hellenism into the Near East. On the one hand, an extraordinary economic and cultural development took place that convinced many Jews, and especially those who belonged to the upper classes, of the necessity of identifying themselves with Greek cultural forms, while on the other hand lower classes, closer to the traditional culture and deprived from the increasing prosperity, remained at a greater distance from Hellenism.

The Maccabean revolt of 167/166 BCE constitutes a turning point in the relationship between Judaism to Hellenism. It also shaped the identity of the Jewish people, and it meant the emergence of tensions and differences which had been latent for decades. The rebellion against the Seleucid power led to the foundation of an "assembly of the just" ['adat-hasidim], which supported the opposition against the Syrian rule. The importance of the Hasidim, the so-called just ones, and their decisive involvement in the emergence of the apocalyptic movement (which may have existed earlier but only acquired relevance after the Maccabean revolt) can be seen in the book of Daniel, whose origins seem to be connected with apocalyptic circles, having been written at the height of the rebellion against the Seleucids.

However, there is a legitimate question about the relationship between the Hasidim and apocalypticism. If the Hasidim were associated with the Maccabean movement which, as it is shown in 1 and 2 Maccabees, does not assume an apocalyptic theology (at least in its basic features), one could wonder about the degree to which they shared certain beliefs. This point is extremely difficult to clarify, first because we should distinguish the historical and political element (agreeing in a common opposition to the Seleucid king and to the challenge posed by Greek rationality) from the theological one. Although both groups might have agreed in their vindication of the Jewish heritage against Greek culture, this does not necessarily mean that they did it in the same way. They might have shared religious and political goals, without adopting the same theology on key issues.

Hengel[38] sees the Hasidim in clear confrontation with the priestly aristocracy of the Temple of Jerusalem. Coming from popular social extraction, they might have won the sympathies of large sectors of the population, who did not identify with the ruling classes in what they saw as an excessively Hellenized Jerusalem. Their proximity to the hopes of the average Jewish man of the time can be visualized in their inclination to granting primacy to the eschatological dimension. In opposition to an interpretation of the religion of Israel centred upon the identity of the people and the cult in Jerusalem, paradigmatic of the official priesthood of Jerusalem (and sanctioned by Ezra and Nehemiah), the Hasidim assumed the inheritance of a biblical tradition (stemming from prophetism) that highlighted the key role of the eschatological future and of the orientation of history towards an end of times in which all human action will be judged by the almighty God.

The upper classes of Jerusalem had no need of an eschatological radicalization in their approach to the Jewish religion, and they were more interested in a moderate hermeneutic approach to the traditions of their parents, compromising with Greek culture and rationality. Popular classes, on the contrary, could have empathized with a vision, that of apocalypticism, which gave them the hope to conceive a future renewal of the world and of earthly existence, when God would deliver justice to his faithful ones beyond any distinction in terms of social classes. In spite of the difficulty of supporting the presence of a fixed binomial involving eschatological emphasis and social class, it seems clear that a lower or higher compromise to present life is going to influence the adoption of one or another perspective: eschatology offers a discourse of liberation for those who suffer in the present, whereas those who enjoy privilege do not seek a transformation of the world from the current status.[39]

Hengel thinks that at first, the Hasidim respected and even promoted the strict fulfilment of the Law. However, the Hasidim gradually chose the way of isolation, as to finally set their own movement, defined by the stress put on penitence (Dan 9:4–19). The Enochic cycle[40] accounts for this inclination towards penitence. The so-called *Epistle of Enoch*

---

38. Cf. Hengel, *Judaism and Hellenism*, 178.

39. On the social and political implications of eschatology, cf. Gutiérrez, *A Theology of Liberation*, chapter 11: "Eschatology and Politics."

40. We will refer to the "Pentateuch of Enoch" in the following section.

The Apocalyptic Conception of History, Evil, and Eschatology 91

(*1 Enoch* 91–108) is in continuity with Daniel's prayer, and according to Hengel it manifests the genuinely penitential spirit of apocalypticism.

The "Damascus Document" (DD) constitutes a valuable testimony in the study of the birth of the apocalyptic movement. It is unknown whether this document tells about the uprising of the Essene movement or if it rather refers to a split inside the Essene movement itself. The document explains that three hundred and ninety years after the destruction of the Temple of Jerusalem by Nebuchadnezzar II of Babylon a Jewish movement claiming for a return to the quintessence of Judaism arose. This might have occurred in the beginning of the second century BCE and before the Maccabean revolt, if we should take the date of "three hundred and ninety years" literally. Perhaps as a response to the increasing Hellenization of the ruling classes in Israel and to the tensions that blossomed in this period, a series of religious groups decided to separate themselves from official Judaism. They might have considered themselves the representatives of the true Israel, in opposition to the perversion/betrayal generated by those sectors in Jerusalem, which compromised with Greek culture and power. Some twenty years later, a figure known as "Master of Justice" joined that separation, acquiring a preponderant role in the definition of the identity of these groups which pretended to recover the true Israel. Later on, this movement might have experienced a rather strict organization.[41]

Those groups separated from the official Judaism found their principal reason of existence in the rejection of Hellenism more than in the illegitimacy of the Hasmoneans becoming high priests. There is considerable evidence, however, that these groups were subject to the assimilation of Hellenistic elements into their theological conceptions (particularly in their emphasis on the individual destiny and in their systematization of history, in a process which Hengel calls "critical enlightenment," inspired by the interaction of Jewish thought with the Greek canons of rationality[42]), which are even manifest in other Near Eastern peoples much earlier than Hellenism.[43]

The phenomenon of the Essenes, also called Essenism, is undoubtedly one of the most relevant movements to bring into consideration in

---

41. Cf. Sacchi, *Historia del Judaísmo en la Época del II Templo*, 251.

42. Cf. Hengel, *Judaism and Hellenism*, 208.

43. Cf. Wilford, "Found," an article about a 2800-year-old monument to the soul of a ruler, discovered in Turkey.

the efforts to understand the separation of some groups from the official Judaism of Jerusalem and the forms adopted by their theological ideas. The communities settled on the shore of the Dead Sea, generally linked to the Essenes of Flavius Josephus, might have created some kind of self-sufficient society, independent of the rest of Israel.

However, after the recent archaeological excavations in Qumran the self-sufficiency and the degree of separation from the official Israel have been questioned. Archaeologists Magen and Peleg are the authors of "The Qumran Excavations: 1993–2004; Preliminary Report," commissioned by the Israel Concil of Antiquities. In their opinion, it does not make sense to think that a series of works demanding large human and material resources such as towers, pools, stables, channels for water supply, and other infrastructures[44] as those found in Qumran could haven been built by a community which, at least in theory, remained in radical opposition to the Hasmonean government. These rulers would have never allowed this division because, on account of what we know from Josephus,[45] they were rather intolerant in religious matters. The economic and social progress experienced in the area of Qumran under the Hasmoneans can only be explained if we admit that those communities had the approval from the governors in Jerusalem.

Magen and Peleg conclude that Qumran was developed by the Hasmoneans themselves, as part of a system of fortresses along the valley of the Jordan River. This military function might have endured until the Roman conquest.[46] There is no evidence to think that Qumran was chosen to accommodate certain groups willing to be isolated from the rest of Israel.

And concerning the scrolls found in Qumran, Magen and Peleg suggest that during the first revolt against the Romans some groups might have moved important documents and deposited them into the Qumran caves. This hypothesis explains the broad range of dates given by carbon-14 on the Dead Sea Scrolls (from the third century BCE to

---

44. The works apparently began in the Iron Age (phase A), and they were carried on by the Hasmoneans (phase B and phase C) and continued from the Roman conquest to the earthquake of the year 31 BCE (phase D). Phase E might go back to the war of 66 CE and phase F to Bar Kokhba's revolt.

45. Cf. *Judean Antiquities* 13.257–58, 398–411; 15.253–54.

46. Cf. Magen and Peleg, "The Qumran Excavations: 1993–2004," 30.

70 CE) and the fact that the biblical texts do not always correspond to a sectarian interpretation of the Bible.

Regarding the sectarian writings, Magen and Peleg think that they were not written by the Essenes alone, but by many other religious sects, and hence the disparity of materials which have been found: apocalyptic, Zadokite, non-apocalyptic writings.[47]

Magen and Peleg do not deny the existence of a separated group of sectarian nature within Judaism, which could be identified with Essenism. They contest the generally held conviction that this group constituted an organized and self-sufficient community separated from the official Israel. In this way, the considerations accumulated from the study of the theology reflected in the Dead See Scrolls (especially in the sectarian documents) are still valid in characterizing certain Second Temple Jewish streams.

If the discussion on the nature of Essenism is far from being closed, the same can be said of the relationship between Essenism and apocalypticism: were the Essenes a subgroup within a movement of broader scope called apocalypticism, or are they different and occasionally coincident movements? Although apocalypticism may be prior to the revolt against Antiochus IV, it is clear that the events surrounding the rebellion against the Seleucid rule created a sociological, theological, and cultural atmosphere that favoured the emergence of apocalypticism. In the beginning of the Maccabean reign apocalypticism and Essenism might have shared a sentiment of rejection against official Judaism.

There are common theological themes and literary genres shared by both apocalypticism and Essenism. An example of this is given by the emphasis on the eschatological wars involving Good and Evil in a scenario which recalls dualism, the importance of the division of time in clearly defined stages, which mark an orientation to the course of history, and the interest in the origin of evil. Essenism, however, seems to stress anticipated eschatology through the belief in the angels living already in the community. Qumran could have adopted the apocalyptic tradition of Daniel and *1 Enoch* in its own, distinctive way.[48]

---

47. Cf. ibid., 65.

48. Cf. García Martínez, "Apocalypticism in the Dead Sea Scrolls," 191. As García Martínez remarks, the relationship between apocalypticism and Essenism depends, to a large extend, on our understanding of the term "apocalyptic": if we admit a vague definition of this phenomenon as consisting of a divine revelation about an imminent

If Qumran was not, as Magen and Peleg suggest, a place of voluntary isolation for religious communities separated from official Judaism, the immediate conclusion coming up is the extreme confusion that existed in the eschatological beliefs of the moment. If groups such as the Essenes experienced a certain degree of toleration from other Jewish streams, with whom they shared much in common, we should not speak of any eschatological doctrine to be exclusive of the Essenes.

It seems necessary to admit the existence of a great variety of eschatological beliefs in Judaism in the third, second, and first centuries BCE. The fact that books with so diverse approaches to eternal life as Qoheleth, Ben Sira, and the different parts of *1 Enoch* were written by this period is a signal that a consensus on Jewish eschatology did not exist until much later. This might also explain the relative ambiguity of the Dead See Scrolls concerning eternal life, which reflect the simultaneous presence of elements taken from traditional eschatology, from realized or anticipated eschatology, and perhaps from transcendental eschatology, too (as suggested by Émile Puech).[49] The same can be said of *1 Enoch*, in which divergent ideas such as immortality of the soul and resurrection find a common place, and only after 70 CE was a more systematic and exclusivist eschatological formulation adopted.

SYSTEMATIC REMARKS: THE NATURE OF APOCALYPTICISM

Characterizing Apocalypticism

Apocalypticism played an essential role in the emergence and development of the belief in the resurrection of the dead in Second Temple Judaism.

Although, as Paolo Sacchi has pointed out, there is no interpretation of apocalypticism which may be regarded as final,[50] it seems clear that this movement possesses a series of characteristic features.

---

end of the struggle between good and evil, it is easy to find apocalypticism in Qumran. However, if the definition of "apocalypticism" is more restrictive, excluding the presence of anticipatory eschatology, it will be hard to find it in Qumran.

49. Cf. Puech, *La Croyance des Essèniens en la Vie Future*.

50. Paolo Sacchi thinks in his book *L'Apocalittica Giudaica e la Sua Storia* that much of the disagreement concerning the term "apocalyptic" is due to the fact that scholars tend to project their own aprioristic categories onto the texts which they study. This systematic and normative interest often generates the incapacity to adopt

Paul Hanson[51] proposes a terminological clarification in order to avoid a misleading use of the word:

1. Apocalypticism as literary genre
2. Apocalypticism as eschatology
3. Apocalypticism as symbolic universe

To these three factors suggested by Hanson one could add the consideration of apocalypticism as a sociological, political, and historical phenomenon: a symbolic universe inserted into a cultural space.

John J. Collins' definition of apocalypticism has become famous: "An apocalypse is a genre of revelatory literature with a narrative framework in which a revelation is mediated by an otherworldly being to a human recipient, disclosing a transcendent reality which is both temporal, insofar as it envisages eschatological salvation, and spatial, insofar as it involves another, supernatural world."[52]

Collins makes a programmatic distinction between apocalypticism and eschatology, which avoids misinterpretations that tend to conflate the two concepts. Apocalypticism as a literary genre consists of a revelation about the heavenly world and the eschatological judgement. Eschatology groups the series of themes referring to the end of history and the future life of the individual. Apocalypticism includes the eschatological themes, but not all the eschatology is apocalyptic.

The scientific interest in apocalypticism goes back to the nineteenth century, with the publication of texts such as *Ethiopic Enoch* in 1821 by Lawrence,[53] who also edited the *Ascension of Isaiah*. Lücke recognized the role of *1 Enoch* in the understanding of apocalypticism, but the principal problem at the time was the lack of apocalyptic literature written in Hebrew, an absence that would only be solved with the discovery of the Dead Sea Scrolls. It was suspected that apocalypticism was not a genuine Jewish movement, a doubt that came to an end with the Qumran texts.

---

a more "flexible" perspective. However, Sacchi himself finds a defining axis of apocalypticism in the problem of evil: man's guilt assumes a cosmic dimension that liberates it from an individualistic frame. Evil is not only the result of man's conscious, responsible transgression but it possesses a cosmic dimension that goes beyond the reach of the individual action.

51. Cf. Hanson, *The Dawn of Apocalyptic*, 11–12.
52. Collins, "Towards the Morphology of a Genre," 40–46.
53. Cf. Collins, *Apocalypticism in the Dead Sea Scrolls*, 2.

There are two types of apocalyptic literature, according to Collins. The first is concerned with the unveiling of history, and it is therefore of great relevance to the theology of history.[54] The second one has the pretension to show the mysteries of the celestial world.[55] Both of them share the common feature of presenting themselves as supernatural revelations mediated by a heavenly being, and both of them deal with topics such as the end of life, the end of history, and the following transformation of creation at the end of times. These revelations exceed the human capacity to know. The fact of basing the authority of these revelations upon legendary figures like Enoch granted credibility.

Regarding eschatology, Collins thinks that apocalypticism represented a turning point, which favored the advent of the belief in physical resurrection, judgement, and punishment and reward after death. Certain writings imagine the end of life in terms of reaching an angelic state, which Collins prefers not to identify with Paul's glorious body. In this way, *1 Enoch* 104 reserves for the just people the destiny of participating in the heavenly, angelic world.

When discussing Gerhard von Rad's thesis[56] which connects apocalypticism with wisdom rather than with prophetic literature, Collins coincides with the majority of scholars in the rejection of this idea, at least in its general terms, but he concedes that there are elements of wisdom present among other functional and structural features of apocalypticism. Anyway, "apocalypticism is not simply late prophecy but is rather a new phenomenon of the Hellenistic age, which drew on many streams of tradition." [57]

However, the question is whether it is legitimate or not to speak in terms of an apocalyptic *Weltanschauung*. As Collins suggests, apocalypticism is not a mere literary movement, because it possesses certain dimensions that go beyond literature, touching society and ideology.[58]

---

54 Wolfhart Pannenberg's work *Offenbarung als Geschichte* includes, in several of its dogmatic theses on revelation, an explicit mention of apocalypticism and of its role in the birth of the idea of a universal history with an eschatological orientation. Cf. Pannenberg et al., *Offenbarung als Geschichte*, 211.

55. Cf. Collins, *Apocalypticism in the Dead Sea Scrolls*, 3.

56. Cf. von Rad, *Theologie des Alten Testaments*.

57. Collins, *Apocalypticism in the Dead Sea Scrolls*, 7.

58. It needs to be noticed, however, that the centrality of eschatology in apocalypticism has been relativized by authors like C. Rowland (in *The Open Heaven: A Study of Apocalyptic in Judaism and Early Christianity*, 1982). In his view, the eschatological

The Apocalyptic Conception of History, Evil, and Eschatology

Regarding the realm of essential characteristics of apocalypticism, Collins mentions historical determinism (although most apocalyptic writings recognize the freedom to choose good and evil) and the belief in divine judgement, both final and individual. If central parts of the Hebrew Bible saw no goal for life beyond earthly existence, and prosperity appeared as prosperity for future generations instead of a future beatific afterlife, apocalypticism understands the meaning of life as a participation in the heavenly and angelic world. However, "it is impossible to say how widely this view was shared. Key elements of it were rejected by some groups (e.g., the Sadducees rejected the judgement of the dead). But neither was it peculiar to a particular sect or the product of a single movement." [59] In fact, during the second century BCE apocalypticism and a more traditional Judaism that is opening its mind to Greek culture do coexist (as can be seen in the contraposition of books like Daniel and Ben Sira). And we should not forget that the apocalyptic movement, in the literary realm, is not limited to a single genre (apocalypses), but it encompasses other genres such as oracles (e.g., the Sibylline Oracles).

Russell[60] finds the essence of apocalypticism in the conviction of being able to reveal divine secrets hidden in heaven: "But there is a God in heaven who reveals secrets [רזין, μυστήρια], and He has made known to King Nebuchadnezzar what will be in the latter days" (Dan 2:28).

In this way, the "apocalyptic" consists of an attempt to unveil what is now hidden in a level of reality higher than the ordinary realm of the

---

element is not the most distinctive feature of the apocalyptic writings, and it should not become the principal focus of the study of this religious movement (cf. ibid., 26). According to Rowland, the essence of apocalypticism is the "disclosure of the divine secrets through direct revelation" (ibid.). In any case, does Rowland's criticism of the traditional conception of apocalypticism refer to the form or to the content? Apocalypticism may respond to Rowland's interpretation in the realm of the "form" through which its content is transmitted, but it seems necessary to admit that in the content itself eschatology plays a very significant role. Rowland warns against the danger of thinking that apocalyptic eschatology constituted some sort of coherent whole (cf. ibid., 37), but few authors would dare to speak in terms of a "coherent eschatology" within apocalypticism, because of the unquestionable variety of its eschatological ideas. What is original to apocalypticism is the idea itself of a transcendental eschatology, which endorses the possibility of life after death. The absence of a unified eschatology may affect the specific content, but not the fundamental concern about a transcendental meaning for human life. For a criticism of Rowland's thesis, cf. Collins, Review of *The Open Heaven: A Study of Apocalyptic in Judaism and Early Christianity*, 465–67.

59. Collins, *Apocalypticism in the Dead Sea Scrolls*, 8.
60. Cf. Russell, *Divine Disclosure*, 82.

world in which humans dwell. It is a kind of knowledge that God alone can reveal.

For Russell, this conscience of revealing the divine, hidden dimensions can be seen in three principal areas: cosmology, the meaning of history, and eschatology.

Concerning cosmology, apocalypticism highlights the role of God as keeper of the order of nature. The *Astronomical Book*, one of the oldest sections of *1 Enoch*,[61] explicitly touches the topic of the laws ruling

---

61. The Enochic cycle, the so-called Pentateuch of Enoch, is a canonical book for some Christian denominations such as the Ethiopian Church. Since R. H. Charles it has been generally divided into five parts:

1. The *Book of Watchers* (chapters 1–36)
2. The *Book of the Parables of Enoch* (chapters 37–71)
3. The *Astronomical Book* (chapters 72–82)
4. The *Book of Dreams* (chapters 83–90)
5. The *Epistle of Enoch* (chapters 91–107)

These five books were written in different periods. The Astronomical Book is normally regarded as the oldest one. It is found in Qumran's cave 4, and paleographical analyses date it around 200 BCE, even though some scholars suggest that it might have been composed under the Persian rule (cf. Nickelsburg, *Jewish Literature between the Bible and the Mishnah*, 48; Vanderkam, *Enoch and the Growth of an Apocalyptic Tradition*, 80). Sacchi dates it later than the Book of Watchers and before 200 BCE (cf. Sacchi, *Historia del Judaísmo en la Época del II Templo*, 195). The Aramaic fragments from Qumran indicate that the Ethiopic version we have is only a summary of a much larger initial book. The Astronomical Book narrates Enoch's cosmic journey, describing the movements of the celestial bodies. Enoch was guided by Uriel (in Hebrew, "light of God"). The Book of Watchers is slightly later than the *Astronomical Book*, although prior to 170 BCE, since we have certitude that it was known before the death of Judas Maccabeus (cf. Sacchi, *Historia del Judaísmo en la Época del II Templo*, 111). Sacchi supports an earlier dating, bringing it back to the beginning of the second Zadokite period (400–200 BCE), due to the density of its theological thought (cf. Sacchi, *Historia del Judaísmo en la Época del II Templo*, 189). However, the continuous references to the so-called giants (possibly related to the wars between the Ptolemies and the Seleucids) and the sophisticated geography of the "afterlife" suggest that the book cannot be as early as proposed by Sacchi. The book offers an eschatological development (in the account of the second journey) that clearly exceeds the cosmological perspective of the Astronomical Book. Chapters 1–5 deal with the imminence of judgement, 6–11 with the rebellion of angels (the so-called watchers), and the reference to battles involving giants might respond to the historical context in which the book was written (the wars between Alexander's generals—cf. Nickelsburg, *Jewish Literature between the Bible and the Mishnah*, 52). In 12–16, Enoch enters the celestial temple, and in 17–19 he travels to the west, to the throne of God. In 20–36 he travels to the centre of the Earth, which is Jerusalem. The Book of Dreams is probably contemporary to the Book of Daniel. It consists of an allegoric apocalypse about the historical moment, and it finishes with a theophany in which God appears to judge the rebel angels, those who have disobeyed

The Apocalyptic Conception of History, Evil, and Eschatology

heavenly bodies and offers a series of mathematical calculations. The almighty God maintains order in the cosmos. Daniel sees "the throne of God" (cf. Dan 7), and Enoch manages to enter the dwelling of the Most High and to contemplate his throne:

> And behold there was an opening before me (and) a second house which is greater than the former and everything was built with tongues of fire. And in every respect it excelled (the other)—in glory and great honor—to the extent that it is impossible for me to recount to you, concerning its glory and greatness. As for its floor, it was of fire and above it was lightning and the path of the stars: and as for the ceiling, it was flaming fire. And I observed and saw inside it a lofty throne—its appearance was like crystal and its wheels like the shining sun: and (I heard?) the voice of the cherubim: and from beneath the throne were issuing streams of flaming fire. It was difficult to look at it. And the Great Glory was sitting upon it—as for his gown, which was shining more brightly than the sun, it was whiter than any snow. None of the angels was able to come in and see the face of the Excellent and the Glorious One; and no one of the flesh can see him—the flaming fire was round about him, and a great fire stood before him. No one could come near unto him from among those that surrounded the tens of millions (that stood) before him. He needed no council, but the most holy ones who are near to him neither go far away at night nor move away from him. Until then I was prostrate on my face covered and trembling. And the Lord called me with his own mouth and said to me, "Come near to me, Enoch, and to my holy word." And he lifted me up and brought me near to the gate, but I (continued) to look down with my face. (*1 Enoch* 14:15–25)

---

him, and the apostates. After this judgement, God builds the New Jerusalem. The argument of the *Epistle of Enoch* is the imminent judgement of God, which will bring eternal blessing for the just, who are encouraged to persevere in order to shine like the luminaries of heaven (cf. 104:2). According to Nickelsburg, the right dating of this book is the late Hasmonean period. The Epistle of Enoch might be similar to other apocalyptic writings in the kind of situation it reflects, the message it transmits, and the aims it has been written for (cf. Nickelsburg, *Jewish Literature between the Bible and the Mishnah*, 149). The *Book of the Parables of Enoch*, *1 Enoch* 37–71, is perhaps the latest section of the *Pentateuch of Enoch*. According to this book, God judges through his Chosen one. The first parable represents the epiphany of the just; the second parable anticipates the judgment and its effects; the third parable anticipates the glorious theophany of light that will cover the just (cf. *1 Enoch* 58). Chapters 62–63 depict the great judgement and the exaltation of the persecuted just. Nickelsburg thinks that the Similitudes of *Enoch* were written before the Synoptic Gospels (in which the title "Son of Man" has a more sophisticated sense than in *1 Enoch*) but after the other parts of *1 Enoch* (cf. Nickelsburg, *Jewish Literature between the Bible and the Mishnah*, 223).

Also, in the *Book of Parables*:

> He carried off my spirit, and I, Enoch, was in the heaven of heavens. There I saw—in the midst of that light—a structure built of crystals: and between those crystals tongues of living fire. And my spirit saw a ring which encircled this structure of fire. On its four sides were rivers full of living fire which encircled it. Moreover, seraphim, cherubim, ophanim—the sleepless ones who guard the throne of his glory—also encircled it. And I saw countless angels—a hundred thousand times a hundred thousand, ten million times ten million—encircling that house. Michael, Raphael, Gabriel, Phanuel, and numerous (other) holy angels that are in heaven above, go in and out of that house—Michael, Raphael, Gabriel, Phanuel, and numerous (other) holy angels that are countless. With them is the Antecedent of Time: His Head is white and pure like wool and his garment is indescribable. I fell on my face, my whole body mollified and my spirit transformed. Then I cried with a great voice by the spirit of the power, blessing, glorifying, and extolling. (*1 Enoch* 71:5-11)

The transcendence of God and His absolute sovereignty, of which the glory of His heavenly throne is a mirror, constitute some of the most relevant aspects of apocalyptic theology. They might have referred at first to God as keeper of the natural order (primacy of cosmology), but a further theological development of the idea of the absolute transcendence of God led to the formulation of a hermeneutics of history and eschatology. In spite of the divergences in certain details or specific elements (such as the acceptance and rejection—and even indifference—of doctrines like resurrection of the flesh in many apocalyptic writings), the apocalyptic theology is guided by the perspective of the transcendence of God. This transcendence is visualized in the lordship of God over nature and its order, in the lordship of God over history in its universality, and in the lordship of God over life and death, with power to judge and to grant eternal reward.

Schematically, we could summarize the evolutionary process of apocalyptic theology in the following way: the conscience of the transcendence of God over the world leads to the conscience of the transcendence of God over history and death. This conscience involves similar convictions regarding the sovereignty of God over these three realms: world, history, and death.

The Apocalyptic Conception of History, Evil, and Eschatology

The conscience of the divine sovereignty is not an exclusive contribution of apocalypticism. As it is well known, it is present in the great writings of Hebrew Bible (cf. Deut 32:39). However, apocalypticism made it possible to integrate partial reflections on divine sovereignty into a global theology centred upon the transcendence of God and upon the unity of world, history (as universal history), and death. In Russell's words, with apocalypticism "we have a picture of a wholly transcendent God, whose great glory is binding in its magnificence and whose presence is portrayed in flames of fire. He is the inaccessible God, guarded by millions and upon whose face is to be seen only by those chosen to behold him by divine revelation."[62]

This hermeneutic frame, based on the idea of the absolute transcendence of God over all things, recognizes the transcendence of God over history. Nonetheless, this divine transcendence over history does not mean, for the apocalyptic *forma mentis*, a radical removal of God from history. God is actively involved in history, because He leads history and history runs according to a plan which is the result of the sovereignty of God. His transcendence over all the events of the world shines in his sovereignty over history. God participates in mankind's history, not just in Israel's history, even though his manifestations in history are progressively less theophanic and miraculous. Instead of breaking the normal way nature works, God reveals himself in his transcendence over history as a whole. This may be seen as an original answer to the dialectics of immanence and transcendence in thinking the nature of the divine: "it is part of the genius of the apocalyptic visionaries that they were able to see, perhaps more clearly than many who had gone before them, that the great God, transcendent in the heavens and seated on his glorious throne, was nevertheless deeply involved in the history of his people and indeed in the history of the whole human race."[63]

The apocalyptic religious genius lies in this intimate unity between nature and history. Divine lordship over the world, over the cosmological dimension of reality, is not separated from divine lordship over history; one leads to another, for: "He changes the times and the seasons; He removes kings and raises up kings; He gives wisdom to the wise and knowledge to those who have understanding" (Dan 2:21).

---

62. Russell, *Divine Disclosure*, 86.
63. Ibid.

World and history are not divergent but convergent spaces tending towards unity: the unity granted by the absolute sovereignty of God over everything that exists.[64]

The apocalyptists were not blind to the historic evidence. They knew that history is an ambiguous reality, in which good and evil, justice and injustice, signs of the presence of God and signs of his absence coexist. Their vision of the transcendence of God over history and of his sovereignty over all worldly events needed an eschatological projection to the future. The key role played by eschatology is essential in the understanding of apocalypticism: only in an eschatologically oriented history God could be the true lord of all the times and He could finally vindicate the victims.[65]

The apocalyptic mind could not refuse the idea that at the end of times God will deliver justice to everyone. This justice will be final, and the ultimate meaning of history will be revealed by then. The ambiguities and the contradictions that we find in history will be followed by the answer about their deepest sense.[66] The God who is ruling creation and history cannot be alien to the contradictions of world and history, and death is the greatest contradiction. The plan of God will be gloriously fulfilled. However, how can this plan be fulfilled if it is constantly challenged by the reality of death and suffering? How can we admit divine sovereignty over a world and a history that frequently reward the impious and punish the just?

All that has not been fulfilled in past or present times will be finally fulfilled in the future. The structure of apocalyptic eschatology is based upon this conviction: creation and history are called to be redeemed, to

---

64. Ibid., 87.

65. Rivkin speaks in terms of a "hidden revolution," fostered by the growing inconsistency between the structure of experience and the structure of the Pentateuch (cited by Schaper, *Eschatology in the Greek Psalter*, 28). The problem of theodicy demanded an answer that exceeded the traditional categories of the faith of Israel. From a Weberian perspective, one could say that too much "rationalization" of God in Israel (in the sense of "humanization," of imagining God as a being who enters into dialogue with humanity and who can be understood in human terms) finally failed, and the eschatological projection emerged as a necessary solution to explain the lack of rationality in the divine action.

66. Kant (*Critique of Practical Reason*) feels himself compelled to admit an infinite "space" after the earthly life in which morality and happiness will be balanced. That space, however, results as a postulate of practical reason and not as a conclusion of pure reason.

be radically transformed by the power of God. The cosmic and social realities of the world will not remain aside from the divine sovereignty, but they will experience a deep change. The plan of God will be gloriously fulfilled, since the glory of God is eternal (cf. *1 Enoch* 63:3). Even the oldest parts of *Enoch*, in which the cosmocentric representation of divine power prevails, hold the conviction that creation is in a progression towards an eschatological end and a final transformation:

> In those days, the angel Uriel responded and said to me: "Behold, I have shown you everything, Enoch, and I have revealed everything to you (so that) you might see this sun, this moon, and those that guide the stars of heaven as well as all those who interchange their activities and their seasons and rotate their processions. In respect to their days, the sinners and the winter are cut short. Their seed(s) shall lag behind, in their lands and in their fertile fields, and in all their activities upon the earth. He will turn and appear in their time, and withhold rain: and the sky shall stand still at that time. Then the vegetable shall slacken and not grow in its season, and the fruit shall not be born in its (proper) season. The moon shall alter its order, and will not be seen according to its (normal) cycles. In those days it will appear in the sky and it shall arrive in the evening in the extreme ends of the great lunar path, in the west. And it shall shine (more brightly), exceeding the normal degree of light. Many of the chiefs of the stars shall make errors in respect to the orders given to them: they shall change their courses and functions and not appear during the seasons which have been prescribed for them. All the orders of the stars shall harden (in disposition) against the sinners and the conscience of those that dwell upon the earth. They (the stars) shall err against them (the sinners); and modify all their courses. Then they (the sinners) shall err and take them (the stars) to be gods. And evil things shall be multiplied upon them: and plagues shall come upon them, so as to destroy all." (*1 Enoch* 80:1–8)

The historical experiences have an influence on the dynamics of the cosmos, because world and history are linked, since they are the work of the same and transcendental God. There exists an intrinsic unity of world, history, and their common horizon: the eschatological consummation, as it can be seen in several apocalyptic texts about the signs preceding the end of times (cf. *2 Bar* 27:70; *4 Ezra* 5:1–13; 6:8–28).

As a synthesis of the nature of apocalypticism, Beyerle proposes a series of statements on its defining features:[67]

1. The interest in divine mysteries
2. The acceptance of eschatological levels
3. A deterministic conception of history
4. The emphasis on divine over human action
5. A pessimistic and dualistic[68] conception of history
6. The Scripture as a tool of consolation
7. Universalism

These defining features show the importance of history in apocalypticism.[69]

Apocalypticism and Prophetism

It seems clear, on the one hand, that there are several elements of continuity between apocalypticism and prophetism, but on the other hand, it cannot be denied that there is an important discontinuity, especially in eschatology.

The fundamental difference that separates apocalypticism from prophecy lies, according to Collins, in the degree of stress the first one puts on the supernatural and mysterious dimensions of revelation.[70] Apocalypticism incorporates new elements that go beyond Old Testament literature, such as angels and devils in an individual sense (so

---

67. Cf. Beyerle, *Die Gottesvorstellungen in der antik-jüdischen Apokalyptik*, 15–16: "Die göttlichen Geheimnisse als Gegenstand; Eschatologische Stuffe; Deterministische Geschichtsauffassung; Betonung des göttlichen Handelns gegenüber des menschlichen; Pessimistisch-dualistische Geschichtsauffassung; Trostfunktion des Schriftums; Universalismus."

68. The dualistic mentality of apocalyptic literature is also emphasized by Kvanvig, *The Roots of Apocalyptic*, 610–13.

69. This can be seen in the Book of Daniel: "Die Theologie der Geschichte bei Daniel ist ein zentrales Thema der Apokalyptik" (Santoso, *Die Apokalyptik als jüdische Denkbewegnung*, 249), for "Die Geschichte ist die Verwirklung des göttlichen Planes," (Santoso, *Die Apokalyptik als jüdische Denkbewegnung*, 250), leading to the advent of the Kingdom of God: "*Die Apokalyptik erwartet am Ende der Welt das königreich Gottes.*" (Santoso, *Die Apokalyptik als jüdische Denkbewegnung. Eine literarkritische Untersuchung zum Buch Daniel*, 253)

70. Cf. Collins, *Apocalypticism in the Dead Sea Scrolls*, 5.

in Daniel and in *1 Enoch*). Both prophecy and apocalypticism share the belief in a future coming of God, who will intervene in history during the so called "Day of the Lord" (cf. Amos 5:18). However, the Day of the Lord in prophetic writings is generally associated with critical situations of the empires and with specific moments in the history of Israel rather than with history as a whole. The apocalyptic literature has an extraordinary interest in the elaboration of chronological calculations and in periodizing history, making use of mathematic and symbolic procedures whose final goal is the prediction of the end of times.

Concerning the relationship between prophetic and post-exilic eschatology, Collins[71] thinks that Mowinckel's differentiation between an earthly, national messiah and a trans-worldly messiah can be held, with qualifications, to account for the principal differences between traditional prophetic eschatology (Isa 11, Zech 1–8) and apocalyptic eschatology (Isa 24–27).[72] Apocalypticism might be seen as the expansion of the eschatological horizon of prophecy via the idea of transcendence. The most important feature of the apocalyptic movement might consist of its progressive transcendentalization of the prophetic contents, which will no longer be restricted to the specific historical situation of Israel, but taken to a truly universal and trans-historical understanding.[73] Under apocalypticism history loses the ethnocentric inclination of prophetism to become universal history.

These considerations offer valuable insight into the study of the belief in the resurrection of the dead. Collins has highlighted the centrality of this doctrine, which cannot be regarded as an accidental motive among the others found in the different apocalypses.[74] Resurrection and judgement after death manifested a deep change in values within

---

71. Cf. Collins, "Prophecy, Apocalypse and Eschatology."

72. Isa 24–27 is dated by most authors in the post-exilic period. Cf. Millar, *Isaiah 24–27 and the Origin of Apocalyptic*.

73. Koziel (cf. *Apokalyptische Eschatologie als Zentrum der Botschaft Jesus und der frühen Christen?*, 636) reiterates this idea: the theology of the Old Testament became eschatological with the advent of apocalypticism, which envisions a future solution to all present contradictions. Eschatology is not a discovery of apocalypticism but apocalypticism emphasizes the dimension of the final action of God, whose intervention is not limited to the fulfilment of specific promises.

74. Cf. Graabe and Haak, *Knowing the End from the Beginning*, 51.

Judaism, because they constituted a transition from the eschatology of restoration[75] to a more cosmic and less ethnocentric perspective.

Grabbe, dealing with the problem of offering a definition of "apocalyptic," prefers to regard this movement as a subdivision of the prophetic genre.[76] The complexity of the question is still higher if we realize that there is no homogeneity of features in prophetism itself, even though this may be considered an advantage rather than a disadvantage: the heterogeneity of prophetism makes it possible for such a particular phenomenon as apocalypticism to fit into its margins.

Prophecy and apocalypticism have many elements in common. Grabbe remarks that both transmit a divine message to men, both are concerned by the interpretation of present situation, both see the invisible, mythic, and heavenly as influential on earthly reality, both expect a transformation whose analog is the idyllic primeval age, both include an important amount of paraenetic materials, in both of them the author is either an individual or the community, and finally, pseudepigraphy plays a significant role in both of them.[77]

As Russell points out, the conscience of the orientation of the world towards a state of eschatological fullness is also present in the *corpus propheticum* (cf. Isa 11:6–8; Ezek 34:25–27), although thanks to apocalypticism it acquires new dimensions and it is inserted into a much more coherent and systematic hermeneutic framework.

Cook supports the idea that apocalypticism, rather than a radical rupture with earlier Israelite traditions (theology of covenant, prophetism, wisdom ...), represented a creative process of cultural reintegration.[78] Native values and symbols were affirmed, not denied. Apocalypticism projected the mythology of cosmic creation onto a future recreation, in which the final Kingdom of God will be established.

Russell has underlined the decisive importance of the theme of universal history in apocalypticism. The treatment of history as a whole constituted a new "method" in itself, and beyond the common points

---

75. Puech, *La Croyance des Esséniens en la Vie Future*, 66–73 regards Isa 26:19 as an expression of individual resurrection instead of national restoration.

76. Cf. Graabe and Haak, *Knowing the End from the Beginning*, 22.

77. Cf. ibid., 23. Grabbe thinks that "mantic wisdom" (common to many ancient Near Eastern civilizations) could have had a decisive influence on Israel's prophetism and apocalypticism.

78. Cf. ibid., 103.

that it is possible to identify between apocalypticism and prophetism, Russell sees a fundamental difference: the hermeneutics of the end of history, a central concept in apocalyptic thought.[79] However, it is hard to deny that apocalypticism stems from prophetic traditions. As Hanson writes, "the apocalyptic literature of the second century and after is the result of a long development reaching back to pre-exilic times and beyond," and "not only the sources of origin, but the intrinsic nature of late apocalyptic compositions can be understood only by tracing the centuries-long development through which the apocalyptic eschatology developed from prophetic and other even more archaic native roots."[80]

The Socio-political Dimension of Apocalyptic Language

One of the most fascinating aspects of apocalypticism is the use of a language that, although it shares important features with earlier theological streams, shows a series of elements which make it, in a sense, unique. A definition of the nature of the apocalyptic language demands the examination of the different functions that it was capable of performing in the various writings, paying special attention to its subversive dimension, associated with a certain historical context and in dialectics with the danger of the Hellenistic cultural hegemony over Palestine. The development of a language provided an instrument for affirming an identity which sought to update fundamental categories of the Israelite faith in order to meet the challenges of the moment.

The apocalyptic language is projected on three principal vectors: mythological, socio-political (as an expression of resistance against oppression and tyranny), and theological. This mythological language finds, however, its most immediate background in certain expressions and symbols of prophetic literature.[81]

---

79. Cf. Russell, *The Method and Message of Jewish Apocalyptic*, 205.

80. Hanson, *The Dawn of Apocalyptic*, 6. In a similar way Kvanvig, who has performed an exhaustive study of the influence of the Mesopotamian traditions in Jewish apocalyptic literature, writes: "the emergence of the apocalyptical traditions and literature presupposes both a direct contact with Mesopotamian culture and the Babylonian diaspora, and the syncretistic tendencies in Palestine in the post-exilic centuries. But these more general conditions are not sufficient to explain why this kind of literature was created" (*The Roots of Apocalyptic*, 611). She concludes that the historical experience of radical evil under the persecution of Antiochus IV had a decisive impact on apocalypticism.

81. Graabe and Haak, *Knowing the End from the Beginning*, 85.

The transition from prophetic into apocalyptic language was slow, but it did not necessarily assume the notes of a deep rupture. In fact, if we look at the book of Daniel we can see that both parts, the prophetic (Dan 1–6) and the apocalyptic (Dan 7–12), pay much attention to the so-called *maskilim* [συνιέντες], "the sages."[82] In both sections the *maskilim* play the role of leaders of the people. In any case, the idea of "prophetism" in Daniel offers significant differences with the traditional idea of prophetism in Isaiah, Jeremiah, and Ezekiel. The symbolic dimension of dreams in apocalyptic literature is oriented to the future (even if we are before a series of *vaticinia ex eventu*).[83]

The continuity between Daniel's prophetic and apocalyptic parts (and, accordingly, the gradual discontinuity between Daniel's prophetic part and the great prophetic literature of the Hebrew Bible) is shown in the sharp dualism that surrounds the fourth chapter. This dualism is materialized in the strong division between earthly and heavenly, or revealed, knowledge. The emergence of a dualistic ontology is one of the distinctive features of apocalypticism.[84]

Santoso[85] proposes a series of fundamental categories concerning the understanding of God and His transcendence in the book of Daniel:

1. God as the God of Eternity [*Gott der Ewigkeit*], with a broader image of the scope of history. The majesty of God rules eternity,

---

82. Cf. the following passages: "Young men in whom there was no blemish, but good looking, gifted in all wisdom, possessing knowledge and quick to understand, who had ability to serve in the king's palace, and whom they might teach the language and literature of the chaldeans." (Dan 1:4); "And those of the people who understand shall instruct many; yet for many days they shall fall by sword and flame, by captivity and plundering." (Dan 11:33); "And some of those of understanding shall fall, to refine them, purify them, and make them white, until the time of the end; because it is still for the appointed time" (Dan 11:35); "Those who are wise shall shine like the brightness of the firmament, and those who turn many to righteousness like the stars forever and ever" (Dan 12:3).

83. While in Ezekiel 37 the cedar of Lebanon serves as a symbol to describe a past event (the fall of Assyria), in Daniel 4 the tree in the king of Babylon's vision serves as a clue to predict *ex eventu* something that has already happened, but that in the eyes of the reader is to be interpreted as a verdict about the future. Cf. Graabe and Haak, *Knowing the End from the Beginning*, 98.

84. Cf. Beyerle, *Die Gottesvorstellungen in der antik-jüdischen Apokalyptik*, 15–16.

85. Cf. Santoso, *Die Apokalyptik als jüdische Denkbewegung*, 243–44.

The Apocalyptic Conception of History, Evil, and Eschatology

in contrast to Antiochus IV, who will perish. The majesty of God, being eternal, is capable of bestowing eternal life:

> "Then the kingdom and dominion, and the greatness of the kingdoms under the whole heaven, shall be given to the people, the saints of the Most High. His kingdom is an everlasting kingdom, and all dominions shall serve and obey Him." (Dan 7:27)

2. God is also the God of justice [*Gott der Gerechtigkeit*], and He will show his majesty through his justice.
3. God is the supreme God [*der höchste Gott*], whose power is universal.
4. God is the God of heaven [*Gott des Himmels*], expression of his universal power on creation and history.

The image of God in Daniel contrasts with that of Antiochus IV. The attributes of God express what the Seleucid monarch lacks. The socio-political dimension of this conception of the deity is clear: God is beyond the powers of all the kings of this world. Daniel's God challenges Antiochus' supremacy, and this affirms the cultural identity of Israel and of Judaism against the danger of Hellenistic dominion. Beyerle sees a "political theology" in Daniel, as he makes the earthly sovereign dependent upon the divine, universal sovereign.[86]

The potential audience of the second century BCE could perceive in the book of Daniel the image of turbulent times. Its content was extremely political and subversive, challenging the cultural hegemony of the Seleucids, which threatened to dissolve the Israelite religiosity. The apocalyptic language capitalized on the constructive and performative function that is inherent in linguistic acts, and at the same time helped deconstruct the cultural hegemony of Hellenism, the symbolic and ideological universe of which is confronted by the apocalyptic worldview by means of an alternative symbolic universe. The apocalyptic *paideia* stood against the Hellenistic *paideia*.[87]

---

86. Cf. Beyerle, *Die Gottesvorstellungen in der antik-jüdischen Apokalyptik*, 120: "Im Sinne des Ergebens des irdischen Herrschers in Abhängigkeit vom göttlichen Weltenherrscher."

87. Cf. Han, *Daniel's Spiel*, 107.

Its language is full of hope in a difficult situation.[88] The doctrine of resurrection in Daniel serves a similar goal, thematizing a very deep conviction: world and history belong entirely to God. The divine victory will take place in the future. The salvation of God has started, but it will be consummated at the end of times. There is a great respect for history as a substantive reality in which the plan of God is realized, and whose true horizon is fullness. The future becomes a fundamental category in apocalyptic thought.[89]

The apocalyptic language has a constructive dimension, which in itself constitutes a revision of history. This revision affected history as a whole and placed God as the principal figure in the thread of the historical development. The attempt at historic revisionism, or at awareness about the other side of history, "is not motivated merely by an interest in taking another look at the past. The apocalyptist's touch of historical inversion is meant to expose the power structure of his time, when the Hellenistic regime may desire to create an atmosphere where Greek hegemony is taken for granted (...) the present has an underlining reality that the apocalyptic writer seeks to uncover in a graphic language."[90] Historical revisionism is aimed at showing that the long struggle will lead to the ultimate victory of God, according to what might be called a "telescopic vision of history." [91] For apocalypticism history is a linear reality whose innumerable events are but the expression of a manifest fate, that of the victory of God, in which the present suffering is an anticipation of the future glory.

The books attributed to Enoch were not limited to expressing a certain worldview, more or less centred upon an exclusively theological scope. They had a strong ideological component.[92] The theological innovations of Enoch substantially modified some fundamental assumptions

---

88. Adela Yabro Collins speaks in terms of "comissive language," which is a language aimed at generating a commitment in the receptor. Cf. Collins, *Crisis and Catharsis*, 144.

89. On hope as a fundamental category in the understanding of Christian faith, cf. Moltmann, *Theologie der Hoffnung*; Schillebeeckx, *Gott—Zukunft des Menschen*, 153.

90. Han, *Daniel's Spiel*, 26.

91. Cf. ibid., 26.

92. Jacob Taubes, in his essay *Die Politische Theologie des Paulus*, edited in 1993 by the renowned German Egyptologist Jan Assmann and his wife Aleida (based on a series of lectures given at Heidelberg), shows the political dimension of Pauline theology in opposition to the *ethos* of the Roman Empire.

of the Judaism of his time, as in the explanation of the origin of evil not only as a result of human responsibility but also as a result of the angels' transgression.

The true novelty of the Enochic thought is its global structure.[93] The Zadokite tradition conceived of God as directly revealing Himself on Earth by means of theophanies. Ezekiel introduced a notable newness to this approach in a famous vision:

> And above the firmament over their heads was the likeness of a throne, in appearance like a sapphire stone; on the likeness of the throne was a likeness with the appearance of a man high above it. Also from the appearance of his waist and upward I saw, as it were, the color of amber with the appearance of fire all around within it; and from the appearance of his waist and downward I saw, as it were, the appearance of fire with brightness all around. Like the appearance of a rainbow in a cloud on a rainy day, so was the appearance of the brightness all around it. This was the appearance of the likeness of the glory of the Lord. So when I saw it, I fell on my face, and I heard a voice of one speaking. (Ezek 1:26–28)

The celestial theme bursts onto Jewish theology with exilic and post-exilic prophetism: rather than expecting theophanic interventions of God in the history of Israel, the new prophetic conscience is encouraged to reflect on the essence itself of the dwelling of God (celestial kingdom). God is beyond all we can conceive of, and no theophanic manifestation can reveal us his true nature.[94] Ezekiel sees the glory of God; he sees his transcendence. The apocalyptic emphasis on transcendence stems from the prophetic tradition, and it expresses the conviction that the divine is beyond all possible representation or categorization in terms of particu-

---

93. Cf. Han, *Daniel's Spiel*, 15.

94. Nonetheless, there are several texts outside Ezekiel, Zechariah, and Daniel in which the celestial world plays a relevant theological and symbolic role, such as Isa 6:5; Ps 89:1–15; Ps 82; Jer 23:18.23.22. A rather explicit text of this orientation is 1 Kgs 22:19: "Then Micaiah said: 'Therefore hear the word of the Lord: I saw the Lord sitting on his throne, and all the host of heaven standing by, on his right hand and on his left.'" It seems clear, anyway, that these references may be regarded as occasional, since they do not correspond to a constant theological insight capable of recognizing the centrality of the celestial realm. The question is not why the authors of the Enochic cycle invented a concept (for it already existed) but why this earlier concept did not become so significant until the emergence of the kind of apocalypticism that stems from the Enochic literature.

lar events. The necessity appears of a universal perspective, capable of going beyond the contingency of the particular, without which it is not possible to fully understand the importance that faith in the afterlife and in the resurrection of the dead will finally acquire.

The apocalyptic depiction of the celestial world presupposes the possibility of achieving real communication with this invisible universe. There is an interaction between the worldly and the celestial, unlike in Zadokite theology, which established a radical separation between the two realms of consequential political and ideological effects.[95] Enoch's symbolism stands out at this point: the Enochic cycle appeals to the figure of Enoch who, according to the book of Genesis, saw the celestial world with his own eyes. His visions actually contradicted the Zadokite postulate of an incommunicability between the worldly and the celestial unless through specific theophanic manifestations. The figure of Enoch challenged the social and religious order in Jerusalem. For a more traditional theology, only Moses had been able to see the face of God (cf. Num 12:6–8). However, Moses did not ascend into heaven: it was God who descended from heaven. There is a passage from the book of Deuteronomy that is very eloquent on this: "For this commandment which I command you today is not too mysterious for you, nor is it far off. It is not in heaven, that you should say, 'Who will ascend into heaven for us and bring it to us, that we may hear it and do it?'" (Deut 30: 11–12).

Apocalypticism, on the contrary, advocates for a theology of ascent, which in the long term will lead to the Gnostic speculation on the elevation of the individual to the knowledge of the divine.[96] This theology of ascent confronts a theology of descent that, of course, was susceptible of falling under the monopoly of the ruling, priestly classes.

Heaven was a danger for the Zadokites and their cultural hegemony. An ideological superstructure, as that of Zadokites in Jerusalem, needs to perpetuate its hegemony by ruling the cultural production and by rejecting those elements that may be subversive against their primacy. Texts from the Zadokite tradition tend to limit the possibility of a direct communication with the celestial realm to the sphere of theophanic mediations, exclusive to Moses. The Zadokites might have appropriated the

---

95. Cf. Han, *Daniel's Spiel*, 18.

96. Concerning the fundamentals of the Gnostic worldview, cf. King, *What Is Gnosticism?*

figure of Moses for themselves.[97] The fact that the Zadokite, priestly sections of the Pentateuch do not exclude explicit references to the celestial ascent of Enoch and Elijah could be seen as the result of a compromise within different internal streams in Second Temple Judaism.

History, Periodization, and Time in Apocalypticism

The same hermeneutic frame that favors the understanding of history in terms of a universal reality favors the emergence of a theological infrastructure capable of embracing the concept of resurrection.

The idea of universal history cannot be understood without the process of universalization and broadening of the traditional notion of divine sovereignty, now applied to history as a whole. Resurrection might be regarded as a corollary of a more ambitious process of re-categorization of Israelite theology regarding the idea of history. This process took place in the context of apocalypticism.

There is a reciprocal relationship between the prevalence of universality in apocalyptic theology (the universal sovereignty of God over history as a universal reality encompassing all the peoples and going through a series of steps towards an end) and the birth of the concept of resurrection as an explication of this universality from the point of view of the lordship of God over life and death.

Beyerle has given great attention to the consideration of the so-called theophanies or manifestations of the divine. Theophanies appear in the principal intertestamental apocalyptic texts. For instance, they play a key role in the *Book of Watchers*, and also in the *Astronomical Book*.[98] The theophany of the *Book of Watchers* is quoted in the New Testament.[99] Enoch's theophany tries to reveal the wonders of God as an expression of his greatness and of his concern for humanity.[100]

Apocalypticism assumes the legacy of prophetism on topics such as the greatness, majesty, and sovereignty of God over all things cre-

---

97. Cf. Han, *Daniel's Spiel*, 33.

98. Cf. Beyerle, *Die Gottesvorstellungen in der antik-jüdischen Apokalyptik*, 55.

99. "Now Enoch, the seventh from Adam, prophesied about these men also, saying: 'Behold, the Lord comes with ten thousands of his saints, to execute judgment on all, to convict all who are ungodly among them of all their ungodly deeds which they have committed in an ungodly way, and of all the harsh things which ungodly sinners have spoken against him'" (Jude 14–15).

100. Cf. Beyerle, *Die Gottesvorstellungen in der antik-jüdischen Apokalyptik*, 81.

ated. The specificity of the apocalyptic approach to the manifestation of divine greatness and of his relation to human history lies in the primacy of universality: divine theophany is not limited to single events, but also includes the self revelation of God in creation and in history as a whole. This process was gradual, and it is not absolutely clear even in apocalyptic literature itself, but both the *Astronomical Book* and the *Book of Watchers* underline the dialectics between the divine and the earthly.

Theophany, the manifestation of God to men, is not limited any more to the physical and mythological dimensions that might have been present in other cultures and in the primitive stages of Israelite religiosity. It refers to God in the totality of historic and salvific events. The idea of "the glory of God" expresses, in Old Testament, New Testament, and apocalyptic writings, the revelation of God. According to Pannenberg, *kabod Yahweh* ("the glory of God" or "the weight of God") and *doxa tou theou* share a common background. In the Old Testament, *kabod Yahweh* is a synonym of revelation, linked to the action of God in history. The glory of God has been present in fundamental moments of the history of Israel, and for Isaiah (cf. Isa 6) the glory of God is everywhere, because God reveals himself every where. After the Exile, the appearance of the glory of God acquires the feature of a future, gradually eschatological event.[101]

In the case of apocalyptic literature, the enlargement of the scope of the revelation of God to history as a whole, together with the progressive emphasis on the transcendence of his manifestation to mankind, can be seen, as Beyerle points out, in the book of Daniel. The fourth chapter deals with the vision of the four beasts as a metaphor of the four kingdoms that will follow each other in the course of history. It is an expression of a linear history oriented to an end and susceptible of being periodized. The central point is not the specific history of Israel but the history of humanity as a whole. The universality of history and the universality of divine action and of divine sovereignty over time are stated here. Beyerle's conclusion is that Daniel is led by an underlying theocentric universalism, in which the action of God is that of a cosmic ruler and no longer concentrated on his salvific intervention over Israel but on a universal, salvific plan.

---

101. Cf. Pannenberg, *Offenbarung als Geschichte*, first thesis on revelation.

Hengel, like Pannenberg, remarks the apocalyptic projection of history under the light of universality.[102] However, it is necessary to take into account that the centrality of universal history is not shared by all the apocalyptic writings: Collins' distinction between two types of apocalyptic literature, the first one being concerned with unveiling history and the second one pretending to show heavenly mysteries, is rather convenient. Given the importance of the theme of history received within apocalypticism, progressively substituting cosmological motives in order to concentrate itself on the reflection about history and about its eschatological orientation, it is in no way an exaggeration to say that apocalypticism underwent a transition from a movement led by the conviction that it was possible to receive supernatural revelations concerning the mysteries of the cosmos and of the human being to a movement that turned cosmic revelation into historic revelation. Revelation does not come from unveiling the secrets of the cosmos and the astronomical laws but from the right understanding of the dynamics of history and the eschatological horizon to which it points.

We should therefore speak in terms of a more "historically-centred" inclination or a more "cosmically-centred" inclination within the apocalyptic movement itself. These different approaches exist, for instance, in the Epistle of Enoch and in the *Astronomical Book*. The *Astronomical Book* resembles a treatise on cosmic and astronomic phenomena,[103] describing Enoch's journey to show the mathematical uniformity of the heavens. *First Enoch* 83–90, possibly written in the times of the revolt against Antiochus IV, stresses the relevance of history as an immediate level of reality that reflects the activity in the divine realm. In Enoch's Epistle, history possesses a truly universal dimension and is no longer under the ethnocentric Jewish frame that had prevailed in earlier writings.

Hengel considers apocalypticism to have allowed a substitution of the frame of particular history by a universal picture of history, incorporating the classical themes of the action of God in history into a new universal, world-historic, and truly cosmic frame.[104] He speaks of "new outlines of universal history," which also assimilate elements from Eastern mythologies and from Hellenism. However, assuming Collins's

---

102. Cf. Hengel, *Judaism and Hellenism*, 180.
103. Cf. Nickelsburg, *Jewish Literature between the Bible and the Mishnah*, 47.
104. Cf. Hengel, *Judaism and Hellenism*, 181.

thesis that apocalyptic literature produced two principal tendencies, it is more convenient to say that the cosmic sphere was finally integrated into the historical dimension.

The triumph of the historically-centered tendency did not cause the disappearance of the cosmic theme but rather its insertion into the frame of history. History will be regarded as the totality of natural and human reality. It comprises the totality of created realities, which fall under the power of God, lord of history. If the *Astronomical Book* reflected the firm conviction of the existence of a uniform structure in material creation, in which everything obeys God (this is also present in the *Book of Jubilees*), the *Epistle of Enoch* postulates uniformity, too, but now in the realm of history. The obsession with periodizing history, possibly due to Hellenistic influence, builds up a specifically Jewish perspective which cannot be taken as a mere assimilation of exogenous cultural motives. To periodize history is to show that in history there is uniformity as well, a path towards an end, and the submission to a divine plan. The universe is under supernatural control, and everything responds to the divine plan. This is the sense of historical periodization, which is also meant to transmit hope: albeit the tragedies of present life, confidence must not vanish, since the wish of God shall be realized.

An attempt of periodization of history is found in the book of Daniel. The seventh chapter is about the vision of the four beasts.[105]

---

105. "In the first year of Belshazzar king of Babylon, Daniel had a dream and visions of his head while on his bed. Then he wrote down the dream, telling the main facts. Daniel spoke, saying, "I saw in my vision by night, and behold, the four winds of heaven were stirring up the Great Sea. And four great beasts came up from the sea, each different from the other. The first was like a lion, and had eagle's wings. I watched till its wings were plucked off; and it was lifted up from the earth and made to stand on two feet like a man, and a man's heart was given to it. And suddenly another beast, a second, like a bear. It was raised up on one side, and had three ribs in its mouth between its teeth. And they said thus to it: 'Arise, devour much flesh!' After this I looked, and there was another, like a leopard, which had on its back four wings of a bird. The beast also had four heads, and dominion was given to it. "After this I saw in the night visions, and behold, a fourth beast, dreadful and terrible, exceedingly strong. It had huge iron teeth; it was devouring, breaking in pieces, and trampling the residue with its feet. It was different from all the beasts that were before it, and it had ten horns. I was considering the horns, and there was another horn, a little one, coming up among them, before whom three of the first horns were plucked out by the roots. And there, in this horn, were eyes like the eyes of a man, and a mouth speaking pompous words. I watched till thrones were put in place, and the ancient of days was seated; his garment was white as snow, and the hair of his head was like pure wool. His throne was a fiery flame, its wheels a burning fire; a fiery stream issued and came forth from before him. A thousand thousands ministered to

Daniel's periodization of history is not restricted to the seventh chapter, generally seen as prophetic, but it is also present in the apocalyptic section of the book, and especially in Dan 11 (in the context of the narration of the wars between the Ptolemies and the Seleucids). According to Niskanen, although many authors have considered apocalypticism and Daniel to be essentially anti-historical, Daniel's eleventh chapter is in fact a historical account with a theological intention.[106]

Daniel links the becoming of history to the power of God over it. All the kingdoms fall under his power, the same as the entire creation. History acquires a linear uniformity under the expectation of an eschatological fulfilment. The kingdoms lead to the final kingdom, to the fourth beast, which will be followed by the triumph of the holy ones of the Lord (cf. Dan 7:18). History is not an autonomous reality that can be interpreted from itself but a reality directed towards the future, asking to be interpreted from its eschatological orientation. The four kingdoms symbolize the time of human arrogance and the persecution of the just people, who expect the advent of the eternal kingdom of God and the final consummation of history.

In the field of systematic theology, Pannenberg has made a considerable effort to reflect on the progressive development of the conscience of universal history in Israel and of its implications for the idea of God. In his view, the emergence of a historic conscience was progressive: its scope grew over time. With Deuteronomistic theology the structure promise/fulfilment suffers a key modification by means of the central role played by the Law. The Law becomes a force capable of determining the course of history. The future is no longer unpredictable, but it will take place if precise conditions are fulfilled. History will be extended to the whole course that mediates between creation and the ultimate, eschatological events.

---

him; ten thousand times ten thousand stood before him. The court was seated, and the books were opened. I watched then because of the sound of the pompous words which the horn was speaking; I watched till the beast was slain, and its body destroyed and given to the burning flame. As for the rest of the beasts, they had their dominion taken away, yet their lives were prolonged for a season and a time. I was watching in the night visions, and behold, one like the Son of Man, coming with the clouds of heaven! He came to the ancient of days, and they brought him near before him. Then to him was given dominion and glory and a kingdom, that all peoples, nations, and languages should serve him. His dominion is an everlasting dominion, which shall not pass away, and his kingdom the one which shall not be destroyed" (Dan 7:1–14).

106. Cf. Niskanen, *The Human and the Divine in History*, 7.

The Law still occupies a significant position, but apocalypticism contemplates it not as a historically proclaimed reality but as an eternally underlying basis of all worldly events. The *Astronomical Book* looks for laws behind the cosmic phenomena, and later apocalyptic writings, like the book of Daniel and the *Epistle of Enoch*, want to find uniformity in history rather than in nature: hence the obsession with historical periodization, in place of the former obsession with identifying the laws of natural phenomena. Under apocalypticism history absorbs nature, and history is reality in its totality. The degree of sophistication of this picture of history is one of the most outstanding characteristics of apocalyptic literature.

Apocalypticism and Determinism

The fascination with the division of time and with the periodization of history was motivated by the necessity that apocalypticism felt to discover an underlying divine plan over the course of time.

Apocalypticism developed a deep awareness of simultaneity by means of setting a symbolic view of time: the figure of Enoch, albeit its antiquity, could be perceived as a present, living reality. The phenomenon of "pseudonyms" can be explained as an effect of the conscience of simultaneity of the past and the present. Enoch, in fact, did not die: he was taken into heaven (cf. Gen 5:24).

This conscience of continuity of time and eternity leaves space, however, for the perception of a differentiation. History has an end, a breaking point in its course. History is condemned to disappearing and to being substituted by a new type of reality. Apocalypticism does not conceive of history as a definitive reality but as a reality claiming for a renewal and for a radical transformation. This aspect has been carefully studied by Hahne[107] who, in the context of a well known text of Paul's Epistle to the Romans,[108] examines the apocalyptic imagination

---

107. Cf. Hahne, *The Corruption and Redemption of Creation*. On the relationship between apocalypticism and the modern ecological perspective (the liberation of nature from the oppression of human action), cf. Primavesi, *From Apocalypse to Genesis*, 71.

108. "For the earnest expectation of the creation eagerly waits for the revealing of the sons of God. For the creation was subjected to futility, not willingly, but because of Him who subjected it in hope; because the creation itself also will be delivered from the bondage of corruption into the glorious liberty of the children of God. For we know that the whole creation groans and labors with birth pangs together until now" (Rom 8:19–22).

on the topic of the urgency for a recreation. Creation needs to be transformed, and this theme can be found in the entire Enochic cycle (*Book of Watchers, Astronomical Book, Book of Dreams*), aside from other relevant apocalyptic writings (*Jubilees, 4 Ezra, 2 Baruch, Apocalypse of Moses, Life of Adam and Eve*).

The apocalyptic conception of history hides a paradox: history and eternity are shown, on the one hand, to remain in continuity, but between history and eternity, on the other hand, a radical rupture takes place, since time has an end: "An order has been issued from the court of the Lord against those who dwell upon the earth, that their doom has arrived because they have acquired the knowledge of all the secrets of the angels, like the oppressive deeds of the Satans, as well as their most occult powers, all the powers of those who practice sorcery, all the powers of (those who mix) many colors, all the powers of those who make molten images" (*1 Enoch* 65:6). "After this he showed me the angels of punishment who are prepared to come and release all the powers of the waters which are underground to become judgement and destruction unto all who live and dwell upon the earth" (*1 Enoch* 66:1).[109]

According to Russell, apocalypticism could not refuse to elaborate a linear vision of history that, as happens with many other significant elements of its symbolic universe, ultimately went back to the most genuine tradition of Israel. The great civilizations of the ancient Near East held a cyclic representation of history.[110] Traces of this cyclic idea of time are also present in the Hebrew Bible, for example when we read: "That which has been is what will be, that which is done is what will be done, and there is nothing new under the sun. Is there anything of which it may be said: "See, this is new"? It has already been in ancient times before us" (Qoh 1:9–10).

In Qoheleth, everything has its own, perfectly defined time and there is no place for true novelty. This existential and cosmic pessimism

---

109. A similar topic can be found in *2 Baruch*: "For they shall see that world which is now invisible to them, and they will see a time which is now hidden to them. And time will no longer make them older. For they will live in the heights of that world and they will be like the angels and be equal to the stars. And they will be changed into any shape which they wished, from beauty to loveliness, and from light to the splendor of glory" (*2 Bar* 51:8–10); "For the first will receive the last, those whom they expected; and the last, those of whom they had heard that they had gone away" (*2 Bar* 51:13).

110. This aspect was analyzed by Mircea Eliade in his classic essay *Le Mythe de l'Éternel Retour*, first published in 1949.

contrasts with the apocalyptic conviction of a radical transformation of world and history. Apocalyptic pessimism cannot be compared to the pessimism we find in certain wisdom literature like Qoheleth, since the first refers to the ultimate destiny of history under the expectation of a great change at the end of times. In Russell's words, "any such theory of time, which involved belief in ever-recurring roles of change, was ultimately incompatible with the Hebrew belief in God as Creator and with the prophets' stress on the *eschaton* as the completion of world history."[111] The perception of the unity of divine plan over world, mankind, and history progressively favored the emergence of a more transcendental representation of God, world, and history.

The cyclic vision of time was, however, maintained in certain key elements of the new worldview. The language of recreation might be interpreted as a connection with eschatology and protology, establishing a parallelism between the end and the beginning. It seems clear that the eschatological emphasis bequeaths a new radicalism upon the apocalyptic idea of history. This new radicalism is one of the most original contributions of apocalypticism to the history of religious ideas: the belief in a linear sense of history and the hope in a future triumph of God. Russell thinks that the unity of history is far from being a discovery of the Enlightenment and of Hegelian philosophy: all of them share a Judeo-Christian background, even though there is a fundamental difference concerning the unifying principle of history (whether the divine plan or the idea of human nature).

The unity of history may be regarded as a corollary of the unity of God. The strict monotheism taught by biblical prophetism, and particularly by Deutero-Isaiah, is also expressed in terms of a unified conception of history. Deutero-Isaiah envisions a universal recognition of Yahweh as God, but this recognition does not necessarily consist of a universal conversion to the worship of Yahweh. Deutero-Isaiah proclaims the highest and universal sovereignty of God over the world, and he contemplates all the nations acknowledging the legitimacy of the God of Israel. However, it is only in the latest strata of Trito-Isaiah that the theological tendency leading to a realization of the universality of God will be translated into a true opening of mind to other nations. From that point, Israel will be regarded as a part within the global dynamics of history. Deutero-Isaiah's language makes use of a kind of vocabulary that emphasizes the

---

111. Russell, *The Method and Message of Jewish Apocalyptic*, 215.

The Apocalyptic Conception of History, Evil, and Eschatology

universality of God, but the author does not show a great deal of concern about these nations themselves and their role in history. Trito-Isaiah, especially in its most recent passages, manifests an interest in the fate of non-Israelite individuals and nations. Deutero-Isaiah's monotheism might have inaugurated a new scope of theological reflection, whose real importance was only perceived when the socio-historical circumstances allowed for an increasing awareness of the role of the Gentiles.[112]

The growing conscience of the uniqueness of God (cf. Isa 43:8–13)[113] and, therefore, of the unity of his design, opened a new theological horizon, capable of broadening and of extending traditional religiosity to the consideration of the role of Israel in the world and in history. The other peoples could not be left aside in the plan of the only God, maker of reality as a whole. Monotheism led to a significant loss of ethnocentrism in the Israelite vision of history. The apocalyptic conception of universal history is the summit of this tendency, but, as Kaminsky and Stewart indicate, this conscience was progressive,[114] and it received a determin-

---

112. Cf. Kaminsky and Stewart, "God of All the World," 140–41.

113. "Bring out the blind people who have eyes, and the deaf who have ears. Let all the nations be gathered together, and let the people be assembled. Who among them can declare this, and show us former things? Let them bring out their witnesses, that they may be justified; or let them hear and say, 'it is truth.' 'You are my witnesses,' says the Lord: 'And my servant whom I have chosen, that you may know and believe me, and understand that I am He. Before me there was no God formed, nor shall there be after me. I, even I, am the Lord, and besides Me there is no savior. I have declared and saved, I have proclaimed, and there was no foreign god among you; therefore you are my witnesses,' says the Lord, 'that I am God. Indeed before the day was, I am He; and there is no one who can deliver out of my hand; I work, and who will reverse it?'"

114. The redemption in Deutero-Isaiah is still linked to the divine election of Israel (cf. Kaminsky and Stewart, "God of All the World," 145). God is the God of Israel, and God and his actions in history are interpreted from the perspective of Israel's singular position among other peoples, as we read in Isa 43:3–4: "For I am the Lord your God, The Holy One of Israel, your Savior; I gave Egypt for your ransom, Ethiopia and Seba in your place. Since you were precious in my sight, you have been honored, and I have loved you; therefore I will give men for you, and people for your life." A careful examination of certain texts from Deutero-Isaiah reveals that the author is invoking the nations as a part of the universal glorification of the God of Israel. The centrality of Zion in the redemption of God also appears in Trito-Isaiah (cf. Isa 60–62), but in some passages the dichotomy is not focused on the opposition between Israel and its neighbours but on the opposition between the just and the impious (cf. Isa 65:13–15). Finally, the vision of Isa 66:18–23 expresses more interest in the fate of the Gentile nations, for "all flesh" will gather in Jerusalem to give praise to Yahweh: "'For I know their works and their thoughts. It shall be that I will gather all nations and tongues; and they shall come and see my glory. I will set a sign among them; and those among them who escape I will

ing impulse from the historical events (in particular, the interaction with Hellenism and the Maccabean crisis).

This universalism finds a soteriological translation in terms of the apocalyptic theology of the universal judgement of God, which will affect all men and women on Earth. The just ones, regardless of their ethnic origin, can enjoy the future glory. This marks a great contrast with the nationalistic tone which is found in former Old Testament writings.[115]

The pioneers in the unity of history, explicated by apocalypticism, are the prophets. The monotheistic faith shines with its most powerful luminosity in prophetic writings: God is called to exert his universal sovereignty over history and over all the nations. However, it is important to note that the prophets, who constantly refer to the historical events involving the cultures surrounding Israel (Assyria, Egypt, Babylon . . .), still attribute to Israel a privileged position in history. They do not manifest a real will to integrate Israel into the dynamics of universal history; on the contrary, they prefer to place it in a parallel *historia salutis*.

An ambiguity persists within late prophetism and within Jewish intertestamental literature. Some prophetic texts still offer a hostile image of foreign peoples, beginning with the traditional idea of "Yahweh's anger" against nations (cf. Isa 34:2), and ending up with certain verses in Trito-Isaiah (who, at least theoretically, should have been more receptive to the role of the Gentiles in history) in which we read the following:

> I have trodden the winepress alone, and from the peoples no one was with me. For I have trodden them in my anger, and trampled them in my fury; their blood is sprinkled upon my garments, and I have stained all my robes. For the day of vengeance is in my heart, and the year of my redemption has come. I looked, but there was no one to help, and I wondered that there was no one

---

send to the nations: to Tarshish and Pul and Lud, who draw the bow, and Tubal and Javan, to the coastlands afar off who have not heard my fame nor seen my glory. And they shall declare my glory among the Gentiles. Then they shall bring all your brethren for an offering to the Lord out of all nations, on horses and in chariots and in litters, on mules and on camels, to my holy mountain Jerusalem,' says the Lord, 'as the children of Israel bring an offering in a clean vessel into the house of the Lord. And I will also take some of them for priests and Levites,' says the Lord. 'For as the new heavens and the new earth which I will make shall remain before me,' says the Lord, 'so shall your descendants and your name remain. And it shall come to pass that from one New Moon to another, And from one Sabbath to another, all flesh shall come to worship before me,' says the Lord."

115. Russell, *The Method and Message of Jewish Apocalyptic*, 268.

The Apocalyptic Conception of History, Evil, and Eschatology

to uphold; therefore my own arm brought salvation for me; and my own fury, it sustained me. I have trodden down the peoples in my anger, made them drunk in my fury, and brought down their strength to the earth. (Isa 63:3–6)

And on the other extreme we find other texts which show hope in the universal salvation for all the peoples:

> Assemble yourselves and come; draw near together, you who have escaped from the nations. They have no knowledge, who carry the wood of their carved image, and pray to a god that cannot save. Tell and bring forth your case; yes, let them take counsel together. Who has declared this from ancient time? Who has told it from that time? Have not I, the Lord? And there is no other God besides me, a just God and a Savior; there is none besides me. Look to me, and be saved, all you ends of the earth! For I am God, and there is no other. (Isa 45:20–22)[116]

Everyone who converts to Yahweh will participate in his salvation, regardless of his ethnic origin. The acceptance of the gradual, progressive emergence of the conscience of the universality of the salvific plan of God is the only way to offer a convincing explanation about the different criteria on the salvation of the Gentiles that can be found in the great prophetic books.

Daniel has a conscience and a theology of universal history.[117] Daniel sees his people as part of a broader history, which responds to the plan of God and which is determined by the perspective of the continuity of past, present, and future times.

History possesses an internal consistency, since it is endowed with a meaning: it is the result of the action of God, and it points to a final consummation, in which the sense of all the particular events will be revealed. The apocalyptists "believed that the happenings of history have

---

116. Verse 22 is eloquent enough: "Look to me, and be saved [פְּנוּ־אֵלַי וְהִוָּשְׁעוּ, ἐπιστράφητε πρός με καὶ σωθήσεσθε]," as eloquent as the following passage: "Also the sons of the foreigner who join themselves to the Lord, to serve him, and to love the name of the Lord, to be his servants—Everyone who keeps from defiling the Sabbath, and holds fast my covenant—Even them I will bring to my holy mountain, and make them joyful in my house of prayer. Their burnt offerings and their sacrifices will be accepted on my altar; for my house shall be called a house of prayer for all nations" (Isa 56:6–7).

117. Cf. Russell, *The Method and Message of Jewish Apocalyptic*, 221.

a meaning and that the meaning is to be understood in terms of the goal toward which history is moving."[118]

The consecration of this dyad, history and sense, by apocalypticism, may be extrapolated to the sphere of individual human life. Human life, in its individual dimension, is also susceptible to a meaning, because it is oriented towards an end. Death, apparently the lack of sense, cannot represent the ultimacy of reality, for "all the events of history were directed toward a single goal—the establishment of the kingdom of God—in which the divine purpose would be vindicated once and for all."[119] Projecting the fundamental problem of theodicy onto the eschatological future is the consequence of the consideration of the divine plan, which has not been fulfilled yet, inasmuch as history has not undergone its consummation. The adoption of a teleological perspective in history is ultimately driven by the fundamental conviction that there is an answer to the "why" posed by the tragedies of this world. The drama of history asks for a substitution of the present *aeon* by the future one. There is, as Woschitz suggests, a utopian component in the expectation of a final end of history.[120]

However, is it right to attribute a deterministic conception to apocalyptic theology? Apocalyptic theology is certainly marked by a deterministic mentality about the course of history, due to the conviction that historic events are not random, but they respond to the divine plan which is realized despite human deeds. Divine justice will triumph over human injustice (and, therefore, over human freedom). The sentence "for what has been determined shall be done"[121] from Dan 11:36 actually means that the end of history has already been written, and it is inevitable. History advances towards its final consummation.

There is a great similarity between this conception and the Hegelian view of history. Every comparison is always subject to qualifications, but both hermeneutics of history (the apocalyptic and the Hegelian) are led by the underlying conviction that history is not left to the realm of randomness but that it follows a plan, an economy. In this sense, it is perfectly coherent to speak in terms of "apocalyptic determinism."

---

118. Ibid., 223.
119. Ibid.
120. Cf. Woschitz, *Parabiblica*, 71.
121. כִּי נֶחֱרָצָה נֶעֱשָׂתָה, γὰρ συντέλεια γίνεται.

The apocalyptic writings comment on the role of human actions. There will be a divine judgement affecting all the human deeds. Hence, the responsibility of the individual in his final destiny is accepted by many apocalyptic works (cf. *1 Enoch* 1:3, 8–9; 61:8). Human actions can determine the historical events in their temporal dimension, but the total process that time undergoes is determined and unified by the realization of the eternal will of God. This dialectics involving two antithetical terms (in this case, human freedom and the will of God) cannot be susceptible to a "linear," univocal solution. Later Christian theology, and in particular the *De Auxiliis* controversy in the sixteenth century, shows the difficulty of offering a final answer to this problem. The apocalyptic authors were compelled to recognize the role of human freedom, while at the same time they believed in the invincible force of divine design.[122] They may have privileged divine design over human action through their insistence on the directionality of the process of history, leading to an eschatological consummation. However, their treatment of the topic was not systematic. It is possible to perceive a convergence between the apocalyptic conception of history and the Hegelian intuition that the plans of the spirit are realized through the actions of individual agents, even unconsciously.

The present age is necessarily pointing towards a future time: "He answered me and said, 'This present world is not the end; the full glory does not abide in it; therefore those who were strong prayed for the weak. But the day of judgement will be the end of this age and the beginning of the immortal age to come, in which corruption has passed away, sinful indulgence has come to an end, unbelief has been cut off'" (*4 Ezra* 7:112–14).[123]

---

122. Cf. Russell, *The Method and Message of Jewish Apocalyptic*, 234.

123. See also *2 Bar.* 44:9, 12: "For everything will pass away which is corruptible, and everything that dies will go away, and all present time will be forgotten, and there will be no remembrance of the present time which is polluted by evils . . . And the period is coming which will remain forever; and there is the new world which does not carry back to corruption those who enter into its beginning, and which has no mercy on those who come into torment or those who are living in it, and it does not carry to perdition." Fourth Ezra, one of the most important literary works of Jewish apocalypticism, was written after the destruction of the Temple of Jerusalem in 70 CE, perhaps in times of Emperor Domitian (81–96). It might be contemporary to the Apocalypse of St. John. According to some authors, 4 Ezra was composed after *2 Baruch*, because of its more developed structure (cf. Aranda et al., *Literatura Judía Intertestamentaria*, 322). On the reception of 4 Ezra in the Christian tradition, cf. Hamilton, *The Apocryphal Apocalypse*.

The present time will be followed by the advent of the paradise, and the end will come which is not a mere repetition of primeval times (although it keeps a narrow parallelism with the beginning of Creation): "What the Creator willed and planned at the time of his creation of the world will reach its fulfilment in the last days when he will redeem his universe, rectifying and restoring what has gone wrong and brining to perfection what has already been created." [124]

However, this question remains ambiguous because certain texts describe the paradise in a way that resembles a return to the initial state of creation,[125] while others choose a more transcendental image, overcoming the protological discourse.[126]

The proximity to an idea of "return" to the original state of created things holds to a more traditional view, whereas the acceptance of a truly transcendental, eschatological depiction of the paradise that definitely goes beyond all protological representation constitutes a more original development within apocalyptic theology.

According to Hengel,[127] there are five principal causes behind the emergence of the idea of history as unity under apocalypticism:

1. The necessity of offering a new interpretation of history capable of going beyond the glorification of the past.

2. The attempt to calculate the date of the imminent end of the world.

3. The decrease of faith in the role of human action in history, as a consequence of the desperation generated by the socio-

---

124. Russell, *The Method and Message of Jewish Apocalyptic*, 282.

125. Cf. *Jubilees* 2:7; *2 Enoch* 30:1; *4 Ezra* 3:6.6:2.

126. Cf. *2 Enoch* 8:1; *2 Bar* 4:3.51:11; *4 Ezra* 6:26; 7:28, 36; 13:52; 14:9. Thus, *1 Enoch* 61 tells us about Enoch's contemplation of the paradise of the just people, which is being measured by angels equipped with large cords. This paradise seems to be imagined as an eternal blessing of the name of the Lord: "All the vigilant ones in heaven above shall bless him; all the holy ones who are in heaven shall bless him; all the elect ones who dwell in the garden of life (shall bless him); every spirit of light that is capable of blessing, glorifying, extolling and sanctifying your blessed name (shall bless him); and all flesh shall glorify and bless your name with an exceedingly limitless power forever and ever. For the mercy of the Lord of the Spirits is greater in quantity, and he is long suffering. All his works and all the dimensions of his creation, he has revealed to the righteous and the elect ones in the name of the Lord of the Spirits" (61:12–13).

127. Cf. Hengel, *Judaism and Hellenism*, 194–95.

The Apocalyptic Conception of History, Evil, and Eschatology

historical context, which might have increased faith in a pre-established divine plan.

4. The necessity of recognizing the importance of individual decisions in order to differentiate apostasy from fidelity in a critical moment for Jewish identity, while simultaneously highlighting the group's responsibility.

5. The triumph of rationalization and systematization of history, opposing Greek cosmopolitanism, and providing the Jewish vision of the world and of mankind with a universal category.

Hengel's five causes are not free of contradiction. It is difficult to make compatible, on the one hand, the decrease of faith in the role of human action in the configuration of historical development and, on the other hand, to point out that the crisis suffered under Antiochus IV was a determining force in the fixation of criteria to distinguish apostasy from fidelity, since both apostasy and fidelity involve the existence of individual responsibility. The complexity of the topic obliges us to move away from univocal, uniform analyses and the acceptance of the presence of paradoxes that resist a harmonization or an easy, superficial conciliation is by all means necessary.

The challenge of Hellenism paved the way for the birth of a new hermeneutic frame in the understanding of the world and of mankind, in the struggle for Jewish self-determination against the Hellenistic spirit.[128] Apocalypticism, however, although closer to the interests of the popular classes and willing to preserve the Jewish identity, assimilated fundamental aspects of the Greek *Weltanschaaung*, and especially the concern for the individual and the development of a cosmopolitan and universalistic vision of history.

Apocalypticism and the Cultural Borrowings

The question about the origin of the apocalyptic conceptions has generated much debate in the study of Second Temple Judaism. The similarities found in several fundamental theological elements of apocalypticism and the beliefs and symbolism of the surrounding cultures has led to the suspicion that there were significant foreign influences.

---

128. Cf. Russell, *The Method and Message of Jewish Apocalyptic*, 196.

While Collingwood considers apocalypticism to have been influenced by Greece, Bultmann holds a more radical position, stating that the apocalyptic idea of history was a betrayal to the Old Testament traditions. According to him, the Old Testament conceived of God as the leader of history, but not of history taken as a whole. The relationship of God to history was limited to the specific history of the people of Israel, with which He had signed a covenant. The other peoples would be excluded from that history, or at most they would play the role of mere accidental spectators. Apocalypticism extends divine action on history to the universality of history itself. For apocalypticism, God does indeed lead the history of other peoples, and the ethnocentrism that prevailed in the Old Testament imagery is now lost. The apocalyptic periodizations of history do not privilege the history of Israel, but rather they integrate it into the global dynamics of the course of times, oriented towards an eschatological consummation.

On the contrary, Pannenberg argues that we should not confuse the notions of *Historie* (Hegel's narrative history or the so-called "factual history") with *Geschichte*, the thought about history (in a more philosophical sense), which could be related to the philosophy of history and, in the case of apocalypticism, to the theology of history.[129] Pannenberg points to the fact that apocalypticism favored the acquisition of a broader idea of history rather than a rupture with former traditions. This broader idea constituted a substantial change in the hermeneutic frame of history, and many could see it as a real separation, but if one analyzes the defining lines of biblical imagination it is possible to admit that an extension of the scope of divine action on history may fit in continuity with the most genuine biblical tradition. The stress put on the transcendence of history in its path towards an eschatological end, beyond the purely intra-historical treatment of classical prophetism, should not be regarded as a betrayal, but as an effective broadening of sense. It is typical of several apocalyptic writings to emphasize the idea of transcendence. Apocalypticism could be defined as an expansion of the eschatological horizon of prophetism through the idea of transcendence. The most notable feature of the apocalyptic movement is the progressive transcendentalization of the prophetic contents, which abandon their former limitation to the specific historical situation of the people of Israel so

---

129. Cf. Pannenberg, "Heilsgeschehen und Geschichte," 259–88; Koziel, *Apokalyptische Eschatologie als Zentrum der Botschaft Jesus und der frühen Christen?* 640.

as to reach a truly universal and trans-historical understanding. Under apocalypticism, history loses its ethnocentric consideration in order to become universal history.

Few authors deny the existence of exogenous influences in the apocalyptic thematization of history. Hengel acknowledges that Dan 7 is the result of the convergence of Babylonian, Iranian, Syrian, and Phoenician conceptions.[130] Daniel uses in abundance the technique of *vaticinia ex eventu*,[131] which is also present in the *Demotic Chronicle*, written in Egypt in the fourth century BCE. These *vaticinia* are interpreted by Russell as a sign of the sense of totality that apocalypticism attributed to history. Also, an apocalyptic stream of political inspiration found a fertile ground in the classical world, as it may be seen in the anti-Roman oracles of Asia Minor. The "internationalist" or cosmopolitan vision of history is eminently Greek.[132]

The Greeks also spoke in terms of a succession of empires, as in Dan 11. This makes Niskanen defend that this chapter of the book of Daniel is strongly influenced by foreign, principally Greek sources. The

130. Cf. Hengel, *Judaism and Hellenism*, 183.

131. Some authors have seen in the text of the "Apocalypse of the Seventy Weeks" (Dan 9:24–27) an oracle of insurrection with political aims rather than a *vaticinium ex eventu*. Cf. Tomasino, "Oracles of Insurrection," 86–111, who asserts that Daniel's prophecy of the seventy weeks had a determining influence in the Jewish revolt against Rome of 66 CE. The text goes as follows: "Seventy weeks are determined for your people and for your holy city, to finish the transgression, to make an end of sins, to make reconciliation for iniquity, to bring in everlasting righteousness, to seal up vision and prophecy, and to anoint the Most Holy. Know therefore and understand, *that* from the going forth of the command to restore and build Jerusalem until Messiah the Prince, *there shall be* seven weeks and sixty-two weeks; the street shall be built again, and the wall, even in troublesome times. And after the sixty-two weeks Messiah shall be cut off, but not for Himself; and the people of the prince who is to come shall destroy the city and the sanctuary. The end of it shall be with a flood, and till the end of the war desolations are determined. Then he shall confirm a covenant with many for one week; but in the middle of the week He shall bring an end to sacrifice and offering. And on the wing of abominations shall be one who makes desolate, even until the consummation, which is determined, is poured out on the desolate" (Dan 9:24–27). According to Tomasino, the oracle mentioned by Josephus in some of his writings as a catalyst of the revolt against Rome was actually that of Dan 9:24–27, since Josephus says that the oracle used by the insurgents came from the sacred Scriptures. However, Dan 9:24–27 might have been widely read in eschatological circles before the First Jewish War.

132. Internationalism in Daniel can be found in the absence of significant references to pre-exilic history. Daniel's concern is not the vindication of his people's past but the integration of Jewish history into the frame of universal history (cf. Niskanen, *The Human and the Divine in History*, 125).

difference, however, is pointed out by Hengel: neither Greece nor Egypt account for the frame of a universal understanding of history. Greece did not assume the linear perspective of history, with a beginning and an end.[133]

The Enochic cycle offers a clear sign of time periodization in the so-called *Apocalypse of the Ten Weeks*.[134] The *Book of Dreams* also contains a division of history into stages, although the orientation of this writing is principally focused on the history of the people of Israel seen a history of salvation. The vision of history goes in parallel to some of the essential moments in the history of Israel: the flood, the patriarchs, Egypt, the Exodus, the judges and the building of the Temple, the two kingdoms,

---

133. Cf. Hengel, *Judaism and Hellenism*, 186.

134. "Then after that Enoch happened to be recounting from the books. And Enoch said: 'Concerning the children of righteousness, concerning the elect ones of the world, and concerning the plant of truth, I will speak these things, my children, verily I, Enoch, myself, and let you know (about it) according to that which was revealed to me from the heavenly vision, that which I have learned from the words of the holy angels, and understood from the heavenly tablets. He then began to recount from the books and said: "I was born the seventh during the first week, during which time judgement and righteousness continued to endure. After me there shall arise in the second week great and evil things; deceit should grow, and therein the first consummation will take place. But therein (also) a (certain) man shall be saved. After it is ended, injustice shall become greater, and he shall make a law for the sinners. Then after that at the completion of the third week a (certain) man shall be elected as the plant of the righteous judgement, and after him one (other) shall emerge as the eternal plant of righteousness. After that at the completion of the fourth week visions of the old and righteous ones shall be seen: and a law shall be made with a fence, for all the generations. After that in the sixth week those who happen to be in it shall all of them be blindfolded, and the hearts of them shall forget wisdom. Therein, a (certain) man shall ascend. And, at its completion, the house of the kingdom shall be burnt with fire; and therein the whole clan of the chosen root shall be dispersed. After that in the seventh week an apostate generation shall arise; its deeds shall be many, and all of them criminal. At its completion, there shall be elected the elect ones of the righteousness from the eternal plan of righteousness, to whom shall be given sevenfold instruction concerning all his flock. For what kind of a human being is there that is able to hear the voice of the Holy One without being shaken? Who is there that is able to ponder his (deep) thoughts? Who is there that can look directly at all the good deeds? What kind of person is he that can (fully) understand the activities of heaven, so that he can see a soul, or even perhaps a spirit -or, even if he ascended (into the heavens) and saw all (these heavenly beings and) their wings and contemplated them; or, even if he can do (what the heavenly beings) do?—and is able to live? What kind of a person is anyone that is able to understand the nature of the breadth and length of the earth? To whom has the extent of all these been shown? Is there perchance any human being that is able to understand the length of heaven, the extent of its altitude, upon what it is founded, the number of the stars, and (the place) where all the luminaries rest?"' (1 Enoch 93:1–14).

The Apocalyptic Conception of History, Evil, and Eschatology

the seventy shepherds ... (cf. *1 Enoch* 89). Immediately after the "seventy shepherds," Enoch envisions four periods: the first period comprises the time from the seventy shepherds[135] (who will deliver the house of the sheep to the beasts) up to the reign Cyrus the Great of Persia; the second period goes from the Persian rule to Alexander the Great; the third period is the dominion of the Diadochi, and the fourth period begins with the Maccabees and covers until the advent of the messianic Kingdom and the New Jerusalem (cf. *1 Enoch* 89:65—90:42).

Niskanen sees continuity between Daniel's theology of history and the biblical traditions, but he recognizes the influence of Greek historiography, and especially that of Herodotus. In any case,

> the truly significant development, however, is the broadened historical focus, which takes in not only Israel and Judah (along with those nations that immediately interact with them), but embraces a truly universal perspective. Commenting on this development, Robert H. Charles said: "the Old Testament prophet dealt with the destinies of this nation or that, but took no comprehensive view of the history of the world as a whole . . ." Hence Daniel was the first to teach the unity of all the human history, and that every phase of this history was a further stage in the development of God's purposes . . . This universal history is markedly different from earlier historical writings in the Bible that followed the story of Israel's election by God.[136]

The book of Daniel reformulates the history of Jewish people, now inserted into the universal history of the great empires of the Earth. The Davidic restoration is no longer sought, because the final and eternal Kingdom of God is the true goal of history.

Some authors have proposed an Iranian trace in the apocalyptic periodization of history. Zoroastrianism developed a linear (not cyclic, like in Greece) conception of history. In the early twentieth century, the so-called *Religionsgeschichtliche Schule* ["school of the history of religions"] defended the hypothesis of the influence of Zoroastrianism on apocalypticism in topics such as messianism and eschatology. Common

---

135. It is generally accepted that the seventy shepherds symbolize the pagan regents of Israel and Judah until the definitive advent of the messianic Kingdom, although some authors regard them as a representation of the seventy angels who will rule Israel until the establishment of the messianic Kingdom. Cf. Díez Macho, *Apócrifos del Antiguo Testamento*, vol. 4 fn. 59 to *1 Enoch*.

136. Cf. Niskanen, *The Human and the Divine in History*, 113–14.

literary motives, like the heavenly journeys of visionaries who are capable of revealing supernatural knowledge and eschatological dualism, have been of great interest to researches. In the ancient times, Theopompus and Plutarch expressed a similar fascination for the beliefs of the Iranian peoples.

Zoroastrianism constitutes one of the most original religious phenomena of ancient Near Eastern civilizations. However, as Hultgard remarks, after two centuries of attempts to identify the exact nature of the influence of Persia on Jewish apocalypticism, there are still reasonable doubts concerning Zoroastrian sources: "no coherent apocalyptic tradition can be restored from the Avesta that has come down to us. It is not until medieval times—that is, the early Islamic period—that we meet with full descriptions of cosmogony and eschatology that enable us to delineate a coherent apocalyptic tradition."[137]

Most texts come from the Sassanid age (third through seventh centuries CE) and from the early Islamic period, although they usually appeal to an authoritative tradition called *den* ("religion"), *agahih* ("the knowledge"), *zand* ("the commentary on sacred texts"), and *abestag* ("Avesta"). In fact, several eschatological passages are preceded by an introductory formula which refers to an authorized revelation. An important eschatological work is *Bahman Yasht*, o *Zand i Wahuman Yasn*, a secondary compilation of apocalyptic materials of diverse origin, which is the only independent, apocalyptic text (the others are fragments of major compositions). It can be argued that several basic beliefs go back to the Achaemenid time: "eschatology, both individual and universal, is from the very beginning strongly integrated in the Iranian worldview."[138]

In Zoroastrianism there are two opposite entities which occupy the realm of the divine reality: Ohrmazd ("Ahura Mazda" in Avestan language), who is omniscient and possesses the light and the good, and Ahreman ("Angra Mainyu" in Avestan), the lord of darkness. Ohrmazd, in his omniscience, knew that the negative spirit would eventually attack him to try to steal his light, and so he created the world as a battlefield to solve the conflict involving both co-principles: good and evil. Ahreman set a bad "counter-creation" with destructive demons. All the good comes from Ohrmazd, and all the evil from Ahreman. The problem of theodicy finds an answer: there is a struggle between Good and Evil and the final

137. Hultgard, "Persian Apocalypticism," 39–40.
138. Ibid., 70.

The Apocalyptic Conception of History, Evil, and Eschatology

resolution of the conflict will come at the end of times. Ohrmazd, by virtue of his omniscience, has been able to anticipate its final victory.

This myth divides history into three periods of three thousand years: in the first one, creation is born in a state of light and purity; in the second one, there is a mixed state of light and darkness; in the third one, the conclusion of history, the resurrection of the death, and the return of the world to its original purity take place.[139] The last period is subdivided into three millennia. *Bahman Yasht* imagines a decay since the appearance of Zoroaster (the golden age), with parallels in both Greece and India.[140]

There is a profound faith in the final defeat of Ahreman and in the elimination of evil out of the world. There will be a restoration of the world (*frasgird* in Pahlavi), accompanied by a general resurrection of the dead (*ristaxez* in Pahlavi), in which the elements of the individual which have been spread out through nature will be reunited. After the resurrection, the souls of the just will go into paradise (*garodman* in Pahlavi) and those of the wicked into hell (*dusox*). The belief in a purification of the wicked souls after the restoration (analogous to Origen's *apokatastasis*) seems to be present.

The similarities with Jewish apocalypticism are too obvious to be ignored: "the Iranian prophet Zarathustra—more generally known under a later, Greek form of his name, Zoroaster—came to see all existence as the gradual realisation of a divine plan. He also foretold the ultimate fulfilment of that plan, a glorious consummation when all things would be made perfect once and for all."[141]

Both Zoroastrianism and Jewish apocalypticism divide history into periods, led by the fundamental assumption that there will be a definitive consummation of history and a victory of Good over Evil. There is a common belief in reward and punishment to each individual. However, although both of them assimilate the perspective of eschatological dualism, radical dualism is absent in apocalypticism, which incorporates a strict theocentric monotheism (devils—Belial, Satan . . .—, probably of

---

139. If we include the initial state of creation in its spiritual form (*menga*) history is twelve thousand years long instead of nine thousand, with four periods instead of three. However, in the Pahlavi tradition history starts with the creation of the world in its material form (*getig*).

140. There are testimonials of this perspective of decay in Hesiod's *Works and Days* (109–201) and in *Mahābhārata* (III, 186–89).

141. Cohn, *Cosmos, Chaos and the World to Come*, 77.

Persian origin, are never placed along with God in power and majesty). For apocalypticism, evil is real and inherent to the world, but it is not set on the same ontological level as good, which is the work of God. There is no time of "co-government": the lordship of God over history is absolute. There are also ritual differences: in Persia, corpses were not buried, but exposed to the air.[142]

According to Hultgard, in order to prove that there has been a substantial influence of one religion on another, two conditions must be fulfilled:

1. The existence of chronological priority of one religion on another.
2. The presence of significant contacts between both religions.

Zoroastrianism satisfies both of these criteria. However, there are reasonable doubts concerning the dating of its sources. Some authors have even postulated Hellenistic, Jewish, and Gnostic borrowings in those books written in Pahlavi.[143] In any case, there is evidence that the basic eschatological beliefs of Zoroastrianism go back to the sixth century BCE or earlier and the contact between both religions is clear from the Persian rule on Palestine after Cyrus's conquest of Babylon.

The problem with the hypothesis of a major influence from Zoroastriansm on Judaism is the fact that, according to biblical and intertestamental testimonials, the Iranian religion never posed a serious cultural challenge for Israel. In contrast with Hellenism, which compelled Judaism to search for its identity and to adopt a more universalistic and less ethnocentric interpretation of its own traditions, Zoroastrianism did not create a comparable impact. Cyrus the Great is called "Messiah" by Deutero-Isaiah (Isa 45:1), but in a political context: the liberation from Babylon.

The presence of exogenous elements in Jewish apocalypticism is well attested. However, the question refers to the degree of those influences, which are not exclusively Zoroastrian.[144] König has carefully examined the Zoroastrian eschatological conceptions in comparison with the biblical traditions, finally rejecting the hypothesis of a substantial

---

142. Cf. Levenson, *Resurrection and the Restoration of Israel*, 158.
143. Cf. Hultgard, "Persian Apocalypticism," 79.
144. Cf. Collins, *The Apocalyptic Imagination*, 79.

influence of Zoroastrianism in the elaboration of biblical thought concerning eternal life.[145] The reasons of this rejection are based on methodology (comparative approaches to religion tend to be centred upon the particularity and specificity of each religion, instead of seeing everything as a cultural borrowing), on thematics (divergent ideas, like the absence of the doctrine of remission of sins in Persia), and on chronology (it is not clear that Zoroastrianism from the Achaemenid age may have been as it is featured in Avesta). On account of this, all the attempts at linking Zoroastrianism and Judaism will face serious problems in the realms of chronology and theology.[146]

Borrowings were not general and direct, but indirect[147] and constrained to specific motives, such as the personification of evil in figures like Satan and Belial, or the cosmic battle between Good and Evil, as found in apocalypticism and in Qumran. Hultgard extends the influence to the idea of resurrection itself; however, this thesis is hard to defend, since intertestamental texts show that the faith in the overcoming of death was originally related to the problem of theodicy and the vindication of the suffering just, a topic stemming from prophetic literature and from the wisdom writings of the Hebrew Bible, which after the assimilation of the cosmopolitan universalism inspired by Hellenism took eschatology beyond the boundaries of the historical Israel and of the restoration of the nation.

These difficulties make Hengel state that the exogenous influence on apocalypticism coming from other religions did not actually affect its overall vision of history, but only certain aspects of it.[148] According to Russell, "however much the details of the two schemes may vary, this much seems plain, that the Jewish apocalyptists were deeply influenced by the Iranian conception of world-epochs and used it to develop, systematize and universalize the idea of the unity of history which they had

---

145. Cf. König, *Zarathustras Jenseitsvorstellungen und das Alte Testament*, 267–85.

146. We should not forget that the theological nature of Zoroastrian eschatology differs from that of Jewish apocalypticism in the fact that history is still linked to mystic and astral static imagery, what prevents from envisioning true newness in the course of time. According to the philosopher Ernst Bloch (in *The Principle of Hope*), in Zoroastrianism the future does not manifest itself as an open and new reality, as a *novum*, but as the fulfilled *quantum* of an already existing light, which Ahriman has obstructed.

147. Cf. Hultgard, "Persian Apocalypticism," 80.

148. Cf. Hengel, *Judaism and Hellenism*, 194.

already received from their prophetic predecessors in the Old Testament tradition."[149] Vanderkam holds that apocalyptic theology exhibits a series of features whose root is definitely biblical.[150] Santoso considers the historic context of persecution, rather than the cultural borrowings, as the most relevant influence in the configuration of the theology of history and of eschatology in the book of Daniel.[151]

The experience of suffering and injustice under Antiochus IV inspired a theology founded upon the idea of a future action of God over history. Against the traditional view, in which the important episodes of Israelite history are seen as events that have already taken place and have already determined the movement of history, apocalypticism leaves the dynamics of history unfinished in order to displace its culmination until the eschatological end of times. The ultimate meaning of history cannot be found in the past, but it will appear in the future.

One could pose the question of why it was the crisis experienced under Antiochus IV, instead of any other historical event, what to a large extent motivated a change in Jewish mentality concerning the afterlife. Antiochus IV's persecution cannot be interpreted as the unique cause, since it seems evident that without the theological reflection favored by post-exilic prophetism and wisdom literature, the "ideological conditions" for the emergence of apocalyptic thought would not have been reached. These "ideological conditions" favored an apocalyptic *forma mentis*.

---

149. Russell, *The Method and Message of Jewish Apocalyptic*, 229.

150. Cf. VanderKam, *Enoch and the Growth of an Apocalyptic Tradition*, 156.

151. Cf. Santoso, *Die Apokalyptik als jüdische Denkbewegnung*, 271.

4

Death

ATHEISM, PANTHEISM, AND THEISM

THE PROBLEM OF EVIL is closely related to the question of the meaning of life, and the question about such a meaning seems to be inevitably bounded to the development of a higher consciousness, as it has happened in the latest stages of human evolution.

Virtually all religious traditions have offered some sort of hope in the form of overcoming death. Even the Neanderthal man believed in some way or another in a future life, which he thought to be rather similar to the present existence. On account of this, Neanderthals buried the dead equipping them with the food and tools that they might need in the afterlife.[1]

The search for a meaning faces the universal experience of death as a reality that pertains to the human condition, but at the same time challenges it. Is meaning only temporal, a meaning within the limits of earthly existence, or is there an ultimate meaning that makes the human being significant even after his death?

Heidegger exposes a series of considerations about death in *Sein und Zeit* that have been highly influential in Western philosophy on account of their depth and richness. Heidegger pays attention to the fact that as human beings we always experience death in others, but we never experience the act of dying itself. And there is no possibility of substitution concerning death: no one can assume the act of dying of someone else, even if this person decides to die in order to save other people (like St. Maximilian Kolbe in Auschwitz). Death intrinsically belongs to the individual, and no one else can assume it: "my death is mine," and

---

1. Cf. James, "Prehistoric Religion," 23–38.

nobody, no institution, no religion, no philosophical system . . . has the right to deprive me of it.

For Heidegger, *Dasein* needs death in order to achieve its fullness, its integrity. While it exists, *Dasein* is lacking something. However, the completion of its integrity makes it become a *Nichtmehrdasein* ["no-more-*Dasein*"], no longer existing. This is the end of the *Dasein*. The resolution of *Dasein* so that it is no longer a "being that is not yet" leads to death, leads to its ceasing to exist as a *Dasein*. The *da* of the *sein* is therefore lost. Death is consubstantial to us, and our existence demands the assumption of the weight of death as something that is a phenomenon of life: death belongs to every *Dasein* and it defines its existence, for death reveals in its most radical way the condition of possibility that accompanies *Dasein*. Death illuminates the true possibilities of *Dasein*. Death is in fact a task which no one can avoid; otherwise, there is the danger of falling into the lack of authenticity: *Dasein* cannot achieve fullness without death. In Heidegger's own words:

> In the publicness with which we are with one another in our everyday manner, death is "known" as a mishap which is constantly occurring—as a "case of death." Someone or other "dies"; be he the neighbour or stranger . . . Death is encountered as a well-known event occurring within-the-world . . . Dying, which is essentially mine in such a way that no one can be my representative, is perverted into an event of public occurrence which the "they" encounters . . . Death, as the end of *Dasein*, is *Dasein*'s ownmost possibility, non-relational, certain and as such indefinite, not to be outstripped. Death is, as *Dasein*'s end, in the Being of this entity towards its end.[2]

In any case and if, as Heidegger says, death constitutes the unsurpassable possibility of *Dasein*, the possibility of the radical impossibility of existing [*Daseinsunmöglichkeit*], doesn't it make more sense to regard it as the frustration of a project rather than as the means of realization of *Dasein*? It seems that death, instead of bringing *Dasein* into its ultimate fulfilment, marks a sudden rupture within *Dasein* itself: *Dasein* could have continued to project onto the future, but its individual existence comes to an end through death, and so do its aspirations and its possibilities. Death, rather than the triumph of *Dasein*, is interpreted by many as its ultimate defeat. Heidegger thinks that an authentic existential project

---

2. Heidegger, *Being and Time*, 296–97.

is based upon the understanding of death as something that belongs to *Dasein*. But, again, it seems that, rather than providing a meaning, death annihilates all possible meaning. Miguel de Unamuno (1864–1936) was extremely worried about the fate of his *ego*, of his identity, and for him it was not enough to believe in some sort of "social survival" in the memory of the future generations, what he calls, using a very strong language, "affective stupidity."[3] Hence, he could understand Kant's emphasis on postulating the immortality of the soul and the existence of God in the realm of practical reason. It was the only way to offer hope and to give an answer to the legitimate worry about the destiny of the individual.[4]

What is going to happen to me as an existential project? Why do I have to live if I have to die anyway? Why was I brought into existence if I had to be brought into death? And if there is no meaning, there is no necessity of conceiving of a fulfilment of the integrity of *Dasein*, or even of an authentic existential project: if there is no meaning, there is no reason to differentiate authenticity from non-authenticity.

The gravity of death is deep indeed. There are different approaches to death, different views on how it should be interpreted.

In atheism, death is regarded as a natural reality. Human beings are natural beings, and death is, therefore, part of them. We engender mortal, not immortal beings. There is a cycle in nature which is built upon the succession of life and death: there is life, because there has been death before (according to the law of "negation of negation" in Engels' dialectical materialism). Death is in fact a means of regeneration, and it favors the renewal in both nature and history. We must die so that other people may live.

One of the few words that Marx wrote about the meaning of death is in his *Economic and Philosophical Manuscripts* (1844): "death is the victory of the genus over the individual." Individuals perish, but humanity persists, and the reality of death speaks about the necessity of inserting the individual into the social dynamics. Marxism conceives

---

3. Unamuno writes, "Todo eso de que uno vive en sus hijos, o en sus obras, o en el universo son vagas elucubraciones con las que sólo se satisfacen los que padecen de estupidez afectiva, que pueden ser, por lo demás, personas de una cierta eminencia cerebral" (*Del Sentimiento Trágico de la Vida*, 20).

4. "El hombre Kant no se resignaba a morir del todo. Y porque no se resignaba a morir del todo, dio el salto aquél, el salto inmortal de una a otra crítica. Quien lea sin anteojeras *La crítica de la razón práctica* verá que, en rigor, se deduce en ella la existencia de Dios de la inmortalidad del alma, y no ésta de aquélla" (ibid., 11).

of a historical solidarity of humanity over time: the sufferings and defeats of the past are to be seen as means to encourage the advent of the utopian, classless society. The meaning of the individual lives must be understood in light of the whole history of humanity and of the deepest goal of history: the freedom of the entire human race. The individual may not drink any more, but humanity will continue drinking the wine of fraternity (Dorothee Sölle).[5]

Other forms of atheism explain that there is a natural impulse to death [*thanatos*], which coexists with the impulse to life, as in Freud. For Nietzsche, the theory of "eternal return" [*ewige Widerkunft*] is a way to avoid nihilism: the meaning of the passing of time is that everything is repeated, and everything happens again and again.

In a pantheistic approach, death is interpreted as the reintegration of the individual into the divine dynamics of cosmos and history. For Hegel (for whom the label of "pantheism" is certainly problematic), individual deaths are steps in the realization of the spirit as absolute spirit. In the *Upanishad*, the idea of an integration of the individual [*atman*] in the totality [*Brahman*] serves a similar goal: death is not to be feared, because it is a form of achieving the union of the singular and the universal; the meaning of the individual cannot be sought by itself: the individual is significant inasmuch as it gets integrated into the totality, which is the true liberation of the individual subject. Once liberation has been achieved, the chain of reincarnation ceases, and the individual penetrates into the eternal and imperishable *Brahma*. Temporal death is not the final answer to the question about the fate of the individual.

The doctrine of reincarnation is associated with this perspective: the self, the individual conscience, will remain alive, adopting new shapes, in a process that manifests the link between all things in nature. The transmigration of souls (a belief shared by Pythagoreanism, Orphycism, Druzism, and to some extent Buddhism)[6] or *metempsycho-*

---

5. Cf. Sölle, *Die Hinreise*, 22. According to Dorothee Sölle (1929–2003), a German theologian, God is suffering with us, and He is powerless in solidarity with us. The human struggle for a more just, more fraternal society is also the struggle of God. The question of whether or not "everything" comes to an end with death is actually an "atheistic" worry, since intrinsic to the definition of a "Christian" is the idea that he or she is not everything for himself or herself.

6. On Buddhism and death, cf. Román, *Un Viaje al Corazón del Budismo*, 77–82. Buddha did not speak about the ultimate nature of nirvana, but it seems that the annihilation of the subject to which his teachings refer is that of the "false subject," identified

sis resembles the notion of reincarnation in major Eastern traditions. Arthur Schopenhauer spoke in terms of *palingenesia*, an impersonal metempsychosis in which the will does not die and is the eternal, permanent reality that unveils itself in the new individuals.[7]

Theistic approaches to death are defined by the belief in a personal God. Death is not a natural reality: in different versions of Christianity, for example, it is the result of sin and fall, and the true destiny of the human being is immortality together with God, the eternal being. As St. Augustine writes in his *Confessions*: "You have made us for yourself, O Lord, and our heart is restless until it rests in you."

Plato developed the doctrine of the immortality of the soul, with its classical proof in *Phaedo*: the soul has no parts, and on account of its simplicity it cannot be divided, in opposition to material things. Death consists of the division of the body into parts which no longer form an organism, but this cannot happen to the soul. Hence, it is immortal:

> I suspect that you and Simmias would be glad to probe the argument further. Like children, you are haunted with a fear that when the soul leaves the body, the wind may really blow her away and scatter her; especially if a man should happen to die in a great storm and not when the sky is calm ... And then we may proceed further to enquire whether that which suffers dispersion is or is not of the nature of soul—our hopes and fears as to our own souls will turn upon the answers to these questions ... Now the compound or composite may be supposed to be naturally capable, as of being compounded, so also of being dissolved; but that which is uncompounded, and that only, must be, if anything is, indissoluble ... And the uncompounded may be assumed to be the same and unchanging, whereas the compound is always changing and never the same ... Is that idea or essence, which in the dialectical process we define as essence or true existence— whether essence of equality, beauty, or anything else—are these essences, I say, liable at times to some degree of change? Or are they each of them always what they are, having the same simple self-existent and unchanging forms, not admitting of variation at all, or in any way, or at any time? ... The unchanging you can only perceive with the mind ... Let us suppose that there are two sorts of existences—one seen, the other unseen. Let us suppose

---

with the external and superficial realities: with wish. Nirvana liberates the true subject, but it does not destroy the human being.

7. Cf. Whittaker, *Schopenhauer*, 43.

them. The seen is the changing, and the unseen is the unchanging ... And, further, is not one part of us body, another part soul? ... And to which class is the body more alike and akin? Clearly to the seen—no one can doubt that ... And is the soul seen or not seen?—Not seen ... And we were not saying long ago that the soul when using the body as an instrument of perception, that is to say, when using the sense of sight or hearing or some other sense ... were we not saying that the soul too is then dragged by the body into the region of the changeable, and wanders and is confused; the world spins round her, and she is like a drunkard, when she touches change? ... But when returning into herself she reflects, then she passes into the other world, the region of purity, and eternity, and immortality, and unchangeableness, which are her kindred, and with them she ever lives, when she is by herself and is not let or hindered; then she ceases from her erring ways, and being in communion with the unchanging is unchanging. And this state of the soul is called wisdom? ... When the soul and the body are united, then nature orders the soul to rule and govern, and the body to obey and serve. Now which of these two functions is akin to the divine? And which to the mortal? ... The soul is in the very likeness of the divine, and immortal, and intellectual, and uniform, and indissoluble, and unchangeable; and that the body is in the very likeness of the human, and mortal, and unintellectual, and multiform, and dissoluble, and changeable.[8]

This vision involves a dualistic conception of human nature, which is also present in Gnosticism, Encratism, and in Descartes' distinction between *res extensa* and *res cogitans*.

But there is another theistic approach: resurrection. In resurrection there is a rebirth, a new coming into existence. Death is not denied: it is overcome. There are three principal types of resurrection: resurrection of the spirit, resurrection of the body, and resurrection of the totality of the person (both spirit and body).

Apocalypticism developed a highly original conception of history, and in this movement the belief in the afterlife, and especially the belief in the resurrection of the dead, found fertile ground. How did this happen? How is it possible that Judaism suddenly adopted a belief that had been absent in it for centuries? Still in late books like Job, Qohelet, and Ben Sira, eternal life is either explicitly denied or simply ignored.

---

8. Plato, *Phaedo*, 78–81.

Nonetheless, resurrection became a canonical belief for both Judaism and Christianity.[9]

THE ORIGIN OF THE IDEA OF RESURRECTION IN JUDAISM

In our opinion, there are three fundamental positions in recent bibliography regarding the origin of the idea of resurrection of the dead in Judaism:

a) Negative hypothesis: separation between resurrection and Israelite tradition

b) Positive hypothesis: continuity between resurrection and Israelite tradition

c) Synthetic hypothesis: novelty of resurrection (integration of both the negative and the positive hypotheses, admitting the originality of resurrection and even the possibility of cultural borrowings, and at the same time defending its deep roots in the Israelite religious traditions)

Negative Hypothesis: Separation between Resurrection and Israelite Tradition

George W. E. Nickelsburg[10] has analyzed the principal references to the ideas of the immortality of the soul and the resurrection of the flex in Jewish intertestamental literature. Nickelsburg's approach is based upon the identification of the great theological themes and literary genres associated with the belief in the resurrection of the dead. This methodology is closely related to *Formgeschichte* ["history of forms"], in an attempt to discover the hermeneutic patterns which lie behind the different texts, in order to answer three essential questions:

---

9. Islam shares with Zoroastrianism, Judaism, and Christianity the belief in a final resurrection of the dead at the end of time. Cf. Abumalham, *El Islam*, 120–23. For an introduction to Islam, cf. Küng, *Islam: Past, Present and Future*.

10. The book *Resurrection, Immortality, and Eternal Life in Intertestamental Judaism*, by G. W. E. Nickelsburg, was first published in 1967, and it has been reedited and extended as *Resurrection, Immortality, and Eternal Life in Intertestamental Judaism and Early Christianity*. The new edition of Nickelsburg's principal work on the development of the belief in the resurrection of the dead has inspired different reviews by Clanton (according to whom Nickelsburg's most outstanding contribution is to show the variety and vitality of Jewish thought on eternal life during the Second Temple period), Blanton, Schutte, and Whitley.

1. Have intrinsically different conceptions such as resurrection of the flesh and immortality of the soul served the same goals?
2. Did these conceptions assume new theological functions over time?
3. Why are they found only in certain texts?

In effect, resurrection of the flesh and immortality of the soul are two divergent, if not antithetical, ideas, reflecting different cultural and religious backgrounds. On account of this, historians of religion face a serious problem when realizing that there is a rather notorious confusion between both notions in several intertestamental texts. This gives the impression that the authors themselves were not fully aware of the full implications of the beliefs they wanted to express.

The elenchus of texts examined by Nickelsburg covers the whole range of Old Testament and intertestamental literature with connections with the belief in the resurrection of the dead, undertaking a rather comprehensive study.

He first analyzes Dan 12:1–3, taking Dan 12:2 as the first absolutely clear mention of resurrection in the Old Testament.[11] There is an almost unanimous consensus that this passage from the book of Daniel goes back to the time of Antiochus IV's persecution, around 164 BCE. His campaigns in Palestine might have provoked not only a political reaction against his figure, but a rejection of the ideas he embodied in the sphere of religious beliefs: a rejection of Hellenistic rationality, including a rejection of the Greek conception of immortality of the soul, which was meant to affect both the pious and the impious. This context of refusal of the Greek *logos* by certain Jewish groups may be interpreted as the frame in which to locate the emergence of an idea that in its beginning had to be bizarre, at least in comparison to the earlier beliefs held by the people of Israel. But, on the other hand, Nickelsburg also attributes the origin of this concept to a gradual individualization of religious practice and of eschatology.

11. Dan 12:1–3: "At that time Michael shall stand up, the great prince who stands watch over the sons of your people; and there shall be a time of trouble, such as never was since there was a nation, even to that time. And at that time your people shall be delivered, every one who is found written in the book. And many of those who sleep in the dust of the earth shall awake, some to everlasting life, some to shame and everlasting contempt. Those who are wise shall shine like the brightness of the firmament, and those who turn many to righteousness like the stars forever and ever."

The association of the idea of resurrection to the dramatic experience under Antiochus IV's persecution seems to presuppose a rather sudden emergence of this notion, without an apparent continuity with the precedent traditions of Israel. We must take into account, however, that the explanation of the birth of the belief in resurrection in terms of two causes (the reaction against Hellenism and the progressive individualization of religious practice) hides a contradiction. It is not easy to reconcile both proposals: on the one hand, a reaction involving important sectors of Judaism in their fighting Greek culture, and on the other hand, a loss of the sense of community that could have converted the idea of *restauratio* ["restoration"] of Israel, which had prevailed in the Old Testament, into the resurrection of the individual.

If we should wonder about the roots of the tendency leading towards an increasing predominance of individualism (that became more intense during the second century BCE), the answer would involve dealing with the infiltration of elements of the Hellenistic rationality. The thought about the individual in the ethical, religious, and cosmological realms found a higher development within Greek philosophy than within Hebrew religiosity, because in the latter the way to understand the individual was connected with his membership to the community, sharing the same beliefs and practices. The rejection of Hellenistic rationality was not therefore so radical, or otherwise it would be difficult to explain why the birth of the idea of resurrection meant, even unintentionally, an assumption of certain elements of that rationality.

Concerning the individualization of eschatology, Nickelsburg emphasizes the novelty of the resurrection doctrine in Daniel. For Nickelsburg, the language of Isaiah's Apocalypse[12] could have offered a decisive inspiration for Daniel's text, but it cannot be forgotten that Daniel presents a truly universal resurrection, affecting both the pious and the impious. It consists of a resurrection that is not imagined as a mere defence or vindication of the just, but as an instrument so that everyone may be judged.

The acceptance of a double eschatological destiny, that of the just and that of the wicked, can be found in Isa 66. Nickelsburg thinks that a new reading of Isa 66 in a context of persecution could have been more

---

12. Isa 26:19: "Your dead shall live; together with my dead body they shall arise. Awake and sing, you who dwell in dust; for your dew is like the dew of herbs, and the earth shall cast out the dead."

relevant for the emergence of the idea of resurrection than Isa 26. This faith was added to the deep conviction about the creative power of God, capable of renewing heavens and earth and of causing the rebirth of a nation. The suffering of the just under the persecution of Antiochus IV posed a dilemma that was not unknown to Hebrew theodicy, although it now appeared with greater intensity: how is it that the wicked can destroy the just person's will to fulfil the law of God? Is the just condemned to a common, natural death, participating in the same fate as the wicked? The contradiction that exists between the thesis of the triumph of the just and the antithesis of the triumph of the impious could have favored a new theological synthesis: the idea of resurrection as a prolegomenon to divine judgement. This divine judgement was represented as a particular judgement, too, following the dynamics of eschatological individualization which has been already mentioned by Nickelsburg. Resurrection emerges as the condition of possibility for judgement to take place.

Resurrection may be seen, in this sense, as an expression of the theological synthesis that a situation as complex as the one experienced under Antiochus IV's persecution demanded and that might have otherwise disputed the religious pillars of Israel. Resurrection is the tool of God to bring judgement into effect. Different authors have shown their disagreement with Nickelsburg's "dialectical" approach, aimed at justifying the birth of the idea of resurrection.[13] They especially focus on the fact that this model is unable to explain why not every Jewish group accepted this belief.

Daniel's structure can be interpreted, according to Nickelsburg, as follows: since judgement is needed, resurrection arises as a condition *sine qua non* for judgement. But it is to be noticed that Daniel does not present a completely universal resurrection: Dan 12:2 speaks in terms of "many of those" [*rabim mishné* . . . ; *polloi ton*], a fact that makes him state that resurrection is a functional notion for Daniel, allowing him to solve the problem posed by those who had an unfair end for their lives. It is not integrated into a systematic reflection on eschatology. The book of Daniel is not a general treatise on theodicy.[14] As it often happens in the history of ideas, in spite of the originally reduced and even provincial

---

13. Cf. Levenson, *Resurrection and the Restoration of Israel*, 194.

14. Cf. Nickelsburg, *Resurrection, Immortality, and Eternal Life in Intertestamental Judaism and Early Christianity*, 23.

perspective from which it emerged, the concept of resurrection finally acquired an undeniable transcendence for rabbinic Judaism.

The contrast between the Hebrew and the Hellenistic mentality can be seen in the recurrent topic of the persecution of the suffering just, which appears in both the Old Testament and intertestamental literature. Wis 1–6 (the justice of God will bring immortality) and the different stories about unfair condemnations (Joseph in Egypt, Ahikar, Mordecai, Daniel, Susanna . . .) reflect a didactic goal, and so do the songs of the Servant in Deutero-Isaiah, themselves an exaltation of the suffering just: "Our analysis has shown that the servant and the protagonists in the wisdom tales are analogous figures."[15] As a matter of fact, Nickelsburg consecrates an important part of his study to the elucidation of the topic of the exaltation of the just with its prophetic, wisdom, and intertestamental parallels (especially *1 Enoch* 62), highlighting the point that resurrection is also a proof of the sovereignty of God above all created realities: He is the One who judges and exalts, and resurrection constitutes an essential part of the systematization of the belief in the universal lordship of God, whose prophetic roots are clear. This approach appears in 2 Macc 7, where suffering does not mean divine abandonment.[16]

Regarding Qumran, we must first notice that Nickelsburg's considerations have been played down by the Émile Puech's far-reaching study.[17] Nickelsburg, just as Collins,[18] thinks that the Dead Sea Scrolls "contain not a single passage that can be interpreted with absolute certainty as a reference to resurrection or immortality." The *Hodayot*, the community's hymns, speak in terms of a "realized eschatology" in the present participation of future life: "The blessings of the eschaton are already a reality for the author of the Qumran hymn."[19] Nickelsburg stresses the fact that the topic of death is infrequent in Qumran, and this might lie behind the absence of a treatment of the idea of resurrection.

In a conclusive way, we might say that Nickelsburg thinks of resurrection as the manifestation of a theological demand, motivated by

---

15. Ibid., 66.

16. The perspective of the exaltation of the just people remains in later intertestamental writings, like 2 Baruch 49–51.

17. Cf. Puech, *La Croyance des Esséniens en la Vie Future*.

18. Cf. Collins, *Apocalypticism in the Dead Sea Scrolls*, 123.

19. Nickelsburg, *Resurrection, Immortality, and Eternal Life in Intertestamental Judaism and Early Christianity*, 190.

the fundamental problem of classical theodicy: the suffering of the just. This problem became intensified during the crisis experienced in times of Antiochus IV. Jewish religion needed new answers of broad scope to resolve a complex and non-peaceful question: the future exaltation of the just people. The idea of resurrection appeared as a bright theological synthesis, incorporating traditional Israelite religiosity into a new frame of understanding. How resurrection is going to take place is not the principal issue (whether in terms of a realistic resurrection of the flesh or of a spiritual resurrection); what matters is the deep meaning of resurrection as a mechanism to vindicate the heritage of the just people on earth, of those who deserve the reward of God.

A similar perspective is adopted by *Hans Clemens Caesarius Cavallin*.[20] The texts he proposes generally coincide with those examined by Nickelsburg. Cavallin mentions Dan 12:2 and Dan 12:13 as the principal Old Testament references to resurrection. He classifies the texts according to their geographical and cultural setting rather than to their topic, identifying two great groups: texts coming from Palestinian Judaism and texts coming from Greek-speaking Judaism of the Diaspora.

Important texts falling into the first category are the Enochic cycle, the *Testaments of the Twelve Patriarchs*, the *Psalms of Solomon* and the Qumran's manuscripts. Cavallin only finds one or at most two texts in the Dead Sea Scrolls which reflect the belief in resurrection (4Q181 1 II 3–6; 4QPsDn 38–40). He also studies the *Life of Adam and Eve* (with the *Apocalypse of Moses*), the *Book of Biblical Antiquities*, Pseudo-Philo, *4 Ezra*, *2 Baruch*, the *Apocalypse of Abraham*, the *Testament of Abraham*, and the *Apocryphal of Ezekiel*. Finally, he goes on to analyze the most significant inscriptions found in Palestine.

The exposition of the texts from the Greek-speaking Jewish community of Diaspora starts with those passages in the Septuagint that deviate from the original Hebrew version (perhaps influenced by the belief in the resurrection of the dead), 2 Macc, 4 Macc, Wis, Philo's writings (concerned with the immortality of the soul), Josephus' testimonies, the *Sibylline Oracles*, *Pseudo-Phocylides*, *Joseph and Aseneth*, the *Testament*

---

20. The first part of the book *Life after Death: Paul's Argument for the Resurrection of the Dead in 1 Cor 15*, by H. C .C. Cavallin, is titled "An Enquiry into the Jewish Background," and it contains a detailed analysis of the intertestamental texts about the belief in the resurrection of the dead.

of Job, *2 Enoch* (*Slavonic Enoch*), and certain inscriptions from tombs of Jews in the Diaspora referring to life after death, although not clearly manifesting a belief in resurrection.

The examination of both sets of texts leads Cavallin to support the idea that a unified anthropology never appeared, but "the writers intend to state that the personality survives."[21] There is no further specification or aim of accuracy about how the personality survives, and a unified perspective on the structure of human being does not exist at all.

Cavallin finds three recurrent motives in intertestamental literature:

1. Astral immortality of the just (Dan 12:13; *1 Enoch* 104:2; Wis 3:7; *4 Ezra* 7:97; *Book of Biblical Antiquities* 33:5), also present in certain Old Testament passages (like Deut 12:3), but principally connected with Eastern *theologoumena*.
2. The assumption or exaltation of the just, recalling Isa 52:13.
3. The topic about the holy ones of Israel, stemming from the Old Testament imagery.

He ends up enumerating twelve important theses as a colophon to his research:[22]

1) *There is obviously no single Jewish doctrine about life or death in the period under consideration.*[23]

The texts examined by Cavallin prove that Second Temple Judaism did not know a uniform eschatology, neither in the Old Testament nor in intertestamental literature. There are at least three predominant perspectives: the oldest one, which conceives of Sheol as the common destiny for all human beings, the idea of resurrection of the flesh, and that of immortality of the soul.

2) *These ideas, partly contrary, partly possible to harmonize, but seldom actually harmonized, do not only change from one stream of tradition to*

---

21. Cavallin, *Life after Death*, 212.
22. Cf. ibid., 199–201.
23. Mowinckel has underlined this aspect: "These ideas were never systematically arranged; and any attempt so to present them would only result in an artificial picture" (*He That Cometh*, 267).

another, but appear simply juxtaposed in the same writings and even in passages very close to each other.

Resurrection and immortality of the soul may appear together in certain works (e.g., 4 *Ezra* 7), indicating that by the time they were written, a systematic reflection on anthropology and eschatology had not taken place. Instead of this, the confluence of ideas from different origins (Greek, Old Hebrew, Eastern . . .) finds a common ground in the belief in the persistence of personality beyond death. The problem grows when we differentiate general eschatology (the consummation of the world) from particular eschatology (individual resurrection, judgement, and reward), both of which are intended to be reconciled in writings like 4 *Ezra* through the idea of an intermediate state.

3) *It is necessary to demythologize texts in order to get their truly relevant meaning, which transcends the specific symbols or representations.*

This thesis must be understood in the context of 1970s dominant theology, and especially after the so-called demythologization proposal of Rudolf Bultmann[24] and the School of Marburg.

4) *Resurrection of the body does not prevail in most documents.*

In fact, few Old Testament and intertestamental eschatological texts may be depicted as containing explicit references to the resurrection of the flesh. The latter is often confused with the immortality of the soul or with the resurrection of the people in a collective sense (as a restora-

---

24. Demythologization advocates for a critical assessment of the mythological elements found in the primitive Christian writings, which make the preaching of the Gospel incompatible with the mentality of modern societies. Bultmann's work assimilates existentialist philosophy (most notably, Heidegger's existential analytics) to Christian theology. Cf. Jaspers and Bultmann, *Myth and Christianity*. Concerning Bultmann's interpretation of the faith in the resurrection of the dead, cf. Greshake, *Auferstehung der Toten*, 109–25. A fundamental problem that every project of demythologization is compelled to address is that of the definition of a "myth." What is, in fact, a myth? Does all human discourses fall into this category? Is it sufficient to characterize it from the study of rites, from a mythopoietic point of view, or from the examination of the unconscious? It seems, as Roland Barthes emphasizes, that mythology offers at least two dimensions: formal-semiological (which could be associated with the synchronic sphere) and historical-ideological (linked to the diachronic sphere; cf. Barthes, *Mythologies*, 112). Every myth exhibits a series of constant structural elements that reproduce universal human situations, but the expression of these situations is mediated by the historical scenario. For a structuralist approach to myth, cf. Segal, *Structuralism in Myth*; Barthes, *Mythologies*, 112.

tion). The majority of these texts might fit in what Cavallin has classified as Palestinian Jewish works (Dan 12:2; *Life of Adam and Eve*, *Book of Biblical Antiquities*, *4 Ezra*, *2 Baruch*).

5) *Resurrection is associated with the divine glorification of the just rather than with a material, bodily dimension.*

Nickelsburg had already remarked that the idea of resurrection, both in the first Old Testament references and in the oldest intertestamental testimonies, possessed a functional nature regarding the exaltation of the suffering just by God.

6) *Palestinian sources do not emphasize the idea of immortality of the soul.*

The most important writings of the Greek-speaking Judaism of Diaspora, such as the works of Philo of Alexandria and the book of Wisdom, do not mention resurrection of the flesh. They gravitate around the idea of immortality of the soul, a concept of far-reaching importance in different Greek philosophical schools (Orphic, Pythagorean, Platonic).[25] Palestinian sources do not bestow such a nuclear position on the notion of immortality of the soul, although this statement should be confronted with different passages from the Enochic cycle, like *1 Enoch* 22,[26] which contain allusions to the imperishable nature of the spirits of the just and the impious.

7) *Qumran shows an anticipated eschatology, in which immortality and resurrection are "realized" realities.*

Cavallin shares the same point of view than Nickelsburg and Collins. This thesis should be compared with that of Puech (1993).

---

25. For an introduction to Pythagoreanism, Platonism, Orphism, and their views on the afterlife, cf. Reale and Antiseri, *Il Pensiero Occidentale dalle Origini ad Oggi: Storia delle Idee Filosofiche e Scientifiche.*

26. In *1 Enoch* 22:9–11 we read: "These three have been made in order that the spirits of the dead might be separated. And in the manner in which the souls of the righteous are separated (by) this spring of water with light upon it, in like manner, the sinners are set apart when they die and are buried in the earth and judgement has not been executed upon them in their lifetime, upon this great pain, until the great day of judgement—and to those who curse (there will be) plague and pain forever, and the retribution of their spirits. They will bind them there forever—even if from the beginning of the world."

8) *Several intertestamental writings attribute great importance to the idea of an imminent end of history, although 4 Macc, Philo, and Testament of Abraham are focused on the destiny of the individual.*

General eschatology and the concept of "consummation of history" are intrinsically linked to the apocalyptic imagination, as we have analyzed in the previous chapter. It is in fact difficult to understand the birth of the belief in resurrection without the parallel development of a theology of history. This development was nurtured by several apocalyptic authors. The eschatological concern of the apocalyptic writings affects history as a whole and the end of the world. Those writings influenced by the Greek cultural environment, such as Philo of Alexandria's works and 4 Macc, do not draw much attention on the topic of the consummation of history which involves a linear perspective in the arrow of time that was not so clear for the Hellenistic mentality. The interest in the fate of the individual goes beyond the interest in the destiny of history as a whole. Anyway, Cavallin has shown how both perspectives, the general and the individual, also coexist in certain writings, generating different problems of interpretation.

9) *These writings account for a harmonization between the common end of history and the immediate salvation of the individual.*

An example of this is *4 Ezra* and his idea of an "intermediate state," some sort of proposal to solve the apparent impossibility of reconciling the judgement and the destiny of the individual with the judgement and the fate of history as a whole.

10) *The so-called intermediate state implies a harmonization between the two perspectives (that of general eschatology and that of individual or particular eschatology).*

In Cavallin's own words, "there seems to be a tendency in 4 Ezra to try to combine and harmonize different eschatological ideas, inasmuch as it describes the intermediate state, harmonizing the end time of resurrection with the immediate retribution after death."[27]

---

27. Cavallin, *Life after Death*, 84.

11) *The most consistent topic in the different texts is the one of judgement and final retribution.*

Cavallin is admitting, as so does Nickelsburg, that the idea of resurrection initially constituted a functional instrument to express the notion of judgement and of vindication of the just people in spite of their earthly suffering. In fact, a majority of the texts place resurrection in parallel to the eschatological judgement.

12) *The rabbinic canonization of the resurrection of the dead is the culmination of a process beginning in early intertestamental literature.*

Just as Nickelsburg, Cavallin brings the origin of the idea of resurrection of the dead back to early intertestamental literature, at the end of the third century BCE. There exists a restricted continuity with the eschatological conceptions of the Old Testament.

Any analysis of Cavallin's work must be aware of the changes of appreciation in the theological and exegetical tendencies during the last decades.[28] However, it is true that his approach offers a perspective that cannot be ignored at all: the differences between the eschatological conceptions of the Old Testament and intertestamental literature make it necessary for both the theologian and the exegete to look for the essential doctrinal basis underlying these conceptions, beyond the particular representations that they may have adopted. This core content could be, according to Cavallin, the divine exaltation or glorification of the just. The resurrection of the dead might consist of a *theologoumenon* aimed at providing with a symbolic representation of the conviction that divine power cannot leave the just person unrewarded after his death.

In a strictly philosophical level, it is interesting to notice how this attempt to reach the essence of pre-rabbinic Jewish eschatology beyond its different symbolic representations keeps a close relation with Hegel's philosophical appeal to transcend the representation by the concept, retaining its universal content. In any case, it is extremely difficult, although not impossible, to separate the symbolism from the idea with the intention of being capable of recognizing the most genuine dimension of eschatology.

---

28. The proposal of a demythologized reading of the ideas of resurrection and immortality of the soul has been defended by Krister Stendahl, too, who thinks that both beliefs demand a creative, demythologizing interpretation if they are to be taken seriously by twenty-first-century thought (Cf. Stendahl, *Immortality and Resurrection*, 5).

Geza Vermes can be said to follow the perspective defined by Nickelsburg and Cavallin, which regards resurrection as an innovation within Judaism, whose goal was to express the idea of an afterlife reward for the just, as a divine exaltation/glorification of those who have been righteous in life. Vermes thinks "resurrection is unquestionably one of the most important and intriguing concepts of the Christian faith . . . In the Judaism of the Old Testament, resurrection made only a few late and foggy appearances, probably not before the end of the third century BCE,"[29] even though it is undeniable that this belief rapidly assumed a central role in Judaism. Vermes supports the idea that the late emergence of the doctrine of resurrection cannot be interpreted in terms of an exogenous borrowing, as if it were an ideological import in the history of religions. We are rather committed to suppose that "resurrection, or more precisely, bodily resurrection, is definitely a Jewish idea."[30]

Vermes shows how the idea of resurrection began as a metaphor of the rebirth of the nation, as it may be seen in Ezek 37: "The dream of the biblical Israelites, especially in the pre-exilic age—before the sixth century BCE—was to enjoy God-fearing, long and happy life amid their families and expect at the end, having reached the fullness of years, to join peacefully their predecessors in the ancestral tomb." However, as it has been noticed by most authors, the traditional theology of Israel developed the hope in a continued presence with God, which can be appreciated in certain Psalms (particularly Ps 73:23). But it is also true that "for most Jews of the Old Testament period—the exceptions belong to the last two hundred years of the pre-Christian era and to the first century CE—the grave marked the final end of a man's story."[31]

A distinction began to appear between the just and the unjust in relation to death, and in Isa 26:19 we hear of the divine victory over Sheol as a way of reanimating the bodies of the just. This means that resurrection would be fulfilling, at this point, the function of representing a reward for the just. Resurrection could be seen as a mechanism for God to deliver justice to those who deserve it. It is with Daniel that resurrection will turn to be an almost universal reality, followed by a divine judgement. Vermes remarks that for Palestinian Judaism resur-

---

29. Vermes, *The Resurrection*, xvi. Some important reviews of this book are Miller's and Byron's.

30. Ibid.

31. Ibid., 14.

rection did not offer such a problematic character as it did for the more Hellenized Jews of regions like Alexandria, in which the influence of Greek philosophy was in every respect greater.

With the advent of intertestamental literature, a radical change in the way of understanding death happens. Works like *Psalms of Solomon* and *2 Baruch* express the belief in the resurrection of the dead, restricted, however, to the just people. Immortality of the soul, instead of resurrection, plays a key role in other intertestamental books, such as Pseudo-Phocylides and Philo of Alexandria's writings. Concerning Qumran, Vermes says that "the outcome of the study of the Qumran texts both of the subject of afterlife in general, and on resurrection in particular, is rather disappointing."[32] Vermes acknowledges the extensive research carried out by Émile Puech in his study of potential references to the eschatological convictions of the Qumran community, but he only sees in 4Q 521 (fragment 2ii, line 12) a possible mention of resurrection: "He heals the wounded and revives the dead and brings good news to the poor."

Positive Hypothesis: Continuity between Resurrection and Israelite Tradition

Klaas Spronk has made a comparative study of the conceptions of the afterlife in Israel and the surrounding civilizations, a necessary tool for the contextualization of Hebrew eschatology.[33]

According to this author, neither Egypt, nor Persia, nor Greece, nor Canaan provide us with an adequate platform to find the roots of the Jewish belief in the resurrection of the dead; it is therefore necessary to explain the birth of this idea in terms of endogenous causes. The question is about the factors which, within Yahwism, fostered the birth of an idea, that of resurrection of the dead, which radically contrasted with the primitive faith in the common destiny of all the individuals. This common fate was seen as independent of the moral value of actions: everyone was meant to go to Sheol, and there was no hope in a future life.

As Spronk writes: "the factors within Yahwism which are usually supposed to have ultimately led to the belief in beatific afterlife can be summarized as a growing sense of individuality next to the belief in

32. Ibid., 44.
33. Cf. Spronk, *Beatific Afterlife in Ancient Israel*. Cf. the review of Spronk's book by Smith and Bloch-Smith.

Yhwh being powerful and just and the hope for a lasting communion with *Yhwh*."[34] The first argument (that of a gradual individualization of faith and religious praxis) is already found in Nickelsburg, although this author has emphasized that the tragedy experienced under the persecution of Antiochus IV Epiphanes played a decisive role in the configuration of Jewish self-awareness.

For Spronk, "Deut 32:39, 1 Sam 2:6, Amos 9:2 and Ps 139:18 are interpreted by most scholars as early indications of the conviction that the power of Yhwh also extends to the dead and the netherworld."[35] These texts offer in fact an open door to the hope in a beatific afterlife.

Looking for Old Testament precedents of the belief in resurrection is not a new goal. Several authors[36] have identified in certain passages from the Hebrew Bible elements which might be connected with this future faith. Sellin, as early as 1919,[37] related the ascent of Enoch and Elijah to Dan 12:3 and to its idea of astral immortality.

The general dynamism leading to individualization that took place in the Israelite religion recalls a phenomenon present in the teachings of Jeremiah and Ezekiel, with their stressing the responsibility of the individual in his own deeds. This might have results in the representation of eschatology finally transcending the narrow category of collective restoration (the triumph of the genus over the individual), as it had prevailed in ancient times, to open itself to the consideration of the destiny of the individual.

At any rate, it is important to realize, as Spronk does, that collectivism and individualism were never totally separated. In fact, the transition from Israel's *restauratio* to the individual's resurrection does not imply an abandonment of the importance attributed to the community

---

34. Spronk, *Beatific Afterlife in Ancient Israel and in the Ancient Near East*, 72.

35. Spronk, *Beatific Afterlife in Ancient Israel and in the Ancient Near East*, 72. Deut 32:39: "Now see that I, even I, am He, and there is no God besides me; I kill and I make alive (*aní amit wahayeh*); I wound and I heal; nor is there any who can deliver from my hand." 1 Sam 2:6: "The Lord kills and makes alive; He brings down to the grave and brings up (*waya'l*)." Amos 9:2: "Though they dig into hell, from there my hand shall take them (*misham yadé tiqahem*); though they climb up to heaven, from there I will bring them down." Ps 139:18: "If I should count them, they would be more in number than the sand; when I awake, I am still with you."

36. Cf. Levenson, *Resurrection and the Restoration of Israel*.

37. We are referring to the article "Die alttestamentliche Hoffnung auf Auferstehung und ewiges Leben," cited by Spronk, *Beatific Afterlife in Ancient Israel*, 73.

of the people of Israel as a whole, because general eschatology still keeps the hope in a new creation that will restore divine sovereignty upon Israel. The inextricable association of community and individuality in the Israelite mentality makes it difficult for Spronk to defend a direct relation in terms of cause and effect with the idea of the resurrection of the dead[38] which, as explicitly formulated, is neither in Jeremiah nor in Ezekiel.

Another factor that could help justify the emergence of the belief in resurrection is the hope in a continuation of communion with Yahweh, acquiring unusual relevance in certain Psalms and wisdom texts.[39] These passages would confront other ones which describe death and Sheol as places of no return.[40]

The former opposition reflects an underlying tension in the Old Testament eschatological conceptions, and it will not be completely solved until the canonization of the idea of resurrection by rabbinic Judaism after 70 CE. It is also interesting to notice, as Spronk does, that it is better not to confuse the tendency leading to individual resurrection (as it appears in Dan 12) with the one guiding to a more mystical and less materialistic view (in the sense of bodily resurrection) of future life.[41]

Spronk has also analyzed the conceptions of the afterlife in ancient Israel. The funerary customs tend to be rather conservative,[42] and "archaeology has also revealed that we cannot speak of a typical Israelite way of burial . . . the way the deceased was buried indicates that the

---

38. Cf. Spronk, *Beatific Afterlife in Ancient Israel*, 73.

39. An example of this appears in Ps 16:10–11: "For you will not leave my soul in Sheol, nor will you allow your holy one to see corruption. You will show me the path of life; in your presence is fullness of joy; at your right hand are pleasures forevermore."

40. This perspective is present in the following passages: "For Sheol cannot thank you, death cannot praise you; those who go down to the pit cannot hope for your truth." (Isa 38:18); "Hear, o Lord, and have mercy on me; Lord, be my helper!" (Ps 30:10); "The dead do not praise the Lord, nor any who go down into silence." (Ps 115:17).

41. Cf. Spronk, *Beatific Afterlife in Ancient Israel*, 75. Another important element, cited by Spronk too is covenantal theology. Resurrection is possible because God has established a perennial covenant with the people of Israel.

42 Cf. Ibid., 237. The expression of mourning in Israel, as recorded in the Hebrew Bible, is rather similar to that of other Near Eastern cultures like Mesopotamia (cf. tale of the death of Enkidy in the Gilgamesh cycle, VIII.ii.19–22) and Ugarit. Those who practiced public mourning in these cultures, just as in Israel, identified themselves with the dead: they stopped washing their faces and they took no care for their physical appearance, as an expression of sympathy with those who had passed away (see ibid., 245).

state of the dead was believed to resemble their life before death."[43] It is difficult to define in concise terms the ancient Israelite beliefs about the nature of the dead: in Deut 26:14 we are told that the dead need to be sustained, resembling the Egyptian conceptions of the netherworld.

On the cult of the dead, Spronk thinks that finding food offerings does not constitute a conclusive proof of the existence of this kind of worship. In any case, it stands in favor of the special care given to the dead: "clear evidence of a cult of the dead practised by Israelites is scarce."[44] We may conclude that "the ancient Israelite funerary customs point to a belief in some kind of continued existence of life after death."[45] Practices such as necromancy (formally forbidden but still frequent) and exorcisms reveal that the dead could have either a positive or a negative effect on the living.

Regarding the Old Testament topics that might have been relevant in shaping the later belief in the resurrection of the dead, Spronk highlights the ascents of Enoch and Elijah (who did not die, but were taken into heaven before the presence of God). It is equally relevant to elucidate which texts can be interpreted as a reaction against certain foreign conceptions which were seen as contrary to the faith of Israel. Spronk underlines the following texts: the already quoted Deut 32:39 and Hos 11:2–3, as a reaction against the Ugaritic idea that Baal heals and revives.[46]

Spronk thinks that the Yahwistic silence on the afterlife might be due to the rejection of Baalism rather than to a deliberate denial of the existence of a future life, because "the belief in *Yhwh* helping and even revivifying the dead, as may have been popular with some groups of the Israelites, could too easily be confused or identified with Canaanite beliefs concerning the yearly resurrection of the Baal."[47] Texts like Deut 32:39 do not hesitate to grant Yahweh the same power than Baal, as it is done in 1 Sam 2:6 and Ps 22:30.

---

43. Spronk, *Beatific Afterlife in Ancient Israel*, 238.
44. Ibid., 249.
45. Ibid., 251.
46. "As they called them, so they went from them; they sacrificed to the Baals, and burned incense to carved images. I taught Ephraim to walk, taking them by their arms; but they did not know that I healed them" (Hos 11:2–3).
47. Spronk, *Beatific Afterlife in Ancient Israel*, 281.

The idea of a rescue from death is an important precedent in the evolution of the Israelite eschatological conceptions before the formulation of the doctrine of the resurrection of the dead. Nevertheless, the predominant view among the authors, at least since Barth,[48] is that of interpreting this literary topic, common to various Psalms, not as a reference to the future, but to the present life. Ps 118:17[49] and Ps 119:75[50] think of life as an act of appraisal of Yahweh. To live is to praise Yahweh, and death deprives from the possibility of worshipping the Lord, the God of Israel. In fact, the rescue is generally aimed at allowing the possibility to continue praising Yahweh.[51] Ps 103:3–5 says that Yahweh rescues and, in parallel, heals: rescue is linked to the healing performed by Yahweh. It is therefore reasonable to suppose that it refers to a rescue before death.[52]

Spronk's work is a valuable contribution to the study of the development of Jewish eschatology from the perspective of the comparative history of religions in the ancient Near East. An interesting contribution of this author is his linking the Jahwistic silence on the afterlife to the opposition to Baalistic cults of Canaanite origin. This would explain why it was not until a relatively late age that the topic of the afterlife became central in Jewish theology.

Émile Puech's[53] considerations offer very interesting insights for current research on the belief in the afterlife in Second Temple Judaism. The principal focus of his work is the Dead Sea Scrolls, but he has also

---

48. C. Barth developed his thesis in *Die Errettung vom Tode in der individuellen Kluge und Dankliedern des Alten Testaments*, of 1947, cited in ibid., 286.

49. "I shall not die, but live, and declare the works of the Lord (*ky ehyeh*)."

50. "I know, O Lord, that your judgments *are* right, and that in faithfulness you have afflicted me."

51. Cf. the following texts: "That I may tell of all your praise in the gates of the daughter of Zion. I will rejoice in your salvation. The nations have sunk down in the pit which they made; in the net which they hid, their own foot is caught" (Ps 9:14–15); "Sing praise to the Lord, you saints of his, and give thanks at the remembrance of his holy name" (Ps 30:4).

52. Cf. Spronk, *Beatific Afterlife in Ancient Israel*, 286. There are different Canaanite and even Egyptian elements in this psalm, in spite of the fact that the Yahwistic conception (monotheism, the eternity of God, and the mortal nature of man) has not been lost. Cf. ibid., 289.

53. Puech's principal work, *La Croyance des Esséniens en la Vie Future* (1993), whose first volume is dedicated to "la résurrection des morts et le contexte scripturaire," has been subject to several academic reviews, by García Martínez, VanderKam, Sacchi, Ausín, and Maier.

analyzed both biblical and intertestamental texts regarding the idea of resurrection.

According to Puech, the examination of the funerary beliefs held by the Mesopotamian peoples shows that this type of practices might have favored the conviction that in spite of the weakening of the body on earth, the *etemmu* of man (his double or, to speak in a more metaphorical way, his shadow or spirit) still exists under the earth, in the country of no-return. The relationship between that shadow and the corpse was, anyway, mysterious.[54] Puech reminds us of the documentary evidence of the knowledge in Qumran of such an important text for Mesopotamian literature as the Epic of Gilgamesh. This is a proof of the high degree of diffusion that certain beliefs or frames of understanding concerning the afterlife achieved in the Near East.

On Syria-Palestine, which has bequeathed to us so significant texts as the "Descent of Baal into hell," in which the name *Baal rap'u* or "Baal the taumaturg" [*Baal guèrisseur*] appears, the belief in Baal's healing power (which could be viewed as a form of salvific power) plays an important role and it is probably referred to the deceased ancestors who remained alive in the memory and in the worship offered by the community.[55] Puech indicates that the fierce opposition found by the worship of Baal in the harsh criticism of the prophets is not but a demonstration of the level of social acceptance that these practices had encountered in Israel.

Regarding Israel, Puech thinks that in the earliest stages of its religiosity the influence from Canaanite and Syro-Phoenician conceptions on the afterlife prevailed. It seems that there was not much evolution in the funerary practice and in the belief in the after-world in the Middle East from Ugarit until the Phoenicians under Persian rule.[56] This statement is sufficiently eloquent, as it highlights the fact that for many centuries

---

54. Cf. Puech, *La Croyance des Esséniens en la Vie Future*, 3.

55. Cf. Ibid., 5. However, it needs to be noticed that in the global eschatological context of the Middle East in the first two millennia BCE it does not seem that the possibility of an afterlife was radically excluded. In any case, it is extremely difficult to compare different religions as the Egyptian and the Mesopotamian on the topic of death and judgement, and it is not easy to clarify the extent that this afterlife existence was associated with the preservation of individuality, or whether the concept entailed simply a vague spiritual presence of the deceased in an equally obscure post-mortem space. As Puech remarks, there is evidence of a Phoenician belief in the journey to the netherworld, to a new existence.

56. Cf. Ibid., 12.

a significant religious and theological development on afterlife beliefs and future life did not take place. The same conceptions inherited from Mesopotamian cultures endured for a long time, being substituted either by Zoroastrianism and its eschatology and by Hellenism. But it only happened by the fourth century BCE. Before this, the same ethereal imagery on the afterlife was predominant in Semitic cultures. As a consequence, the fact that the biblical mentality did not represent a clear subversion of earlier beliefs on the future life until the emergence of apocalypticism (a movement that incorporated, as it has been remarked by different authors, essential elements from prophetic and wisdom religiosity) cannot be interpreted as an exclusive Israelite phenomenon.[57] It was not the result of an excessive religious zeal that made Israel incapable of giving birth to new eschatological ideas. It was, on the other hand, quite a common feature of Near Eastern cultures.

According to Puech, there were two principal Jewish answers to the problem of death: the denial of a future life and the belief in a future victory over death. The second option was subject to different categorizations (immortality of soul, resurrection, and even eschatological anticipation of future life), but the conceptual basis remains untouched: human life does not end with death. On the term "resurrection," Puech makes the following remark about its ambiguity: does it refer to a return to the previous life or is it to be understood as an entry into eternal life? If this were the case, under which form would it happen?[58] This detail has not been specified by intertestamental eschatology, at least if we take into account that in a "recent" apocalyptic book like 4 Ezra, written around year 100 CE, the seventh chapter still wonders about the state of the bodies once they have resurrected.

The Old Testament texts examined by Puech are generally coincident with those studied by authors like Nickelsburg and Cavallin. First, Puech analyzes the resurrections performed by Elijah and Elisha, concluding that this type of resurrection did not constitute a definitive salvific event (a strict resurrection), but were reanimations meant to manifest the power of God upon death and Sheol.[59] They should not be confused with the eschatological concept of resurrection, which is

---

57. Cf. Levenson, *Resurrection and the Restoration of Israel*, 207.
58. Cf. Puech, *La Croyance des Esséniens en la Vie Future*, 33.
59. Cf. ibid., 38.

associated with the final incorporation into future life, and not with the return to an earthly existence, falling again under the domain of death.[60]

His examination of the Septuagint gives him the opportunity to offer a series of examples that show a double dynamism: the dynamic of eschatological concretion, on the one hand, through the doctrine of the overcoming of death and, in some cases, by means of the idea of resurrection; and the dynamic of generalization and abstraction, on the other hand. This second dynamic can be observed in the transition from the concrete name "grave" to the abstract name "corruption." At first glance, both dynamics could seem contradictory to each other: specification and generalization. We think, however, that there is not such a sharp incompatibility, at least if we assume that the doctrine of the overcoming of death and its concretion in the idea of resurrection implies an approach to the final problem of existence from the point of view of an "abstraction" from earthly life: the life we enjoy on Earth is broadened in order to reach the further step of our presence in the world. This phenomenon of the "eschatological extension of earthly life" incorporated the imagery of the worldly existence, with notions such as judgement and reward that were the result of an abstraction. This abstraction was common to many other religions (and especially to the Egyptian and the Zoroastrian creeds), and it was a manifestation of the process of anthropomorphization whose goal is to symbolize judgement and afterlife retribution.

We may therefore consider the development of the eschatology of victory upon death, and its highest expression in the doctrine of the resurrection of the dead, as an extension of the primitive concept of life, so as to make it capable of encompassing an existence after the earthly death. This perspective passed on to the Greek translations of *Tanakh*,[61] as it has been underlined by Cavallin and Puech (among others), although from the point of view of the pure biblical analysis it is impossible to

---

60. Puech mentions three prophetic texts: Hos 6:1–3; Ezek 37:1–14; and Isa 52:13—53:12. The first one shows Israel's hope in a return to life, whereas Ezekiel accounts for the restoration of Israel. The text from the Servant Songs expresses the hope in the rehabilitation of the Servant, in the triumph of life, which cannot be seen, as Puech points out, as an individual retribution but as a grace manifested in the fulfilment of the divine plan (cf. ibid., 44). These texts can be interpreted as testimonies of the hope in the continuation of life, which progressively shaped the Israelite *forma mentis*. Without this hope it is not possible to understand the emergence of the idea of resurrection, which is a thematization of the idea of the continuation of life.

61. See the Septuagint version of Prov 15:24. Cf. Cavallin, *Life after Death*, 103.

determine which other factors (sociological, political, cultural) were also influential in such a decisive turn in the Israelite theology.

The doctrine of the resurrection represented an integration of previous religious and theological traditions into a social and historical context that demanded a new eschatology: the theology of the covenant, Isaiah's prophetic theology of the Servant of Yahweh, the apocalyptic notion of a new world and a consummation of history, the wisdom literature critical questioning of the traditional doctrines regarding evil and justice, the hope in a continued joy of the presence of God, etc. Resurrection was therefore a theological synthesis framed by apocalypticism which, far removed from meaning a radical rupture with earlier traditions, assimilated some of their key elements. Notwithstanding the possible exogenous influences in the birth of the doctrine of resurrection, biblical scholarship and the analysis of Jewish literature make it legitimate to state that such a doctrine did not necessarily have to involve an absolute separation or alienation from the religiosity of the people of Israel.

In his study of Old Testament apocrypha, Puech chooses a philological classification: books written in Semitic languages,[62] and books written in Greek.[63]

---

62. Puech mentions the references to the belief in the resurrection of the dead that can be found in the Enochic cycle, the *Testaments of the Twelve Patriarchs*, the *Psalms of Solomon*, the *Testament of Moses*, the *Life of Adam and Eve*, the *Apocryphon of Ezekiel*, the *Book of Biblical Antiquities* (Pseudo-Philo), and *2 Baruch*. Second Baruch undoubtedly assumes the idea of resurrection, but the question is: how and under what form is this resurrection going to take place? *Second Baruch* insists upon the fact that resurrection will lead to the former state of the body, re-establishing the earthly corporality. Puech considers this statement anti-Sadducean and anti-Hellenistic (cf. Puech, *La Croyance des Essèniens en la Vie Future*, 139). Nonetheless, the transformation of those who have been justified after the judgement echoes an angelic or a starry glorification. The reward of the just will consist of a totally renewed world, and this is a firm conviction of the great writings of Jewish apocalypticism. The faith in the resurrection of the dead appears in the *Testament of Abraham* too, which refers to the end of the life of the just par excellence: Abraham, and it is explicit in *4 Ezra* 7.

63. The Greek apocrypha includes writings like the *Sibylline Oracles* and *Pseudo-Phocylides*, in which the influence of Hellenistic thought is patent (we participate of divine immortality through *psyche* or *nous*); the *Testament of Job*, written between 40 BCE and 70 CE (Nickelsburg, *Jewish Literature between the Bible and the Mishnah*, 247, dates it back to the first century in Egypt), with explicit mentions of resurrection (such as 4:9 and 40:3), 4 Macc (which seems to substitute resurrection with a more spiritualized belief in immortality—Puech, *La Croyance des Essèniens en la Vie Future*, 173), and *2 Enoch*.

Concerning the non-literary testimonies, like ossuaries and certain inscriptions found in Palestine, Puech is categorical: in its earlier stages they do not prove anything about resurrection, because of the scarce eschatological references they contain, but in the latter ones there is clear evidence of the existence of this belief. Their use covers from the first century BCE up to the third century CE. And concerning the targumim, Puech thinks that the diversity of approaches to the afterlife (with the exception of the doctrine of reincarnation, which is absent) makes it difficult to offer general statements, even though the atmosphere in which these translations were born was not alien but rather favorable to the doctrine of the resurrection of the dead.

According to Puech, the belief in the resurrection of the righteous took shape in certain Jewish circles during the third century BCE.[64] However, it was a selective resurrection, exclusive to the just, since biblical literature gives no conclusive evidence of a universal understanding of resurrection.

Simcha P. Raphael also supports the idea that the doctrine of the resurrection of the dead appeared in continuity with the fundamental theological convictions of the Israelite religion. Raphael sees the doctrine of resurrection of the dead as the next organic and necessary step in the development of biblical conceptions regarding the afterlife.

Raphael identifies two great theological lines that might have progressively led to the formulation of the doctrine of resurrection: the collective redemption of the whole nation, stemming from prophetism, and the individualization in morals and eschatology that had been taking place since the sixth century BCE, especially with Ezekiel. Resurrection has to be regarded as a philosophical integration of all the previous ideas,[65] and it finds its background in the Hebrew conception of the organic unity of the human being, in opposition to a radical separation of body and spirit. For Raphael, while Ezek 37 (the vision of the valley of dry bones) has a clear collective sense (the resurrection of the nation), Isa 26:19 (dated by Raphael in 334 BCE) expresses an individual resurrection.

The book of Daniel represents the definitive advent of apocalyptic thought in the theological horizon of the people of Israel. In it, the Jewish teachings on the afterlife become apocalyptic and dualistic. Sheol, which

---

64. Cf. Puech, *La Croyance des Esséniens en la Vie Future*, 98.
65. Cf. Raphael, *Jewish Views of the Afterlife*, 69.

in Old Testament eschatology was rather inert and lacked vitality, being shared by both the just and the impious, is transformed under apocalypticism into an intermediate space, and it is not anymore an eternal and neutral place.[66]

The evolution of Jewish eschatology cannot be properly understood without studying the influence of Greek philosophy in the Jewish world.[67] In fact, the book of Wisdom (written in the first century BCE) does not speak in terms of resurrection or of intermediate eschatology, but it tries to integrate several fundamental Jewish and Greek conceptions.[68]

However, this development was not uniform. 1 Enoch, the Pentateuch of Enoch, contains a variety of approaches to eschatology, reflecting a complex and multidimensional view of eternal life. Books like *2 Enoch* and *3 Enoch* manifest that a solution to the tension between the individual and the collective notions of judgement and post-mortem survival was never achieved.[69] A late work like *3 Enoch* does not refer to the collective dimension of the judgement: its theological epicenter resides upon the idea of an individual judgement. The triumph of resurrection within Judaism might be due (as Raphael believes) to the strong emphasis on the unity of body and spirit stressed by Hebrew anthropology.

The idea of resurrection must be examined in continuity with the earlier eschatological conceptions. This is Raphael's view. It cannot be denied, however, that resurrection constituted an innovation in comparison to precedent post-mortem ideas. How should we explain its success and its quick implantation into the Jewish mentality so as to become a canonical doctrine under rabbinism? For Raphael, its success stems from its capacity to integrate the collective and the individual dimensions of the afterlife. Primitive Israelite eschatology had recognized both dimensions, but not without tensions. We find constant references to the restoration of the collective Israel, and over time we identify more

---

66. In *1 Enoch* 17 (a part of the *Book of Watchers*), which some authors date back to the third century BCE (cf. Milik and Black, *The Book of Enoch*), some of its sections being older than the book of Daniel, we find a description of Enoch's journey to Sheol. Other parts of the cycle envision a glorious future for the just who have suffered injustice on life. *Second Enoch* contains highly detailed depictions of the afterlife (cf. *2 Enoch* 8:1–7).

67. Cf. Raphael, *Jewish Views of the Afterlife*, 102.

68. Cf. Wis 3:1–4.

69. Cf. Raphael, *Jewish Views of the Afterlife*, 109.

explicit concerns about the destiny of the individual. The doctrine of resurrection made it possible to unify into a common frame of understanding both the idea of national redemption and the idea of individual retribution, and at the same time it pointed to the future.[70]

In Raphael's view, there is a clear prevalence of the thesis of an organic and evolving development of Jewish eschatology until the advent of the idea of resurrection (as the logical result of a process of vital and practical reflection which brings us back to centuries earlier).[71]

Jon D. Levenson supports the idea of the continuity of the doctrine of the resurrection of the dead with the earlier ideas of the Hebrew Bible.[72] His work may be seen, in fact, as a reaction to those streams in biblical scholarship that postulated a radical rupture between both conceptions.

For Levenson, "it is too often forgotten that the classical Jewish doctrine of resurrection does not represent a belief that death can be avoided, averted or minimized. All the contrary, it takes the gravity and tragedy of death with full seriousness and represents a belief that death will be—miraculously, supernaturally, graciously- overcome."[73] The doctrine of resurrection is therefore capable of expressing in its integrity the faith in the promises of life given by God to his people. These promises, as Levenson will argue to a larger detail, are already present in some of the principal texts of Hebrew Bible.

---

70. Cf. ibid., 74.

71. However, this methodological approach to the idea of resurrection cannot hide, as Raphael remarks, the fact that "younger" books like 2 Baruch still see death as a natural reality. Jubilees 23:1 speaks in terms of "sleeping with the parents," in connection with the older conception, although in other passages from this book the notion of judgement appears. In the book of Jubilees the fate of the just resides in his living in happiness rather than in a transcendent afterlife reality: "And their bones will rest in the earth, and their spirits will increase joy, and they will know that the Lord is an executor of judgement, but he will show mercy to hundreds and thousands, to all who love him." (*Jubilees* 23:31) However, one might think that the gradual assumption of the doctrine of resurrection involved the introduction of a dualistic anthropology, in opposition to the primitive Hebrew imagery. A manifestation of this phenomenon is in the *Apocalypse of Moses* 32:4, in which we read: "Adam has left his body."

72. Cf. the reviews of Levenson's book *Resurrection and the Restoration of Israel* by Tiemeyer, Gnuse, Lenzi, Hagedorn, and Gignilliat.

73. Levenson, *Resurrection and the Restoration of Israel*, x.

Levenson wonders about the causes that might have led many great modern Jewish thinkers to abandon a formerly canonical belief of their religion. He finds two principal reasons behind this phenomenon:

1. The predominance of rationalism, which interprets resurrection as a sudden interruption of natural laws.
2. Traditionalism, for which the belief in the resurrection of the dead is a late creation within Judaism, alien to the primitive spirit of this religion.[74]

The problem with traditionalism is its difficulties at explaining why this late belief was destined to become a fundamental concept for rabbinic Judaism.[75] Rabbinic literature is derashic and does not follow the patterns of historical-critical methods, but it provides us with precious information on what rabbis saw as the *sensus plenior* of the biblical text. Also, we must not forget that the Hebrew Bible often overlaps on both the individual and the collective levels, for instance in the superposition of Jacob and Israel. This might explain why prophetic and traditional eschatologies were focused on the perspective of the restoration of Israel in a collective sense rather than on the individual resurrection, and how it was possible to move from the eschatology of restoration to a new eschatology (namely, resurrection) that brought together restoration and individual resurrection.

Concerning the examination of traditional Israelite eschatology, Levenson warns against the immediate identification of Sheol and Gehenna with hell (Gehenna being associated with violent deaths, as a way of divine punishment). He also remarks that the Temple "was thought to be an antidote to death, giving a kind of immortality to those who dwell there in innocence, purity and trust."[76] One could, however,

---

74. Ibid., 23–24.

75. According to Levenson, the principal problem with the interpretations that view the experience of the suffering of the just as the catalyzing factor in the emergence of a new synthesis expressed in terms of resurrection is that not all Jewish groups accepted this new doctrine as an overcoming of the dialectics of a thesis (divine justice in life) and an antithesis (the suffering of the just and the success of the impious), similar to the Hegelian *Aufhebung* (cf. ibid., 194). We do not find a trace of this doctrine in *Ben Sira*: the relation of cause-effect between the traumatic events of Antiochus IV's persecution and the meditation on theodicy do not constitute the sole basis for a satisfactory explanation of the undeniable triumph of the idea of resurrection in the Jewish religion.

76. Ibid., 90. Levenson argues that there is growing evidence of the practice of spiritualism, mantic wisdom, and cult of the dead in ancient Israel, even though he admits

think of this reference to the Temple as a mere literary ploy, in no way invested with the same degree of realism as Dan 12:1–3. There is always legitimacy in the fundamental suspicion that these texts are referring to immortality rather than to resurrection. Levenson believes that this doubt may be resolved if we realize that they tend to unveil a redeeming action by God which contrasts with the peaceful and calm continuity of immortality.[77]

The Babylonian exile envisioned the hope for a restoration of Israel, for a return to the protological state.[78] Levenson mentions the view of the valley of the dry bones in Ezekiel, a basic text for the articulation of the doctrine of the restoration of Israel.[79] Against those who identify

---

that we still have too many questions. Torah forbade these practices (cf. ibid., 47), but it is necessary to differentiate the Hebrew Bible from the popular religiosity of Israel: "biblical sources, to reiterate, proscribe necromancy (e.g., Deut 18:9–14), deliver prophetic indictments of those who engage in it (Isa 8:19–22), and express contempt for 'sacrifices offered to the dead' (Ps 106:28–31), to give just three typical examples" (ibid., 58). However, the formal clarity of the biblical laws does not mean that these kind of religious practices had been entirely abandoned in the popular religiosity.

77. Ibid., 106.

78. This feeling can be found in paradigmatic texts from Deutero-Isaiah and Jeremiah: "Yet hear now, O Jacob my servant, and Israel whom I have chosen. Thus says the Lord who made you and formed you from the womb, who will help you: 'Fear not, O Jacob my servant; and you, Jeshurun, whom I have chosen. For I will pour water on him who is thirsty, and floods on the dry ground; I will pour my Spirit on your descendants, and my blessing on your offspring; they will spring up among the grass like willows by the watercourses.' One will say, 'I am the Lord's'; another will call himself by the name of Jacob; another will write with his hand, 'the Lord's,' and name himself by the name of Israel." (Isa 44:1–5); "Thus says the Lord: 'A voice was heard in Ramah, lamentation and bitter weeping, Rachel weeping for her children, refusing to be comforted for her children, because they are no more.' Thus says the Lord: "Refrain your voice from weeping, and your eyes from tears; for your work shall be rewarded, says the Lord, and they shall come back from the land of the enemy. There is hope in your future, says the Lord, that your children shall come back to their own border" (Jer 31:15–17).

79. Collins (*Apocalypticism in the Dead Sea Scrolls*, 110) reads Isa 26:19 under the inspiration of the theology of Ezekiel 37 (the restoration of Israel): "Your dead shall live (יִחְיוּ מֵתֶיךָ); together with my dead body they shall arise. Awake and sing, you who dwell in dust; for your dew is like the dew of herbs, and the earth shall cast out the dead." However, Levenson indicates that there are disagreements about this interpretation. Some authors think that the text from Ezekiel is not speaking of the restoration of a nation but of reviving the members of a nation, as can be observed in the use of the expression "your dead" (*metejá*). According to Levenson, the key to understanding the passage resides in the idea of confidence in the Lord as the God of life, who fulfils his promises to Israel: "Indeed, the hope that death may be reversed predates the emergence of Israel itself and constitutes an important aspect

Zoroastrian influences in Ezek 37, Levenson underlines the key differences between the religion of Israel and Zoroastrianism. Ezekiel refers to the restoration of Israel and the "promised land," and it uses the Hebrew verbs *he'ĕlâ* ("getting them up") and *hebî'* ("to bring"), which recall the promise of liberation from Egypt. In this way, "although Ezekiel's vision of the valley does not attest to the expectation of resurrection in the later sense, it does constitute a significant step in the direction of the later doctrine."[80]

The Hebrew Bible shows a deep tension between the universality of death and the belief in the God of life, capable of saving his chosen ones from annihilation. Resurrection hence "reflects certain key features of the deep structure of the theology of pre-exilic Israel."[81] The latter thesis can be regarded as a programmatic statement of Levenson's position: the doctrine of the resurrection of the dead does not appear in a disruptive and unconnected way within Judaism but finds its roots in the profoundest aspirations of the people of Israel. There is continuity between the primitive conceptions of Israel and the eschatology of resurrection, even though Levenson admits that the events related with the persecution of Antiochus IV endorsed the definitive transition to the doctrine of resurrection.

Regarding Dan 12:1–3, Levenson sees Daniel's principal novelty in the binomial *hayyê'ôlah*, "eternal life": those who have been resurrected by the power of Elisha die again, but those who resurrect in the book of Daniel will be raised to the eternal Kingdom of God.[82]

---

of the legacy of ancient Canaan. Without this hope, the religion of Israel would have assumed a very different shape" (Levenson, *Resurrection and the Restoration of Israel*, 202). The influence of the religiosity of Canaan reaches some texts from Hosea, whose background is in the different myths about Baal. Levenson believes that the principle governing texts like Hos 5:14—6:3 is that of the capacity of God to revive, whose effects may be felt in nature too.

80. Levenson, *Resurrection and the Restoration of Israel*, 163.

81. Ibid., 180.

82. In 2 Kgs 4:31, in the narration of Elisha's miracles, we read: "Now Gehazi went on ahead of them, and laid the staff on the face of the child; but there was neither voice nor hearing. Therefore he went back to meet him, and told him, saying 'the child has not awakened.'" And in Job 14:12: "So man lies down and does not rise. Till the heavens are no more, they will not awake nor be roused from their sleep." Levenson is critical of the interpretations that consider Daniel 12 an assimilation of Zoroastrian conceptions. He shows that in Zoroastrianism there is no identification between the verb "to sleep" and death, as in Daniel, which must be understood in light of the previous Jewish tradition.

Levenson takes the figure of the "divine warrior" as an essential element in the later configuration of the doctrine of resurrection: the divine warrior is not a violent fanatic, but texts speak of him when referring to the enthronization of God in justice and righteousness. In fact, the enthronement of the divine warrior is followed by the joy of nature.[83]

His analysis of the figure of the divine warrior makes Levenson conclude that "our exploration of the rabbinic doctrine of resurrection has traced its ultimate origin to the transformation that nature undergoes as a result of the divine warrior's astonishing victory."[84] This statement may be interpreted at first glance as risky because of its excessive dependence upon the exegesis of the figure of the divine warrior. Levenson himself has remarked that it is impossible to identify any monocausal explanation for the emergence of the idea of resurrection.[85] The topic of resurrection is too complex to be reduced to a single factor. However, it makes sense to recall of the deep connection that exists in biblical thought among the ideas of restoration, resurrection, and regeneration of life. This much should be acknowledged about Levenson's work.

Levenson's research stands in a privileged position in contemporary literature on the origin of the belief in resurrection in Jewish religion. As Bakhos explains, much of the strength of Levenson's work lies in his capacity to rigorously cope with the multiple aspects of the notion of eschatological resurrection: while several scholars have underlined the differences between the Bible and the systematic Judaism of rabbinical literature (and it is true that there are many), Levenson has detected resonances. He has therefore contributed to remarking continuity rather than disruption.[86]

---

83. "Let the heavens rejoice, and let the earth be glad; let the sea roar, and all its fullness; let the field be joyful, and all that *is* in it. Then all the trees of the woods will rejoice before the Lord. For He is coming, for He is coming to judge the earth (לִשְׁפֹּט הָאָרֶץ). He shall judge the world with righteousness, and the peoples with His truth" (Ps 96: 11–13).

84. Levenson, *Resurrection and the Restoration of Israel*, 217.

85. "The development of a belief in resurrection is too deeply and thickly rooted in early Israelite and other ancient Near Eastern tradition for any monocausal explanation to do justice" (Ibid., 196) It cannot be justified as a result of "religious engineering," as if a certain theologian or ideologue had thought of resurrection as the perfect synthesis to transcend the contradiction involving divine justice and unfair earthly suffering.

86. Cf. the review of Levenson's book by Bakhos. Levenson reiterates his view in Madigan and Levenson, *Resurrection: The Power of God for Christians and Jews*.

Synthetic Hypothesis

John J. Collins [87] has studied the belief in the resurrection of the dead in the context of the history of apocalyptic ideas in Second Temple Judaism. The intrinsic variety of eschatological representations in the apocalyptic writings makes it necessary to pose the question about what is truly essential in the apocalyptic conception of the afterlife. For Collins, "the belief in the judgement of individuals after death is one of the crucial elements that distinguish apocalyptic writings from earlier biblical tradition."[88]

Nickelsburg had spoken of the gradual individualization of Jewish religious practice and the reaction against Greek rationality as the catalysts for the idea of resurrection. Collins thinks that before the emergence of the doctrine of resurrection as a fundamental teaching of Jewish eschatology there were two great lines that might have led to the conviction that earthly life does not end with death: the wish to enjoy the presence of God and the theology of the restoration of Israel. The wish to enjoy the presence of God appears in biblical writings such as Ps 73, but Collins does not consider these texts to be a *de facto* expression of the belief in life after death, because they might be interpreted as referring to a successful and full life in this world. Concerning the restoration of Israel, Collins sees Ezek 37 (the valley of dry bones) as a representation of the whole House of Israel. Collins is sceptical about the possibility of interpreting Isa 26:19 as a reference to individual resurrection and not to collective restoration. He therefore concludes that it is not until Dan 12 that we can be sure of an explicit mention of resurrection in the Hebrew Bible.

The complexity of the problem grows, since for Collins the resurrection mentioned in Daniel is not necessarily a bodily resurrection but could consist of a spiritual resurrection. Daniel does not conceive of the resurrection as a universal reality, at least if we take the text in its literary sense ("many of those who sleep in the dust of the earth," but not "all shall awake"). And concerning the expression "dust of the earth," it is not easy to understand its meaning. It could be referring to Sheol, because Collins points out that in *Jubilees* 17:16 Sheol and dust are taken in parallel. It is in 2 Macc where we do find a reference to the resurrection of the

---

87. Cf. Collins, *Apocalypticism in the Dead Sea Scrolls*, 2. Cf. the reviews of Collins' book by Harrington, Barrer, and McKay.

88. Collins, *Apocalypticism in the Dead Sea Scrolls*, 110.

flesh and not simply to a vague resurrection of the dead which does not clarify much regarding the anthropological structure of the individual.

The text from the book of Daniel does not indicate the way in which resurrection will be performed. It seems to be speaking of a kind of elevation to the angelic world, similar to the one mentioned in *1 Enoch* 104. We must therefore ask this legitimate question: which idea was born by the time of Daniel, that of resurrection of the dead in a purely spiritual or generic sense (the resurrection of a personal identity, with no further specification), or that of resurrection of the flesh? Is there a physical realism in Daniel's idea of resurrection? Collins prefers the first option, for he finds no conclusive arguments in favour of Daniel's mentioning the resurrection of flesh. This belief might have emerged much later.[89] If we should admit that the idea of immortality of the soul is Greek rather than Hebrew, the idea of a spiritual resurrection would be outstandingly original, in deep contrast to the Hellenistic anthropology. But the notion of resurrection of the flesh goes still beyond, as it broadens the doctrine of resurrection so as to include the body and not only the spirit. An anthropology tending to affirm the unity of body and spirit (as the Hebrew one) could not really accept a separated resurrection for both constitutive elements of the human being.

It is true, however, that a text as relevant to the issue of the future life as *1 Enoch* 104 does not mention the resurrection of the flesh, but the resurrection of the spirits and their transformation into some sort of angelic state. Notwithstanding this fact, and since the expression "dust from earth" does not have to be necessarily identified with Sheol (in spite of the parallels that Collins has found within the scope of intertestamental literature), it is by no means strange that most authors have actually accepted Dan 12 as containing an explicit reference to the physical resurrection of the flesh.[90]

Concerning Qumran, Collins underlines that the sectarian writings show an evident eschatological ambiguity: "this does not necessarily mean that there was no place for resurrection in the eschatology of the

---

89. Cf. Ibid., 113.

90. Cf. Cavallin, *Life after Death*, 200. Collins does well in remarking that the explicit allusions to the bodily resurrection are scarce, and that it is therefore very difficult to determine whether certain intertestamental texts are speaking in terms of a general resurrection of the dead, of a spiritual resurrection, or of a resurrection of the flesh. Each of these three perspectives represents, in any case, a novelty inside Judaism and in the context of Hellenistic thought.

Dead Sea Sect. But it does mean that the hopes of the sectarian community were not formulated in terms of resurrection."[91] These hopes consisted of anticipating the angelic life in the community and of taking that anticipation beyond death.

An interesting contribution of Collins' work resides in his systematization of the principal ideas that might have lead to the emergence of the belief in resurrection of the dead. He finds two principal theological lines: the wish to enjoy the presence of God and the hope in a final restoration of Israel.

Sharing an analogous perspective, aimed at integrating the doctrine of the resurrection of the dead with the theological frame in which it participates, *Stefan Beyerle*[92] has analyzed the phenomenon of apocalypticism in its multiple dimensions: literary, theological, sociological, and political. He proposes a frame in which to articulate the criteria of identification of what can be called "apocalyptical." These criteria are taken from the theological imagery that emerges from eschatology and from the theology of history.[93] The author has given more attention to certain texts than others,[94] but the structure of his work has been designed to cover almost all the relevant aspects concerning the idea of God in apocalypticism.

In Beyerle's study, apocalypticism in its fundamental dimensions is interpreted as a question about the hidden nature of God, about its mysterious reality, and this questioning was capable of creating a theology of history in which the eschatological orientation of time prevails. With apocalypticism a "vertical" or metaphysical hope arises, according to which the divine condescendence is not limited to the history of Israel but is now interpreted as a means in the way towards the final revelation of God.[95] The emergence and development of the idea of resurrection of the dead cannot be seen as an isolated phenomenon within the history of religious ideas of Israel; they belong to a general frame of understand-

---

91. Collins, *Apocalypticism in the Dead Sea Scrolls*, 123.

92. Cf. the reviews of Beyerle's book *Die Gottesvorstellungen in der antik-jüdischen Apokalyptik* by Oegema, Brooke, Kraus, and Henze.

93. Cf. Beyerle, *Die Gottesvorstellungen in der antik-jüdischen Apokalyptik*, 15–16.

94 As Kraus indicates in his review, Beyerle gives special relevance to the *Book of Watchers* and to the *Astronomical Book*.

95. Cf. Beyerle, *Die Gottesvorstellungen in der antik-jüdischen Apokalyptik*, 45.

ing the divine, the human, and the historical realities, a frame which was inaugurated by apocalypticism.

The advent of the apocalyptic vision of reality favored the idea of God as the God of history, invested with universal sovereignty and lordship. In fact, Beyerle defends that Judeo-Hellenistic apocalypticism united the concept of the wisdom of God with that of the historicity of God [*Geschichtlichkeit Gottes*].[96]

In Beyerle's opinion, the consideration of the multicultural influences in the Hellenistic times forces us to relativize all categorical statements about the origin of this idea, although the hypothesis he works with states that the genesis of the hope in the resurrection in ancient Judaism was fundamentally based on the perception of the transcendence of God, inasmuch as it described a development from *restauratio* to *resurrection*.[97] The emergence of the belief in resurrection should not be separated from the progressive emphasis given by apocalypticism on the transcendence and universality of God over world and history. The essential aspect of God is no longer his particular theophany in specific moments of Israelite history, but his theophany as lord of history and as an absolutely transcendental being, whose mysteries will be only known in the eschatological horizon.

Beyerle identifies a series of pre-apocalyptic texts which could be regarded as precedents of the idea of resurrection because of their connection with the belief in an afterlife. However, these texts are concerned with the restoration of Israel rather than with the resurrection in an individual sense, as Beyerle himself indicates.

A text like Hos 6:1–3 uses certain words (*hyh, qwm*) which, in the context of Hos 5:8—6:6 (*hyh* in *pi'el* with *qwm*), point to the notion of people's restoration. In the same way, Ps 73:17 contains the word אַחֲרִיתָם, of eschatological connotations, although it does not reflect a hope in resurrection. Verse 17 plays a similar role in the theophanic moment, in which God breaks the borders between heaven and earth to bring salvation. Psalm 49:20 expresses the image of light: "He shall go

---

96. Cf. Ibid., 315.

97. "Die Genese der altisraelitischen bzw. Antik-jüdischen Auferstehungsvorstellungen ist wesentlich an die Transzendenz Gottes gebunden, insofern sie eine Entwicklung von der restauratio zur resurrectio beschreibt" (Beyerle, *Die Gottesvorstellungen in der antik-jüdischen Apokalyptik*, 191).

to the generation of his fathers; they shall never see light [*ló yró-or*]."⁹⁸ In Beyerle's opinion, the vision of light is linked to the astral imagination imported from the Hellenistic culture. The Hellenistic background might also lie in the dualism that prevails in Ps 49.

Beyerle's approach primarily concentrates on the analysis of the great theological concepts of apocalypticism, and his work constitutes a valuable contribution to the study of the ideological substrate from which the idea of resurrection emerged. It shows how this idea belongs to a certain theological imagination which was defined, in its general principles, by the progressive assumption of the transcendence of the divine over world and history.

CONCLUSIONS

The examination of the current streams in the research on the origin of the idea of resurrection shows three fundamental orientations: the consideration of the idea of resurrection as a sudden and radical rupture with the earlier beliefs on the afterlife, the perspective of continuity between traditional Jahwism and the resurrection of the dead, and a third perspective which adopts some sort of compromise, admitting a relevant degree of agreement between the belief in resurrection and the Israelite traditional theology, and at the same time accepting the originality of this new faith, shaped by important influences coming from foreign cultures (principally, Iran and Hellenism).

The texts used by the different authors do not differ in a substantial way. On account of this, the divergences in approaches should not be attributed to the sources analyzed by the scholars, but to the adoption of divergent interpretations of biblical and intertestamental texts.

The cornerstone of the first position is represented by the work of Nickelsburg, followed by, among others, Cavallin and Vermes. Nickelsburg's principal contribution consists of his elucidation of the three predominant forms adopted by the Second Temple Jewish eschatology:

1. Eschatology in the context of the exaltation of the just[99] (Isaiah, Daniel, book of Wisdom)

---

98. תָּבוֹא עַד־דּוֹר אֲבוֹתָיו עַד־נֵצַח לֹא יִרְאוּ־אוֹר.

99. The topic of the exaltation of the just has been analyzed by Ulrich Kellerman, in the context of 2 Maccabees, in his book *Auferstanden in den Himmel*. In spite of

2. Eschatology in the frame of the scenes of the judgement (Daniel, Enoch's *Epistle, Testament of Judah, 4 Ezra*)

3. The theology of the two ways (Wisdom, Testament of Asher), which stems from the Old Testament idea of covenant. According to this theology, human beings have two ways to choose: that of good and that of evil, obedience to the law of God and its rejection. Some people chose the first way, others preferred the second one (leading to injustice and evil).[100]

In the diachronic sphere, although Nickelsburg acknowledges the importance of certain prophetic motives underlying the apocalyptic and intertestamental belief in resurrection, he thinks that this latter idea emerged in a rather sudden way, as a result of Antiochus IV Epiphanes' persecution and the theological reasoning inspired by this event. Authors like Nickelsburg, Cavallin, and Vermes see resurrection as the answer to the problem of the suffering just. Resurrection constitutes a *theologoumenon*, ornamented with strong religious symbolism, designed to express the conviction that the almighty God cannot consent to the abandonment of the just. God will welcome his faithful people after death. Resurrection has a functional utility: it serves the exaltation of the suffering just, and it must be placed in the frame of a broader eschatology, of apocalyptic roots, whose core idea is the divine judgement of human actions. This "subsidiary conception" of resurrection will gradually yield to a more substantive representation, by means of a later theological systematization.

Another historiographic stream seems more in favor of looking at resurrection in accordance with the primitive Israelite eschatology. A paradigmatic example of this second thesis is Puech's research, who

---

the Hellenistic background of the tale of 2 Maccabees, particularly in the rhetorical level, Kellermann notices that 2 Maccabees 7 shows an explicit intention of relating the resurrection to the theology of the Torah. Its idea of resurrection offers a more celestial, transcendent conception than Daniel 12. Kellermann indicates that, in contrast with the belief in resurrection in ancient Egypt, 2 Maccabees 7 does not interpret resurrection from a cosmic and biological perspective: it rather emerges as the result of a concern about theodicy (the unfair suffering of the just people on earth). Resurrection in 2 Maccabees 7 is not the consequence of the cyclic nature of worldly phenomena but of the linear vision of history that sees a narrow union between the beginning (creation) and the eschatological consummation of time.

100. A good example of this theology can be found in *the Testament of Asher* (God has given two ways to humanity: that of good and that of evil).

interprets resurrection in terms of the thematization/concretion of the hope in the continuation of life. This hope was already present in biblical prophetism. The resurrection, as it appears in the book of Daniel, is rooted in the theology of the Servant of Yahweh of Deutero-Isaiah, a figure later generalized to encompass all those who are suffering from unfair persecution. Faith in the resurrection of the dead integrated numerous former religious and theological traditions, a testimony that this idea did not necessarily have to mean a radical rupture with earlier Israelite beliefs.

Within this line of work, some authors like Raphael think that the resurrection could have emerged as a great theological synthesis, capable of integrating both the individual and the collective dimensions of Israelite imagery. Such a synthesis was deeply rooted in the principles of Hebrew anthropology and its insistence on the unity of body and spirit. However, Levenson believes that resurrection should not be regarded as a theological synthesis planned *ad hoc* to solve the inherent contradictions of the earlier theology, for this position is unable to explain why resurrection was rejected by large sectors of Judaism until Rabbinism. According to Levenson, the idea of resurrection is connected with the symbolism of the "divine warrior," whose victory transforms nature, and it is based upon the deep link among restoration, resurrection, and regeneration of life that can be identified in biblical thought.

All of these authors agree in the impossibility of considering resurrection as a result of the cultural borrowings from foreign civilizations. The earlier silence about the afterlife and the netherworld was due, according to Spronk (who has carefully analyzed the afterlife beliefs in Near Eastern civilizations), to a tacit rejection of Canaanite Baalism.

The third tendency represents a certain compromise between the first two orientations: it does not deny the fact that resurrection stems from the fundamental beliefs of the people of Israel, but it still thinks that there was a considerable degree of discontinuity, too, mediated by the assimilation of religious and symbolic motives from the surrounding cultures.

Collins sees the emergence of the doctrine of resurrection of the dead as a result of the conjunction of two earlier theological traditions: the wish to enjoy the presence of God, on the one hand, and the hope in the restoration of Israel, on the other hand. However, it also involved a simultaneous assimilation of external religious motives (especially that of astral immortality). Beyerle has commented on the importance of examining apocalyptic idiosyncrasy as a whole in order to understand the meaning of resurrection. Resurrection does not appear as an isolated belief, but as a concept integrated within a certain theology. This theology is defined by the emphasis put on divine transcendence over world and history, with an eschatological faith directed towards the final Kingdom of God.

Concerning the belief in resurrection in Qumran, there is no academic consensus among scholars. Nickelsburg's and Collins' theses support the idea that Qumran accepted an anticipated eschatology, in which the post-mortem problem did not play a central role. On the opposite side of the spectrum, Puech finds in certain texts from the Dead Sea Scrolls an expression of faith in eternal life and resurrection.

The presentation of the principal streams in current research on the origin of the idea of resurrection of the dead in Judaism brings us to a further step: which factors in the historical, social, and theological orders promoted the emergence of the concept of resurrection? Is it possible to locate this phenomenon inside a broader frame of religious and cultural creativity that might relate this notion to a certain theological paradigm?

To formulate an answer to the questions we have just posed, it is first necessary to know the social and historical substrate in which the resurrection eschatology was born. It is true that resurrection did not constitute a radical separation from the deepest hopes of the faith of Israel, and in particular from those assumed by late prophetism and wisdom writings, but it is also true that resurrection did mean an important novelty in comparison with the understanding of afterlife that had prevailed in traditional Israelite religiosity.

Social changes can be interpreted as the necessary but not sufficient conditions of the processes taking place in the realm of ideas. The approach of social sciences makes it extremely difficult, not to say impossible, to keep some kind of parallel history of ideas (in this case, of religious ideas) flowing independently from the history of social, political, and cultural processes.[101] Just as the transition from nomadism into sedentary life left an important trace in the religion of Israel (as in the sphere of laws and ritual costumes),[102] and in political terms the exile in

---

101. Cf. Berger and Luckmann, *The Social Construction of Reality*, 117.

102. Cf. De Vaux, *Les Institutions de l'Ancien Testament*, vol. I "Le nomadisme et ses survivances. Institutions familiales. Institutions civiles," with a detailed study of the

Babylon constituted a turning point in Israel's self-conscience, the situation of Palestine in the third century BCE, and especially the increasing presence of Hellenism in social life, could not be alien to the boom of apocalypticism as the movement behind the notion of resurrection that we learn from Old Testament and intertestamental literature.

A double perspective, both philological-literary and social-historical, is necessary since most authors have concentrated on the critical examination of biblical and intertestamental texts about the belief in resurrection and afterlife in general, with only occasional references to the context in which these religious convictions arose. Several authors grant much importance to the Maccabean revolt against Antiochus IV and the influence of Hellenism in Palestine, but the analysis of these events leads them (Nickelsburg, Cavallin) to regard resurrection as a sudden appearance, motivated by the problem of the suffering just in the context of Antiochus's persecution. There is not, however, an attempt to delve into the consideration of the social dynamics that shaped the frame in which resurrection emerged and how this belief was linked by many groups to the Israelite traditional religiosity.

In fact, the sociological approach to the beliefs of the different groups during Second Temple Judaism, and especially to those held by apocalypticism, offers valuable information about the nature of their eschatology. And, in an inverse way, the careful study of apocalyptic eschatology helps elucidate their sociological situation. How certain groups viewed resurrection helps us understand how they saw themselves and how they faced social and political realities.[103]

The examination of the sociological context in which the belief in resurrection was born, together with the determining presence of Hellenism in Palestine and the reaction it provoked, encourages us to ask the following question: can resurrection be interpreted as an idea aimed at answering the challenges created by Greek philosophy and, in particular, by its conception of the immortality of the soul, or is it rather a continuation/concretion of the prophetic hopes in the restoration of Israel? There is a contradiction between both views: it is not easy to

---

relationship between nomadism, family, and the civil institutions of the primitive Israel. The social evolution of the Israelite civilization gradually created a legal *corpus*, as Max Weber noticed when characterizing the laws of Israel as an index of social development. Cf. Weber, *Ancient Judaism*, 61–70.

103. Cf. Setzer, *Resurrection of the Body in Early Judaism and Early Christianity*, 1.

integrate two opposite explanations on the origin of the idea of resurrection, the first one connecting resurrection with the reaction against Hellenistic *forma mentis*, and the second one putting resurrection along with the religious traditions of Israel which, by means of a process of individualization, emphasized the fate of each single person over that of the community (namely, Israel). The second option acknowledges the imprint of the Greek vision of the human being and the world, with the importance they attributed to individuality, while the first one gives more relevance to the reaction against the Greek image of human being and history.

The analysis of written sources does not allow for the elaboration of a satisfactory solution to the problem of the origin of the belief in resurrection. It helps us become aware of the variety of eschatological ideas found in intertestamental literature. It also tells us about the absence of the idea of resurrection in Jewish literature prior to the third century BCE, and it favors the study of the diachronic evolution of this belief, but it does not reach the truly relevant aspect: why did this idea emerge?

The examination of texts must be therefore integrated into a historical and sociological study, as limited as it may be. Beyerle's work represents a great contribution to this perspective, since it approaches the belief in resurrection of the dead not as an isolated idea, but in relation with the new theology that began to emerge around the third century BCE, acquiring great relevance after the revolt against Antiochus IV and Hellenism: apocalyptic theology.

Resurrection cannot be understood without paying attention to the meaning of the apocalyptic worldview, with its original *forma mentis* in so transcendental aspects as the conception of history oriented towards an *eschaton*, universalism,[104] and the sovereignty of God over world, history, and death, which might have influenced the belief in resurrection itself.

The belief in resurrection was born in a social and historical context shaped by the opposition between Hellenism and Judaism. Resurrection, however, assimilated fundamental elements of the Israelite faith within the frame propitiated by apocalypticism and featured, in its most general terms, by a gradual emphasis on the idea of transcendence in the conception of the sovereignty of God over world, life, and the human being. Apocalyptic cosmopolitanism inherited much from the Greek cultural

---

104. Cf. Beyerle, *Die Gottesvorstellungen in der antik-jüdischen Apokalyptik*, 15–16.

paideia,[105] which stressed the universality of the human world over ethnic particularities. God is not, in apocalypticism, the God of Israel, but the universal God who rules history as a whole, and Israel participates in this universal history as one of its many members. Inspired by the Greek cosmopolitanism, apocalypticism developed an idea of universal history which deprived eschatology from its former ethnocentric condition, promoting a transition from *restauratio* (the collective "resurrection" of the nation of Israel) into *resurrectio*: since the membership in the nation of Israel is no longer essential, an answer concerning the fate of the individual is needed. This, together with the apocalyptic emphasis on divine transcendence, promoted the belief in the resurrection of the dead.

The transcendence of God and His absolute sovereignty are the two defining elements of apocalyptic theology. *Prima facie*, they might refer to God as keeper of the natural order (primacy of cosmology), but the idea of the absolute transcendence of God edified, in a later development of apocalyptic thought, a hermeneutics of history and eschatology, both of them closely linked.[106] In spite of the differences in details (the acceptance, rejection, or silence before doctrines such as resurrection of the flesh in several writings), apocalyptic theology unveils a perspective that underlines transcendence: God is the lord of nature and the ultimate maker of its order and measure; God is the lord of history taken as a whole; God is the lord of life and death, with power to judge and to grant an eternal reward.

---

105. As Schaper indicates, although apocalypticism and other Jewish movements reacted against Hellenism, this political opposition does not invalidate the fact that they actually assimilated important elements of the Greek vision of world, of humankind, and history. Cf. Schaper, *Eschatology in the Greek Psalter*, 143.

106. Cf. Russell, *Divine Disclosure. An Introduction to Jewish Apocalyptic*, 86.

5

The Kingdom of God

THE BELIEF IN THE persistence of life after death is not a goal in itself. People who believe in immortality of the soul and in resurrection of the dead do not do so just to state that personal identity will endure. They do so in order to state that the personal identity will endure in a different world, in a different kind of life. The belief in life beyond death is therefore meant to affirm that there is a new world waiting for us, and that life on Earth is not the definitive, final reality.

It would be quite pointless to believe in immortality and in resurrection if this did not specify, at the same time, what type of life we are going to enjoy. Let us assume that there is permanence of the personal identity, but of which nature? Is it going to consist of a mere reproduction of earthly life, but with the gift of immortality? Are evil, conflicts between human beings, selfishness, finitude, ignorance, and the lack of answers to so many questions that we pose going to remain?

The Judeo-Christian response says that the future life is not any kind of life, but a life in the Kingdom of God. We shall awake for the Kingdom, in order to become members of a kingdom in which God, the absolute being, reigns. Resurrection is integrated into a broader frame, that of the Kingdom of God, which suggests the idea of a consummation of history, of a completion of its development. Resurrection points towards a certain philosophy of history, in which the notion of a Kingdom of God plays a central role.

Scientific, artistic, political, and social utopias are always, up to a point, relative utopias. Even the utopia of absolute knowledge is bounded to the limits of this world and of our experience of the world. The same can be said of beauty: the utopia of the highest artistic beauty, which has inspired so many creators throughout the centuries, is confined to the structures of this world. It is beauty according to the parameters of what, as a result of our experience of the world, we may consider to be beautiful. Analogously, social and political utopias promise us a world in which many of the aspects of our current life which we regard, and with reason, as negative (such as non-peaceful relations between men and women, discrimination, hatred, inequality...) will be overcome. However, such an overcoming will not exceed the limits of this world: it will not consist of a definitive, final overcoming of every human problem, and of the limitations that our condition as finite beings imposes. As Paul Ricoeur wrote in "Tâches de l'Educateur politique," "utopia can provide economic, social and political action with a human scope," but this scope is still very limited.

The utopia of the Kingdom of God is, on the contrary, an absolute utopia. It dares to state the most radical transformation that the world can undertake. It points towards an actual overcoming of the limitations generated by our condition of finite beings. By joining the Kingdom of God, the communion with the God of all things, we break the chains of limitation and finitude and achieve perfection in all the dimensions we can think of (knowledge, beauty, fraternity/sorority). It also goes beyond individual utopias, as it not only offers a utopian end for the individual life, but a utopian end for the collective history of humanity. It postulates a final end in the history of mankind, integrating both the individual and general dimensions of eschatology. If certain religious and philosophical movements in the ancient world, such as Orphism,[1] could conceive of a utopian world for the individual soul, the perspective of a collective utopia for the whole of humanity, once its historic course has been taken to an end, seems to pose the most radical, encompassing goal that one can imagine.

Of course, for many people such a utopia constitutes a rather naïve dream, a set of *desiderata*. As Freud remarked, dreams can exert such an enduring influence on ourselves that they become real for us.

This critique is legitimate and necessary to purify, in a cathartic way, the anthropomorphisms and, paraphrasing Nietzsche, the "humane, too humane" discourses that we tend to project onto the sphere of religious imagination, which often hide alienations of all sorts (social, economic, gender, racial, psychological).

However, it is also necessary to try to understand the idea of the Kingdom of God as the summarizing, "recapitulating" concept of Judeo-

1. Cf. Bernabé and Jiménez San Cristóbal, *Instructions for the Netherworld*.

Christianity: what is actually the Kingdom of God? It certainly occupies a central position in Jesus' teachings. Jesus did not make of himself the focus of his preaching and mission. He did not speak about himself, but about the reality of the Kingdom of God [*basileia tou theou*].

There is a paradox in Jesus' preaching on the Kingdom of God because, as the recently deceased Dutch theologian Edward Schillebeeckx (1914–2009) has remarked, despite the centrality of this idea in the New Testament, Jesus never defined it: he never said what it actually was. In fact, the expression "Kingdom of God" appears 63 times in the New Testament and only 5 times in Matthew, who seems to prefer the construction "Kingdom of heavens" [*basileia ton ouranon*], which occurs 31 times, even though both of them keep a rather close relationship. The expression "Kingdom of heavens" means that God is actually reigning there (in the celestial, transcendental dimension) now. The expression "Kingdom of God" refers to the kingdom that is to come (but is initiated in the present).[2]

The centrality of the Kingdom of God in the teachings of Jesus of Nazareth has not been equally emphasized in the Christian tradition. The Nicene Creed does not even mention it. The Nicene-Constantinopolitan does: οὐ βασιλείας ουκ εσται τέλος "whose kingdom shall have no end" [*cuius regni non erit finis*], but it is not, so to speak, the core theological concept of this profession of faith.

It is a merit of contemporary theology, as we shall see, to have recovered the importance that the Gospels themselves, and especially the oldest strata (the so-called Q source, the source of *logia* or sayings of Jesus, which might have been used as a material by Matthew, Luke, and the *Gospel of Thomas*), attribute to the Kingdom of God in the teachings of Jesus.

The Kingdom of God refers to eschatology, and we do not live in times favorable to eschatology. There is a general suspicion about everything that may suggest a transcendental existence beyond the boundaries of this world. However, it seems paradoxical that it is precisely in the last two centuries, when the suspicions against eschatology have dramatically increased, that Christian theology has given more attention to the idea of the Kingdom of God, and that in earlier times, when Western civilization was more willing (at least apparently) to listen to an eschatological

---

2. For a deeper understanding of the ideas of "Kingdom of God" and "Kingdom of Heaven," cf. Schnackenburg, *God's Rule and Kingdom*.

The Kingdom of God

speech on the belief in the afterlife, the message of the Kingdom of God was somehow diluted into other theological considerations which, to be sure, did not play such a key role in Jesus' teachings. Christianity seems to constantly contradict the *status quo* of things.

REFLECTIONS ABOUT THE KINGDOM IN MATTHEW

If there is a canonical Gospel which highlights the centrality of the Kingdom in the teachings of Jesus, it is the Gospel of Matthew.

There are five long speeches in Matthew:

1. The speech on the inauguration of the Kingdom (chapters 5-7)
2. The speech on the duties of those who belong to the Kingdom (chapter 10)
3. The parables of the Kingdom (chapter 13), about the mystery of the growth of the Kingdom (like the parable of the seed and the sower)
4. The speech about forgiveness in the context of the Kingdom of God (chapter 18)
5. The eschatological discourse about the coming of the Kingdom (chapters 24-25)

As it is frequently remarked, the Gospel of Matthew constitutes a *midrash*, a commentary on the Hebrew Bible. The constant citations of the prophets are intended to show that Jesus is the Messiah that had been promised from the ancient times.

Let us focus our comments on the first speech, which contains the famous "Sermon on the Mount." The conceptual epicentre of this speech is the Kingdom that has been promised. The text seems to be, according to most exegetes (and particularly to Ulrich Luz, whose work in four volumes is perhaps the finest and most comprehensive study on this Gospel),[3] Matthew's own composition, although he uses external *logia* as sources. In fact, the material used here differs from that of Luke 6:20-49 (the speech with the beatitudes in Luke).

In Matt 5, the beatitudes go as follows:

---

3. Luz, *Matthew: A Commentary*.

> Blessed are the poor in spirit, for theirs is the kingdom of heaven.
>> Blessed are those who mourn, for they shall be comforted.
>> Blessed are the meek, for they shall inherit the earth.
>> Blessed are those who hunger and thirst for righteousness, for they shall be filled.
>> Blessed are the merciful, for they shall obtain mercy.
>> Blessed are the pure in heart, for they shall see God.
>> Blessed are the peacemakers, for they shall be called sons of God.
> Blessed are those who are persecuted for righteousness' sake, for theirs is the kingdom of heaven.
>> Blessed are you when they revile and persecute you, and say all kinds of evil against you falsely for my sake. (Matt 5:1–12)

In Luke, on the contrary,

> Blessed are you poor, for yours is the kingdom of God.
> Blessed are you who hunger now, for you shall be filled. Blessed are you who weep now, for you shall laugh.
> Blessed are you when men hate you, and when they exclude you, and revile you, and cast out your name as evil, for the Son of Man's sake. (Luke 6:20–22)

In Luke there is no qualification of the term "poor" [οἱ πτωχοι], whereas in Matthew we read: "the poor in spirit" [πτωχοὶ τῷ πνεύματι]. Does this mean that Luke is addressing a community with more economic difficulties, or does it mean the opposite, namely that the community to which Luke is writing is pretty prosperous and he wants to insist on the importance of showing solidarity towards the poor? It is difficult to know. However, in the tradition of the prophetic denunciation of social injustice, which stems from the earliest writings of the Hebrew Bible (let us recall Amos, probably the earliest part of the Hebrew Bible), the reference to sociological poverty seems reasonable as Jesus' original teaching.

The spiritualization of poverty has been a constant temptation in the Christian tradition, which has served as some sort of immunization against facing the cruel reality of economic and social poverty (using charity—instead of justice—as a mirage, as a delusion in order to avoid the critical questioning of the structures of power). In this way, for instance, religious orders could say about themselves that they were keeping the vow of poverty while owning, at the same time, huge amounts of wealth in lands and properties (in Spain, approximately one third of the land belonged to the Catholic Church before the so-called Desamortización de Mendizábal or ecclesiastical confiscation of the properties of monastic orders between 1835 and 1837, decreed by the prime minister Juan Álvarez Mendizábal).

There is also a risk in the exclusive fixation on material poverty, because human life is extremely complex, and material wealth does not always mean happiness, particularly spiritual happiness. But in our present world, in which social inequalities are so scandalous, the real danger is that of minimizing the importance of material poverty and of the impact of Jesus' teachings on this point, as some sort of psychological consolation that helps maintain the Christian faith without assuming the necessary political, economic, and social commitments demanded by the attempts to overcome these situations.

The content of the speech on the inauguration of the Kingdom of God in Matthew has caused everlasting and continuously growing admiration for Jesus and his teaching, since many have found in it an expression of the highest moral ideals that humanity can develop.

The Sermon combines a theology with a moral praxis. It is both theoretical and practical. It is theoretical inasmuch as it constitutes an interpretation of the biblical Law. Jesus is interpreting the biblical Law, *Torah*, to grant centrality to the precept of love. The centrality of love was not alien to the Hebrew tradition and to Judaism in general, and it cannot be, in this way, seen as a Christian discovery.

Jesus' teachings are meant to fulfil the Law and the prophets, and to formulate the demands required to access the Kingdom. As Ulrich Luz has indicated, Matthew stresses the continuity between the Kingdom and the Law. It was probably written in the 80s in Syria, and its audience was principally composed of people coming from Judaism. This might explain the insistence on the biblical Law and on the prophecies of the Hebrew Bible. In this sermon, Matthew conceives of the Kingdom as the hidden presence of God, which contrasts with an old world that has become blind to it. The question immediately arises: is this conception Matthew's own interpretation, or he has been faithful to Jesus' real teachings?

This concern is inexorable, and it constantly reappears when examining any passage from the Gospels. To reach the so-called real Jesus (to adopt John P. Meier's terminology),[4] different from the "historical Jesus" and from the "Jesus of faith," is impossible. We cannot seek to know the real Jesus. It is a legitimate aspiration to go back to Jesus beyond the later traditions that have so many times betrayed the spirit of the Gospel. Martin Luther's Reformation wanted this, and it had a very positive effect in liberating Christianity from the chains of authoritarianism and dogmatism. But it is extremely naïve to think that we can actually know the real Jesus.

The historical-critical research, and in particular the sociological approach to the Jewish context in which Jesus lived, a tendency that has become predominant since the 1970s and 1980s, is valuable indeed, but there is always a danger of forgetting that the scholar is never completely objective and that it seems inevitable to project pre-conceptions from our own time onto the time of Jesus. One of Hans-Georg Gadamer's principal contributions to the development of hermeneutics in continental philosophy is the centrality he attributes to the fact that all possible understanding always bears a pre-understanding.[5]

In this sense, Albert Schweitzer's suggestions (every age has looked at Jesus from its own cultural categories: a master of morality for the Enlightenment, a creative genius for Romanticism)[6] are still relevant, although the progression in our knowledge of the historical and sociological context of Jesus invites us not to fall into pessimism (like Bultmann's radical suspicion of all the attempts to learn about the historical Jesus), but at the same time to keep a realistic mentality: every age has the right to look back at Jesus and to make new discoveries and interpretations, so let us not believe that the conclusions we have reached now are going to be final. This would be unfair to the future generations, as it means the virtual exhaustion of critical inquiry and the death of theology.

---

4. John P. Meier is the author of the monumental work *A Marginal Jew: Rethinking the Historical Jesus*, in which he outlines the distinction between three Jesuses: the real Jesus, the historical Jesus, and the Jesus of faith.

5. This idea constitutes a central philosophical concept in Gadamer's *Wahrheit und Methode* [*Truth and Method*], of 1960, which is the principal expression of his attempt to create philosophical hermeneutics (as the "science of understanding").

6. Cf. Schweitzer, *Von Reimarus zu Wrede*. Jaroslav Pelikan's *Jesus through the Centuries* is inspired to a large extent by Schweitzer's thesis.

Let us return to Matthew. In Matt 6:1–18, we are taught a superior form of justice, which consists of the inner acceptance of the Law, rather than the fulfilment of external norms: "Take heed that you do not do your charitable deeds before men, to be seen by them. Otherwise you have no reward from your Father in heaven.

"Therefore, when you do a charitable deed, do not sound a trumpet before you as the hypocrites do in the synagogues and in the streets, that they may have glory from men. Assuredly, I say to you, they have their reward."

This denunciation of hypocrisy is also present in the prophets, as in Hosea 6:6: "For I desire mercy and not sacrifice, and the knowledge of God more than burnt offerings," which reappears in Matt 9:13.

The way in which Jesus speaks is structured on the bases of a negative part (what we should not do) and a positive antithesis (what we should do): "And when you pray, you shall not be like the hypocrites. For they love to pray standing in the synagogues and on the corners of the streets, that they may be seen by men. Assuredly, I say to you, they have their reward.

But you, when you pray, go into your room, and when you have shut your door, pray to your Father who is in the secret place; and your Father who sees in secret will reward you openly" (Matt 6:5–6).

There is a clear contraposition between an external, merely formal fulfilment of the Law, which seeks to please men instead of pleasing God, and an honest acceptance of the Law by a pure heart.

In the context of Jesus' teachings about the superior form of justice, we find the "Our-Father," which for Ulrich Luz represents the center of the Sermon of the Mount (6:9–13). The "Our-Father" is widely regarded as original to Jesus.[7] The usage of the Aramaic word *abbá* is one of the

---

7. There are three principal versions of this famous prayer. In addition to Matt 6:9–13, we find Luke 11:2–4 and *Didache* 8:2 (an anonymous work of the late first century or the early second century CE that contains some basic Christian teachings, rediscovered in 1873 by Philotheos Bryennios, the Greek Orthodox metropolitan bishop of Nicomedia—in present-day Turkey—and found in the Greek Codex Hierosolymitanus, written in the eleventh century, which included other important early Christian writings). Matt 6: 9–13: "Our Father in heaven, hallowed be Your name. Your kingdom come. Your will be done on earth as it is in heaven. Give us this day our daily bread. And forgive us our debts, as we forgive our debtors, and do not lead us into temptation, but deliver us from the evil one. For Yours is the kingdom and the power and the glory forever. Amen." Luke 11:2–4: "Our Father in heaven, Hallowed be Your name. Your kingdom come. Your will be done on earth as it is in heaven. Give us day by day our

factors pointing to that direction. In the three versions of the prayer there is a petition for the coming of the Kingdom. However, we are not told about the exact nature of the Kingdom.

It is in the following verses of Matthew, namely 6:19–24, where we find an indication about the nature of the Kingdom. There is a warning against the accumulation of wealth, and the heart is understood the centre of man and woman, in which the true treasure lies. The Kingdom refers to that centre: it is the true treasure which goes beyond external appearances. It is, so to speak, a centre beyond all peripheries, beyond all superfluous realities: it is the ultimate reality itself.

In 6:25–34 there is a further clarification about the Kingdom, perhaps the most important of all: the narrow link between Kingdom and justice. The passage is summarized in verse 33: "But seek first the kingdom of God and His righteousness, and all these things shall be added to you."[8]

The expression "His righteousness" refers to God: the justice of God, not of the Kingdom, since the article accompanies the noun *dikaiosyne* ("justice"). The theological interpretation of this refers to the strict connection between the Kingdom of God and His justice.

The rest of the passage possesses an extraordinary poetic beauty, certainly comforting in the midst of the distresses of our life:

> [26] Look at the birds of the air, for they neither sow nor reap nor gather into barns; yet your heavenly Father feeds them. Are you not of more value than they?
>
> [27] Which of you by worrying can add one cubit to his stature?
>
> [28] So why do you worry about clothing? Consider the lilies of the field, how they grow: they neither toil nor spin.
>
> [29] and yet I say to you that even Solomon in all his glory was not arrayed like one of these.

---

daily bread. And forgive us our sins, for we also forgive everyone who is indebted to us. And do not lead us into temptation, but deliver us from the evil one." *Didache* 8:2: "Our Father, which art in heaven, hallowed be Thy name; Thy kingdom come; Thy will be done; as in heaven, so also on earth; give us this day our daily bread; and forgive us our debt, as we forgive our debtors; and lead us not into temptation, but deliver us from the evil one; for Thine is the power and the glory for ever and ever."

8. The Greek text says: ζητεῖτε δὲ πρῶτον τὴν βασιλείαν [τοῦ θεοῦ] καὶ τὴν δικαιοσύνην αὐτοῦ.

> ³⁰ Now if God so clothes the grass of the field, which today is, and tomorrow is thrown into the oven, will He not much more clothe you, o you of little faith?
> ³¹ Therefore do not worry, saying, 'What shall we eat?' or 'What shall we drink?' or 'What shall we wear?'
> ³² For after all these things the Gentiles seek. For your heavenly Father knows that you need all these things.

The beauty of the speech, however, contrasts with the negative judgement that it has found among moderns scholars, some of whom view it as a naïve expression, far away from the reality of life. The great biblical scholar Johannes Weiss, one of the founders of the so-called consequential eschatology, said that any sparrow that dies of hunger contradicts Jesus.

In any case, it seems that the theological context in which this passage should be understood is that of the expectation of the advent of the Kingdom. Jesus is depicting a new scenario: that of the Kingdom. *Basileia* is therefore referring to a future reality: the future Kingdom, and in order to participate in this Kingdom, a judgement must first take place (as in apocalyptic theology). *Dikaiosyne*, "justice," might be, in this way, the behavior that fits the requirements of God and his Kingdom.

What is, therefore, the Kingdom of God, but an active expectation, referring to a future reality which will contrast with the present state of things, but whose achievement demands *praxis* here and now, since not all behaviour, not all ethical conduct is equally acceptable to reach the Kingdom? The Kingdom seems to be the goal of the just person: the righteous action.

The "Our Father" juxtaposes the coming of the Kingdom and the fulfilment of the will of God (second and third petitions, respectively). The coming of the Kingdom cannot be separated from the implementation of the will of God. This coming is also understood as an appeal to God, since the initiative belongs to him.

In order to properly understand what Jesus means by "Kingdom," it is necessary to consider the audience he is addressing to: who are his addressees? According to the German scholar Gerd Theissen, widely regarded as a pioneer in the application of sociological methods to the study of the New Testament,[9] Jesus is speaking to itinerant radicals. But this cannot deny the fact that, since the beginning, the message of Jesus

---

9. Cf. Theissen, *The First Followers of Jesus*.

was interpreted as a general truth, and not only as a teaching for radicals. Ulrich Luz thinks that the original message of Jesus might have been tamed, in order to make it susceptible of generalization.

Certainly, the apocalyptic theological context in which many of Jesus' teachings are set could be understood as radical at the time. However, the influence that this theology (notably in the realm of eschatology, for instance through the idea of resurrection) achieved, helped it lose its radical character. What was initially radical became even conservative, as it happened with Christianity: an originally prophetic religion alien to the structures of power of the Roman world finally becomes the religion of the empire. The radical message of Jesus loses its radicalism, and this seems to have happened very early.

It is reasonable to remark that some fundamental teachings of Jesus, and preeminently that of the Kingdom of God, possessed a potential of subversion and challenge to the established order that would be later lost.

The speech about the inauguration of the Kingdom continues in chapter seven of the Gospel of Matthew. Matthew 7:1–5 is a famous exhortation to avoid hypocritical judgements that do not see "the plank" in our own eyes, while seeing the speck in our brother's eye.

Almost no single verse of the New Testament, and possibly of the whole Bible, has passed on indifferent to history. All of them have been influential, one way or another, not only on theology, but also on art, politics, and social life. Matthew 7:1 is a great example: "Judge not, that you be not judged."

What could seem a rather innocent phrase is, nonetheless, difficult to interpret. Should we take it literally, like the Anabaptists in Münster in the sixteenth century and Leo Tolstoy himself, denying the judicial power to the state? Again, in the context of the previous preaching about the Kingdom, the text might be meant to establish a contrast with this world, highlighting the primacy of the eschatological dimension: the advent of the Kingdom will end with trials between humans. But, of course, this position might be accused of "taming" the original spirit of the text.

The primacy of eschatology in certain verses does not hide the centrality of the present time. Matthew 7:7–11 includes an exhortation to a present action: "Ask, and it will be given to you; seek, and you will find; knock, and it will be opened to you." The present tense is used (Αἰτεῖτε καὶ δοθήσεται ὑμῖν).

This exhortation does not refer to the *eschaton*, but to the present: we must ask now. There is a hope that God is listening to us, humans, joined to a present hope in the future coming of the Kingdom. The tension between the present and the future is never lost, but the idea of the Kingdom suggests that it is a reality that begins now, in this present time.

This passage is followed by the famous golden rule: "So always treat others as you would like them to treat you; that is the Law and the Prophets" (Matt 7:12).

This rule constitutes a summary of ethics. It seems to come from the Q source. However, Matthew could have added "that is the Law and the Prophets," because of his theological intention of connecting the teachings of Jesus with Judaism. The rule is not exclusive to Jesus. It was in the teachings of Rabbi Hillel, who lived during the time of King Herod. It is also in the universal wisdom of the peoples of the Earth. It consists of a truth that must be performed *"semper, ubique et ab omnibus"* ["always, everywhere, and by everyone"]. In the philosophy of Immanuel Kant, it takes the form of a categorical imperative. The rule is to be understood within the radical demands imposed by the sermon of the mount.

In fact, 7:13 warns us about the existence of a "narrow gate," a reminiscence of the so-called "theology of the two ways," which can be found in Deut 30:19: "Today, I call heaven and earth to witness against you: I am offering you life or death, blessing or curse. Choose life, then, so that you and your descendants may live." This teaching reappears in many apocalyptic writings, like the Testament of Asher, and in early Christian literature, like *Didache* 1:1.

The gate to access the Kingdom is narrow: there is a demand of justice. According to Ulrich Luz, there might have taken place an "ethicization" of eschatology, a transformation of eschatology into ethics, by linking Kingdom and justice. A sign of this is visible in Matt 7:21: "It is not anyone who says to me, 'Lord, Lord,' who will enter the kingdom of Heaven, but the person who does the will of my Father in heaven."

The relationship between ethics and eschatology is always difficult. On the one hand, eschatology seems to suppress ethics, since ethics would be linked to a present world which is going to experience a radical transformation. But, on the other hand, as humans we find it very difficult to conceive of the Kingdom of God as a radical suppression of our world. Does this mean that all our efforts for achieving a greater degree of humanization will have been in vain, that our highest ethical concepts—solidarity, love, fraternity/sorority, tolerance, equality—were actually useless, because they shall disappear with the coming of the Kingdom? Does humanization contribute or not to the advent of the Kingdom of God? The pastoral constitution *Gaudium et Spes* of the Second Vatican Council clearly remarked that human progress is not alien to the Kingdom. But doesn't this impose a certain degree of continuity which ignores the mystery of the Kingdom, and how the Kingdom may radically challenge our current ethical conceptions? Is God (and his Kingdom as well) a "Totally-Other" who totally challenges our present assumptions—including those which may stem from the struggle for a more humane, fraternal world; or is He at the end of our present efforts to edify a better society, a better world?

I must confess that I am unable to offer an answer, and I do not think that the Gospels themselves do. The tension between eschatology and ethics is always there. Maybe eschatology does not mean that our ideals of humanization will be cancelled or suppressed, as a means of challenging the world and of subverting the order of "this world." Eschatology could mean that the supreme and radical limitation that we experience in this world, namely finitude and alienation, will be overcome, and hence our ethical conceptions will be ultimately opened to new horizons and scopes that we cannot even imagine. But it is hard for me to believe that the highest ethical ideals for which humanity has struggled over the centuries are going to be in vain. No. What may happen is that, as historical experience itself shows, they will be set in a broader context. History itself relativizes some of our ethical conceptions and many times opens our minds to larger, more encompassing and more humanizing concepts. Maybe it means that we can still expect even higher, more humane ethical concepts, and that there is still place for surprise and novelty, against the so-called "end of history."

What seems clear out of the Gospel of Matthew is that Jesus, when speaking about the features of the Kingdom that is to come but that is inaugurated with his teachings, is expressing a contrast, an alternative: it is an ethics of contrast, which is also present in intertestamental literature, like *1 Enoch* 108 and the *Assumption of Moses*. The contrast is graphically described in the following parable:

> [24] Therefore, everyone who listens to these words of mine and acts on them will be like a sensible man who built his house on rock.
> [25] Rain came down, floods rose, gales blew and hurled themselves against that house, and it did not fall: it was founded on rock.
> [26] But everyone who listens to these words of mine and does not act on them will be like a stupid man who built his house on sand.
> [27] Rain came down, floods rose, gales blew and struck that house, and it fell; and what a fall it had!'
> [28] Jesus had now finished what he wanted to say, and his teaching made a deep impression on the people
> [29] because he taught them with authority, unlike their own scribes.

As a final remark, in Matt 5–7 the Kingdom is depicted as the object of an active expectation. Expecting the coming of the Kingdom cannot be passive. Men and women have to perform justice, and this justice is born in the heart of each person, but it is at the same time universal. The working of justice in our actions contributes to the realization of the Kingdom, but it does not exhaust the scope of the Kingdom. We are invited, in fact, to trust in the advent of the future Kingdom. This confidence is also an appeal to the Father.

The Kingdom begins with the acceptance of these teachings, basically concerned with the working of justice. But the Kingdom grows: the parables in Matt 13 show that the Kingdom is a reality that can grow or diminish. It demands some sort of "cultivation." The eschatological dimension of the Kingdom, which is certainly present in Matthew, does not invalidate the attempts to anticipate the Kingdom in present history through justice. Modern theology, and especially liberation theology, has underscored this point with particular strength, as we shall see.

CONTEMPORARY THEOLOGY AND THE KINGDOM OF GOD

As the great Spanish theologian and martyr Ignacio Ellacuría (1930–1989) once remarked, if Jesus came to proclaim the Kingdom, this concept should be the unifying object of all Christian theology and of all Christian *praxis*. If, as Christians, we want to follow Jesus, we must therefore pursue the greatest possible realization of his message, which principally consisted of the annunciation of the coming of the Kingdom of God.

However, its centrality in theology is recent. Although Patristic thought dealt with it, from St. Augustine onwards the vision of the two cities prevailed, as found in *De Civitate Dei*, with an increasing spiritualization of the Kingdom, which lost its impact on the current life and its critical potential with respect to the present structures of the world.

Nineteenth-century theology rediscovered, up to a great extent, the idea of Kingdom of God. In 1892, Johannes Weiss (1863–1914) published *Die Predigt Jesu vom Reiche Gottes* ["Jesus' Proclamation of the Kingdom of God"], in which he considered the Kingdom to be the "ultimate reality," the *eschaton*, in opposition to Adolf von Harnack and to liberal theology, which, from Kant and Schleiermacher to Ritschl and Harnack himself, had tried to offer an interpretation of the Kingdom in ethical terms, designed at making it acceptable to the moral ideals of nineteenth-century European bourgeoisie. Harnack emphasized the ethical, present teaching of Jesus. Jesus would have expressed the highest aspirations of mankind.

Albert Schweitzer (1875–1965), the renowned theologian, activist, and Nobel Prize winner, wrote his celebrated *Vom Reimarus zu Wrede* in 1906, following the perspective opened by Weiss, namely "consequential eschatology." Jesus' message about the Kingdom of God could not be regarded as a formulation of an ethical program for the present life, in consonance with the Kantian reduction of religion into morality (as it appears in *Religion within the Limits of Mere Reason*, of 1793), but an eschatological reality that will come at the end of the world. Jesus was therefore an eschatological, apocalyptic preacher who spoke about the imminent advent of the Kingdom. His failure, manifested in his death on the Cross, would have forced his disciples to "tame" his message about the approaching end of the world.

According to Weiss and Schweitzer, Jesus did not preach the universal essence of humanity that can be discovered by reason (by Kant's "rational religion," of which the historical religions tend to be an expression, and sometimes a betrayal). The Kingdom is actually a critique of any historic and social structure, which is not ultimate. Only the eschatological is ultimate. The Kingdom is not an "eschatological reserve," some sort of utopian ideal that we can constantly preserve to maintain an ever growing concept of our aspirations. The Kingdom is something that has not come but will come in the future, and it leaves no place for easy compromises or for comfortable, calming considerations. Schweitzer's own life is a proof of it.

Against this view Charles Harold Dodd (1884–1973), author of *The Parables of the Kingdom* (1935), interpreted the Kingdom as a present, ethical reality which grows within us. His theological scope has been associated with the so-called "realized eschatology": eschatology, rather than a future reality that is to come, is a present reality which can be lived within us. The Kingdom of God, so to speak, is inside us.[10]

Oscar Cullmann (1902–1999), a Lutheran theologian and an important figure in the ecumenical movement, author of *Christus und die Zeit* [*Christ and Time*] in 1946, tried to integrate both perspectives, that of consequential and that of realized eschatology, the future and the present, in his famous formulation of what the Kingdom of God is: "already but not yet." The Kingdom has already begun, but only in the future will it come in a definitive way.

However, and as the Spanish theologian working in Latin America Jon Sobrino (1938–) points out in his book *Jesucristo Liberador: Lectura Histórico-Teológica de Jesús de Nazaret* [*Jesus the Liberator: A Historical Theological Reading of Jesus of Nazareth*], of 1991, if we want to know when the Kingdom will come, we must first of all know what it is, its nature.[11] According to Sobrino, there are three basic categories to take into account:

1. Jesus and the Kingdom: Jesus is the mediator and the Kingdom is the mediation of God. The Kingdom mediates between God and His will for the world. The Kingdom is not God (we always speak in terms of "the Kingdom of God"), but the expression of the plan of God. Now, who accomplishes the plan of God? Who brings it into effectiveness? -The mediator, a central concept in the Old Testament theology. The king, the prophets . . . , they

---

10. Leo Tolstoy wrote a famous essay, *The Kingdom of God is within You*, of 1894, whose goal was to interpret the Christian message in a radical way. The phrase "The Kingdom of God is within you" is in Luke 17:21: ἡ βασιλεία τοῦ θεοῦ ἐντὸς ὑμῶν ἐστιν. This view reappears, with qualifications, in the so-called School of Philadelphia and in the hypothesis that the Q source, in its oldest strata, reflects a wisdom perspective, to which the eschatological-apocalyptic level would have been added later. Cf. Kloppenborg, *The Formation of Q*.

11. Cf. the chapters called "Jesus and the Kingdom of God" and "The Kingdom of God in Present-Day Christologies" in Sobrino, *Jesus the Liberator*.

were all regarded, at some point, as mediators, since they built a bridge between God and humanity. Christ is the mediator between God and his Kingdom, since he proclaims his Kingdom. Origen defined Christ as the *autobasilea* of God, the personification of the Kingdom of God, but we should be careful not to identify Jesus and the Kingdom.

2. The signs and reality of the Kingdom: there are signs of the Kingdom, but they do not constitute the reality of the Kingdom. Jesus' healings have not made sickness disappear, as Sobrino says.

3. A new understanding of Cullmann's "already but not yet." The Kingdom has come on the level of the mediator (although this does not mean that Christ be the only mediator), but not on the level of the reality of the mediation. In other words: the Kingdom, as such, has not come yet, but its mediator has. We have not reached yet the state in which "all is in all": "When everything has been subjected to him, then the Son himself will be subjected to the One who has subjected everything to him, so that God may be all in all ($\pi\acute{\alpha}\nu\tau\alpha\ \acute{\epsilon}\nu\ \pi\hat{\alpha}\sigma\iota\nu$)" (1 Cor 15:28).

One of the most important remarks that Sobrino makes in his book is the contraposition of the Kingdom and the anti-Kingdom. The idea of Kingdom has often suggested some sort of ecclesiastical triumphalism, as if the Kingdom could be addressed and reached directly, without considering the reality of negativity in the world. There is a future Kingdom, but there is a present anti-Kingdom. The reflections we made about the problem of evil show the dramatic reality of the anti-Kingdom, and the permanent challenge that it represents for religions and in particular for Christianity. The negativity in reality, deeply analyzed on the philosophical level by the Frankfurt School, cannot be forgotten. The exaltation of the positive dimensions of reality, without paying the necessary attention to the reality of negativity, of evil and suffering, is a concession to a conservative, paralyzing view of the world.

Some important moments from the second half of the twentieth century in Christian theology's understanding of the Kingdom of God are those represented by Bultmann, Pannenberg, Moltmann, and liberation theology.

Bultmann does not stress the centrality of the Kingdom. In fact, he distrusts the New Testament, which he sees as the fruit of the faith of the community. However, he accentuates an existentialist-individualistic approach in which he admits the human need for salvation. For him, it is not the Jesus of history, but the Jesus of *kerygma*, the Jesus crucified and raised from the dead, who defines a new man and a new life, what compels us to take a decision. The ultimate, the eschatological, arrives in our inner subjectivity and not in the exteriority of history. The ultimate does not consist of the realization of the Kingdom in history, but of the inner acceptance of the kerygma and of its existential consequences. Let us recall that Bultmann follows Heidegger's philosophy, according to which history is not a substantive reality but a possibility of *Dasein*. Analogously, for Bultmann the Kingdom is not a substantial reality that is going to take place as a culmination of history, since there is no history independent from our "histories." The Kingdom is our subjective, existential acceptance of the challenge meant by the kerygma.

Pannenberg, as we have seen, reacted against Barth, Bultmann, their insistence on the exclusive revelation of God through the word, and their negligence to view the substantiality of history. Pannenberg relates the Kingdom with a futurity that forces us to unveil our intrinsic openness. We are called to live by the future of God: what is not yet already generates reality in the present in the form of trust, hope, and unconditional surrender. The Kingdom has come in Jesus' resurrection, which is a *prolepsis*, an anticipation of the common fate that awaits us all, at the eschatological end of times.

Pannenberg interprets the future as a power over the present. The Kingdom of God is the acting of a unifying power which will definitively unite all what now seems to be divergent and even contradictory. The future liberates history from the present determinations. The existence of the future inspires the hope in a new world. The unity of the present world resides in its future unity: the future founds that unity. Unity is not given in an eternal, immutable cosmic order, as in the Greek representation, but it is a unity that will come in the future, attracting the present towards itself. Unity has to be conquered through the development of history, in a process of reconciliation of former oppositions, divisions, and dividing abysses. Creation has not been completed but is expecting a definitive reconciliation in the eschatological future. Apocalypticism, Christian theology, and Hegelian philosophy (for which nature and history are not final realities to be understood from their *hic et nunc* but serve a higher goal, that of the universal spirit seeking to achieve the absolute conscience of its freedom) agree on this point.

The future that attracts the present is a unifying power. For Pannenberg, God is that unifying power of the future. Hence, the proposition "God exists" will be possibly true only when history has reached its eschatological future. Revelation takes place at the end of times, and only then we will be able to say with full legitimacy that God exists. God is freedom because the future is freedom: the future liberates the present from the chains it has acquired, overcoming all determinations. There is a sociological implication in viewing God as the unifying power of the future: humanity must converge onto a greater, growing unity. The trace of Teilhard de Chardin is clear. The Kingdom of God is not alien to the human efforts to build a better world, but only in the eschatological Kingdom will it be possible to overcome the present antagonisms, and in particular those which oppose the individual and the society.

The consummation of society in the eschatological Kingdom of God will be possible only if all the individuals that have existed throughout history are able to participate in it, or otherwise they would have been mere means in the transition towards the future. Unlike Hegel, Pannenberg does not want to conceive of the individual beings as transient moments. He postulates an eschatological resurrection of the dead, anticipated in Jesus' resurrection.

Jon Sobrino, like other contemporary theologians (for example, Andrés Torres Queiruga),[12] has criticized Pannenberg, despite acknowledging the originality of his theological thought. Sobrino dislikes Pannenberg's insistence on the "eschatological reserve" [*der eschatologische Vorbehalt*], which relativizes the historical realization of the Kingdom. As Sobrino indicates, the fact that there is an eschatological reserve (meaning that the eschatological as ultimate reality does not get exhausted in the specific historical and social situations, and constitutes a constant "beyond" or "ulteriority") does not mean that all historical realizations are equally compatible with the Kingdom. The Kingdom helps us judge history under its own light. The Kingdom relativizes the historical achievements, but also grades them.

Sobrino remarks that Pannenberg does not give much importance to the anti-Kingdom, to the dialectical relationship that the Kingdom

---

12. Cf. Torres Queiruga, *Repensar la Revelación*.

establishes with its opposite. In a harmonic and peaceful contemplation of reality no anti-Kingdom seems to exist. But the critical analysis of reality, and especially if it is done from the perspective of the marginalized people of this world, shows that there is an anti-Kingdom, a true negativity in the world, that claims to be overcome. We cannot obliterate the reality of conflict in the world, adopting a comfortable position under the shape of theological aesthetics. The crucifixion of Jesus is not a mere prelude to his resurrection, since there are still what Ellacuría called "the crucified peoples of the Earth," who have no hope of resurrection.

Sobrino regards Pannenberg's idea of the Kingdom as too individualistic, in which Christology is an address to personal trust and hope, but not to the people of God. For Sobrino, such a personal and transcendental hope needs to be historicized as the hope of the people, the hope of the entire humanity. It is useless to find the meanings of our individual lives if we do not find our meaning as humanity. We would be deceiving ourselves, since there is no reason to suppose that we, as individuals, can have a meaning, even an ultimate meaning, without thinking that the reality in which we participate (humanity) does not have a parallel degree of meaningfulness.

Jürgen Moltmann is the principal exponent of the so-called "theology of hope," inspired, among others, in the works of Ernst Bloch and in the Frankfurt School. One of his principal books is *Theologie der Hoffnung* ["Theology of Hope"]. His theology stresses the primacy of hope in the Christian life. The orientation towards the future is therefore preeminent.

According to Moltmann, the ultimate is a contradiction of the present. But the present is not innocent: it has sin. There is negativity in history. The ultimate must contradict this negativity, must overcome it. In this way, resurrection is the contradiction of the negative reality of a crucified man. The future, for Moltmann, exercises a critical function with respect to the present: it is a power against the present.

However, hope operates on the future not as a mere expectation, but as *praxis*. The centrality of praxis in philosophy is, of course, indebted at a large extent to Marx. Let us recall a fragment from his famous first thesis on Feuerbach: "The main defect of all hitherto-existing materialism—that of Feuerbach included—is that the Object [*der Gegenstand*], actuality, sensuousness, are conceived only in the form of the object [*Objekts*], or of contemplation [*Anschauung*], but not as human sensuous activity, practice [*Praxis*], not subjectively. Hence it happened that the active side, in opposition to materialism, was developed by idealism—but only abstractly, since, of course, idealism does not know real, sensuous activity as such. Feuerbach wants sensuous objects [*Objekte*], differentiated from thought-objects, but he does not conceive human activity itself as objective [*gegenständliche*] activity."[13]

Praxis unveils the possibilities of reality. By acting, by transforming the world through *praxis*, as limited as this transformation may be, we are actually unfolding the possibilities of reality. Mankind, in this sense, has an ontological responsibility: reality is now unveiled through human action. As Heidegger said, although in a different but convergent context, we are the "shepherds of being," and this is a task.

For Moltmann, hope is a "praxic" hope. The resurrection is the hope of the victims, "that the executioner may not triumph over his victim." This hope is shared, as we saw, by apocalypticism. Resurrection is an expression of justice to the victims of history, who can be raised with Christ and change the present. The Kingdom is the ultimate expression of a better world in which all forms of slavery and alienation have finally disappeared. The relationship between the Kingdom and the liberation from slavery stands clear in light of the New Testament. As we read in Luke 4:18–19 (the speech of Jesus at the synagogue of Nazareth): "The spirit of the Lord is on me, for he has anointed me to bring the good news to the afflicted. He has sent me to proclaim liberty to captives, sight to the blind, to let the oppressed go free, to proclaim a year of favour from the Lord."

This statement stems from the prophetic tradition: "The spirit of Lord Yahweh is on me for Yahweh has anointed me. He has sent me to bring the news to the afflicted, to soothe the broken-hearted, to proclaim liberty to captives, release to those in prison, to proclaim a year of favour from Yahweh and a day of vengeance for our God, to comfort all who mourn" (Isa 61:1–2).

The Kingdom is the good news to the oppressed. We can notice here that the Kingdom contrasts with the anti-Kingdom: the news is addressed to the oppressed, to the captives. There is a captive because there is a captor. There is an oppressed because there is an oppressor. The dialectical confrontation is not an artificial expression of some sort of class struggle, but a sign of justice to a reality that is contradictory in

---

13. Translation by Cyril Smith, based on the work done jointly with Don Cuckson.

itself. In a world in which knowledge and ignorance, wealth and poverty, power and dispossession, love and hatred coexist, there is contradiction. To pretend to hide it is to favor one of the parties. It is true that reality is complex and that we are all susceptible to oversimplifying if we reduce its dynamism to an antagonistic confrontation between contenders. But it would be naïve to deny that such a confrontation, even if diluted and not always susceptible of being attributed to single individuals, exists.

Moltmann conceives of the Kingdom as a present reality in a collective way, in the edification of a new world capable of overcoming negativity. The Christian Churches should be present where Christ is waiting for them: in those who suffer. There is a legitimate historicization of the Church on the basis of its service to the edification of the Kingdom.

Let us now examine the principal contributions of liberation theology to the understanding of the Kingdom of God. It could be said, without exaggeration, that liberation theology constitutes the most innovative approach to the understanding of the Kingdom of God. The utopia of the Kingdom becomes a concrete utopia in liberation theology. By making the poor the veritable *locus theologicus*, the whole theological task becomes reoriented. The Kingdom of God is no longer an abstraction, but the reality of a possible liberation of those who are now enslaved by the chains of ignorance, material deprivation, and marginalization. The distinguished Peruvian theologian Gustavo Gutiérrez (1928–) says that the Kingdom of God is the most appropriate reality for expressing the utopia of liberation.[14]

The reasons for thinking of the Kingdom as the ultimate, eschatological reality are summarized by Jon Sobrino in the following way:

1. There are pre-theological reasons: the specific situation of the Third World. This generates, quoting Sobrino, what Hans-Georg Gadamer called a "fusion of horizons" between objective reality and subjective interpretations. Theology cannot neglect the challenge of the Third World. It can no longer focus on *theological gloriae* and forget *theologia crucis*, the cross of our present world, in which so many people are deprived of the basic human needs. This theological methodology could seem improper in light of the traditional principles of Scripture and Tradition (at least in orthodox Catholic theology), but what do these prin-

---

14. This idea plays a central role in Gutiérrez's celebrated *A Theology of Liberation*.

ciples actually mean? Aren't they aimed at expressing the message of God, the will of God for humanity? And isn't that will in flagrant conflict with the reality of poverty and deprivation?

2. Liberation theology is historic and prophetic, praxic and popular. Such is the Kingdom of God: the Kingdom is a reality which begins in the *hic et nunc* of history, but which is also a prophetic calling to change reality by individual and collective action. In Sobrino's words: "liberation theology, then, claims to have found in the Kingdom of God a totality from which it can deal with all theological subjects and also rank them in accordance with their closeness to the ultimate mystery, now formulated as Kingdom of God."

3. Also, the Kingdom of God as the central category for expressing the utopia of liberation helps avoid certain dangers, like equating the Kingdom with the Church. It also encourages us to criticize the sinful structures.

4. And there are christological reasons too: the fundamental proclamation of Christ was the Kingdom of God, and this is the heart of the Christian narrative.

Why the Kingdom instead of the resurrection of the dead? Both of them show an ultimate meaning of history, but as we have seen, resurrection cannot be taken as a goal in itself: resurrection is for the Kingdom. It does not have the same explanatory power regarding history as the idea of Kingdom of God. It also poses a danger of individualism, of transcendence without history. Resurrection does not say much about the present history.

In liberation theology, the Kingdom of God is in radical conflict with the anti-Kingdom. The Kingdom is interpreted as a utopia whose first focus is the eradication of the anti-Kingdom. In other words: without fighting to defeat the anti-Kingdom there is no possibility of anticipating the Kingdom. The Kingdom, as Sobrino usually repeats, is not built from a *tabula rasa*, but from the present struggle against the anti-Kingdom.

This Kingdom belongs to the poor. It has to be interpreted from the analogy of the poor. Poverty is multi-dimensional, but its basic dimension is that of material deprivation. Poverty goes beyond the Marxist category of "Proletarians," because it also assumes what Marx and Engels pejoratively called *Lumpenproletariat* in *Die Deutsche Ideologie* (1845), the "rag proletarians," the segment of the proletarian class that would never acquire class consciousness and was unable to initiate a revolutionary struggle. Poverty is more encompassing and less discriminatory.

The poor have what Gutiérrez has called a "power in history."[15] They can assume their own destiny, by realizing first the gravity of their situation and by fighting to overcome it and lose the condition of "impoverished" (a situation due to the fact that some segments of society are "enriched" and take for themselves the fruits of other people's labour). The poor sells his labour force to the person who has enough capital to buy it. He finds himself inserted in a social system that compels him or her to do so.

The question naturally arises: after the fall of real socialism in 1989, is there an alternative to this system? The existence of a developed (and often insufficient) welfare state in many European countries shows that it is at least possible to diminish the impact of impoverishment and exploitation, even though it still only constitutes a partial solution to the problem. It is possible, however, to speak in terms of a "radical reformism" (Habermas),[16] since, as Norberto Bobbio noticed, after the Fall of the Berlin Wall the same problems that inspired the revolutionary spirit of socialism persist, as so many people are condemned, still today, to live under the most oppressing injustice,[17] and capitalism seems to have lost, according to Eric Hobsbawm, the fear that was behind some of its historic concessions to the working classes, at least in the Western world.[18] Maybe communism is not, just as for Marx, the solution to the enigma of history, but it is necessary to edify history in such a way that it may be meaningful for everyone, and the utopia of human solidarity is still in our horizon.

However, no social system can exhaust the condition of absolute utopia of the Kingdom. The Kingdom is utopian, never realized in history, but it nonetheless represents a source of inspiration in moving history forward.

---

15. Cf. In fact, the title of one of Gutiérrez's books is, in English, *The Power of the Poor in History*.

16. Cf. Habermas' essay "What Does Socialism Mean Today? The Revolutions of Recuperation and the Need for New Thinking," in Blackburn, *After the Fall*, 25–46.

17. Cf. Bobbio's essay "The Upturned Utopia in ibid., 3–5.

18. Cf. Hobsbawm's essay "Goodbye to All That," in ibid., 115–25.

The Kingdom of God is a political reality. This is not a shame for the idea of Kingdom. The term "political" seems to be vitiated, as if it were better not to use it at all. But "political" refers to the *polis*, to the idea of a human community and of how we want to organize ourselves as social beings. Philosophy is also political, inasmuch as it embodies a vision of the human community. Rudolf Schnackenburg (1959) stressed the religious dimension of the Kingdom of God, but this does not mean that we have to marginalize its political horizon. The Kingdom challenges present reality. Its message is neither neutral nor innocent. Religion is political because it offers a vision of society and history. If by "political" we understand something that refers to the human community, it is hard to find any human, rational activity which does not have an effect on the social life, and on how we conceive of ourselves as beings that live in a community. Of course, this goes beyond reducing politics to a partisan confrontation between machineries of power.

The Kingdom, according to liberation theology, is not an expression of the sum of individual salvations. The Kingdom is addressed to the people of God. Salvation cannot take place outside history and humanity. Moreover, as Sobrino titles one of his books, there is no salvation outside the poor (*extra pauperes nulla salus*). The Kingdom is both qualitative (it is fundamentally aimed at the poor) and quantitative (the immense majorities of the earth).

So, what is the Kingdom of God for liberation theology? It primarily consists of the just life of the poor. In the Third World, life is not given. Life is not taken for granted. The German idealist philosopher Johann Gottlieb Fichte (1762–1814) formulated in his *Wissenschaftslehre* ["The Science of Knowledge"] the idea that the "I," *das Ich*, needs to posit itself (the German verb is *setzen*), going outside itself in order to assert its own self-identity. This primeval movement of the "I" is equivalent to what the Third World has to do. The Third World has been deprived of its condition of subject. In the Third World, the "I" needs to assert its self-consciousness, it needs to come out. As the noted Brazilian pedagogue Paulo Freire (1921–1997) taught, first of all, it is necessary to become aware of our situation in order to take life in our hands. The role of education is therefore urgent: education must be designed for helping people become aware of their true capacities.

Liberation theology does not limit the Kingdom of God to history. There is always a "surplus" in history that points towards transcendence. However, the perception of the theological transcendence of the Kingdom does not mean that it can be diluted in the idea of an abstract God as *Ipsum Esse Subsistens*. God is the God of the Kingdom. It is not any type of God: God is the God of life, the God of those who suffer, the God of the Kingdom. God is *kenosis*, who empties himself to reach humanity and as Jon Sobrino has written: "building the Kingdom is walking toward God."

There is a problem, I think, with liberation theology. It has little to do with the traditional conservative criticism which is often done by accommodated people in the first world who show no spirit of solidarity with the social and political struggle of liberation theologians, many of whom have put their lives at risk. The critique is, I believe, more fundamental. Liberation theology takes evil for granted, as a *factum*, and it does not ask God why He allows it. Liberation theology needs to be complemented with a philosophical and theological inquiry into the nature of the Judeo-Christian God and of the process of history. God could have made a world without poverty, without oppression between humans or could He not? What is the meaning of our having to fight, as humans, for a better life and for a better world?

This question brings us back to our first chapter: the problem of evil and the meaning of history. It seems that we have the responsibility to edify, to build a sense for history, to create a history which may be meaningful to all human beings. This is perhaps a manifestation of our freedom and autonomy. Our legitimate perplexity before the reality of a world and of a history which we do not understand, since we do not know why we are here, may leave place to our capacity to assume the responsibility of living and of building a world and a history. If we think of God not as the beginning or as the end, but as something or someone that is accompanying us, and that shines like us in the realizations of knowledge, justice, beauty, and love which we have been able to create, then there is hope in history.

CONCLUDING REMARKS

To believe in God involves, in one way or another, to go beyond the scope of reason. It is a risky enterprise, but many men and women have given to it an important part of their spiritual energy throughout the ages.

For some people, this option will seem rationally illegitimate; for some others, it will constitute a true necessity, in spite of the multiple arguments, counter-arguments, historical examples, specific situations, and other various expressions of scepticism that may come out. It is not exaggerated to say that religion is, first of all, a vital experience. Rudolf Otto, in his far-reaching book *Das Heilige* ["The Idea of the Holy"], first published in 1917 and regarded as the most successful German book of the twentieth century in the field of philosophy of religion (it has never gone out of print), described religion as *Erlebnis*, "vital experience," the experience of a tremendous and fascinating mystery [*mysterium tremendum et fascinans*].

Religion emerges rather than as a product of social and historical structures as a human necessity that is derived from our contemplation of the world and from our wondering about our position in the universe. Religion can be interpreted, too, as a feeling that makes us dependent upon a reality which theoretically transcends us. The German theologian Friedrich Schleiermacher wrote in his *On Religion: Speeches to Its Cultured Despisers* (1799): "Religion is the result neither of the fear of death nor of the fear of God. It responds to a deep necessity in man. It is not metaphysics, either morals, but first of all and essentially an intuition and a sentiment [*Gefühl*] ... Religion is the miracle of the direct relationship with the infinite; and dogmas reflect this miracle."

According to Schleiermacher, religion is a sentiment of dependence on the infinite.[19] We experience ourselves as parts of a whole that transcends our particularity and our contingency. This vital experience is in many cases the starting and not the final point for most people who call themselves believers.

Faith is not usually the result of a rational, discursive process, capable of showing with clarity the truth of the thematic enunciations of faith. Through tradition, education, or personal will many people "unthematically" (to cite Karl Rahner's famous expression) open themselves to faith. This openness to faith is later concreted, specified in the par-

---

19. Schleiermacher's conception of religion dramatically contrasts with that of Hegel, who explicitly rejects an idea of religion which privileges the sentimental over the rational dimension. Cf. Hegel, *Philosophie der Religion*, 33. For Hegel, religion is the conscience of the absolutely true [*Bewusstsein des absolut Wahren*], and Christianity is the "religion of freedom" [*die Religion der Freiheit*], because the principle of the absolute freedom of God becomes a subjective, human freedom by virtue of the Incarnation. On the importance of Christianity in Hegel's philosophy, cf. Pannenberg, "Die Bedeutung des Christentums in der Philosophie Hegels," In *Gottesgedanke und menschliche Freiheit*, 78–113.

ticular enunciations of the different religions. But in the acceptance of the enunciations which correspond to an epistemological, linguistic, and historical articulation underlies a previous predisposition to religious experience as such. The human will to transcend the finite and concrete helps us open ourselves to the vital experience of the infinite.

It is by all means understandable that this religious experience may have been criticized by some of the brightest minds of philosophy as a projection (Feuerbach, Marx), as a self-alienation, and as a childish illusion (Freud), even though for other thinkers it consists of a "fundamental projection" (Pannenberg). There is always place for the suspicion that the content of this experience could be merely psychological or sociological, internal to the human subject and an expression of his desperation. Neither the thesis nor the antithesis can be truly proved. The suspicion is legitimate and it probably represents the most serious objection against religions, going back to the pre-Socratic philosophers and their criticism of Greek religion.

However, it is surprising to realize that in spite of the power of these objections (which, if ignored, it is normally because of an attitude of "self-catharsis" and of blinding mental restriction) religions continue to persist.

What is happening here? Do we live in such a state of despair that we cannot avoid being religious? The objections are too serious to be dismissed. And there are more objections: if there is a provident God, why did He let so many millions of years of evolution pass until humans emerged as the only beings capable of believing in Him and of acknowledging Him as creator and sovereign of the world? Why have the great advances in the realm of human progress taken so much sacrifice and so much suffering? Isn't the suspicion about the radical autonomy of world, nature, and history justified? Why isn't God present in world, nature, and history? Isn't God the expression of a wish rather than of a reality? Why hasn't the belief in God generally come out of individual freedom but has been imposed by violent and inhuman methods?

These questions do not constitute a blasphemy or a lack of reverence. As St. Irenaeus said, *gloria Dei vivens homo*: the glory of God is our being truly, authentically humane, and there are few things as humane as posing questions.

If many people, in spite of various and powerful objections, still believe in God, they do so perhaps because they appreciate in all the signs of human progress, and especially in the discoveries of science, in the great works of philosophy, in the beauty of the arts, and in the human capacity for cooperation, creativity and solidarity, something eternal and hence divine, something that transcends the finite and contingent, the particularity of the *hic et nunc* of history, lifting us to the horizon of what is truly universal. This reality goes beyond the historical forms adopted by systematic religions and brings us back to the essence of religion in itself, to the essence of the supernatural and mystical: the elevation above the concrete and particular, the quest for the universal, the rebellion against contingency.

Religions do not experience the absence of God in history, but his presence through the mediation of spiritual and ethical figures who have promoted important movements of followers. The cultural, intellectual, and ethical creativity they have favored is a sign of the human longing for the absolute, of the human quest for plenitude, of the hope in a future of transcendence which is already anticipated in all that is true, good, and beautiful (*verum, bonum, pulchrum*, to refer to the famous Medieval trilogy). It is true that the contradictions of history may eclipse all possible vision of transcendence, but it is also true that the great achievements of history, and especially those connected with knowledge, love, and beauty, can open for us a perspective of transcendence. "*Ein Gott den gibt es, gibt es nicht,*" as the theologian and martyr Dietrich Bonhoeffer said: if God were evidently perceived in the reality of the world, He would not be God. We perceive God beyond the world, but anticipated in some realities of the world. Maybe God is walking in history and His most intimate will is not alien to the dynamism of the times. This is a hope shared by many believers, which has to be manifested in the love for humanity, in the confidence in its future, and in the commitment to an action in and over world and history.

Resurrection might be seen, from this perspective, as a sign of our rebellion (useless and vain for many) against death and as the symbolic expression of the collective aspirations of humanity, endowed with a huge emancipatory potential, since it consists of a critique of the present status of humanity, of our present indigence: it is a sign of protest. God is nothing other than the eternal and permanent reality, which is appealing to us here and now, and to which we appeal in search for a universal meaning that may guide both our actions and our thoughts.

The Kingdom of God

Most people will pass unrecognized, with no vindication, and they will be simply forgotten in the shadow of history. Those men and women who have suffered and struggled, those anonymous names that no one remembers and which humanity has taken throughout the centuries, need a vindication. The past needs a vindication in a perennial present of hope. Humanity deserves a God.

In a memorable philosophical exchange between Horkheimer and Walter Benjamin, Benjamin expressed his deep conviction that the past was not closed. Against all the evidence, the past had not been consummated, finished, deprived from any possible modification. Horkheimer made the point that the injustice of the past is immutable: no one can change the evils of the past, unless driven by the idealistic power of faith, and the victims have no future, for no one is going to resurrect them. However, Benjamin, in his *Theses on the Philosophy of History* [*Über den Begriff der Geschichte*], rejects the idea that the victims of history can have no hope, no future, no salvation, and he adheres to some sort of weak Messianic hope, in which the angel of history will raise the dead.[20] But it is difficult to find such an angel outside the biblical traditions and their supremely utopian promises. Benjamin inherits the questions posed by the biblical tradition, but he cannot accept the answers.

I do not know if we are strong enough to assume the weight of history. There is some kind of utopian wish in trying to keep alive the memory of all human beings that have existed, bringing justice to all those who did not enjoy it in life. It is frustrating indeed to think that so many names that humanity has taken will simply vanish, obliterated like the traces on the sand when the wind comes, and that we will not know anything about them. Where are they? Humanity poses this question. Our world will not be just until it preserves the memory of all the names that humanity has taken. Only if we assume the responsibility of carrying our collective memory we can build a just world.

Art is an extraordinary source of justice. Literature immortalizes the memory of those who died without experiencing the greatness of life. Poets, writers, and painters, all of them have the task of witnessing the different names that humanity has taken. That old woman who died after decades of suffering and indefatigable work, and who saw no reward in life, must be vindicated by the power of art, because our greatest treasure is compassion. We can suffer with her, assumer her pain,

---

20. Cf. Benjamin, "Theses on the Philosophy of History," in *Illuminations*.

and share the consolation that tomorrow we shall create something new which may challenge both the present and the past.

It is difficult to reject the following utopia: in the future, we shall remember all the names that humanity has taken. No one will fall victim to forgetfulness. All the anonymous men and women who have edified our history will be in the gallery of our collective memories, alongside the great scientists, the great musicians, and the great leaders. Each memory will be vindicated, and we will feel proud to recognize in the power of memory our real richness.

I can hardly imagine a higher manifestation of concord and union of humanity's hearts and minds. No one will be forgotten, and no one will have lived in vain. They will all be in the library of our memories, whose size will surpass that of all present and past libraries. The beggar who died in the corner of the street will also find a place in that library. And the future generations will often visit it to remember their ancestors. Children in the schools will pay tribute to the anonymous people who built up humanity. They will learn about their successes and their failures, and they will be ready to forgive their mistakes, because compassion is pardon. Such a dream may resemble madness, but madness has inspired creation, and it has encouraged us to open the window facing the unexplored scenario.

The utopia of the Kingdom of God is, in a sense, the utopia of the collective solidarity of humanity: it is the utopia of the possibility for history to have a final meaning in which all its members, past, present, and future, will find a significant place, and their memories will be utterly vindicated, and even those whose remembrance is obscured by the results of their dehumanizing actions will be forgiven. All our lives will have been meaningful. Eschatology orients history towards a definitive fulfilment in which this final sense will be unveiled.

However, eschatology constitutes the denial of history as such. Once eschatology has taken place, history must disappear in order to become substituted by eternity. If eschatology arrives, it is because history is over. The principal problem of Judeo-Christian eschatology is its postulating a final stage, a final fate for history: history will have to be over in order to be fulfilled. But, how can we possibly conceive of an end of history? How can we possibly conceive of a final stage in history in which no further historical movement would be viable? How can we conceive of humanity without history? Would we be truly human if we were not inserted in the dynamics of history? Can eternity ever correspond to our human condition without compelling us to abandon our humanity? Isn't it more appropriate to think of history as a potentially endless process, in which every future generation will have the chance to define new goals and to open new scenarios, now unimagined? And, could we really bear immortality? Could we really bear the possibility of not dying, of living for ever, were it not a utopia, a non-place and a non-time, which we sometimes imagine to grant us hope in the midst of the uncertain course of history?

Religions try to introduce the eternal and immutable in history, bringing security in the midst of variability, but humanity must learn to open itself to the uncertainty of the historical change as a source of new possibilities that allow us to create our own destiny.

We can, of course, conceive of common goals, of collective aspirations for humanity as a whole, but we cannot deny the possibility of a future broadening, of a future extension and even of a radical transformation of those goals into even more humanizing, more emancipatory objectives. We cannot, after all, pretend to exhaust the future: we have to see the future as the greatest treasure of humanity, as a true instrument of liberation, and as the space in which all we can think of now becomes actually opened, "enlarged" by what now seems to be impossible or even inconceivable.

Some religions, like Zoroastrianism, Judaism, and Christianity, have dreamed of future end of history in which final justice might be achieved. The contradictions of the present seemed to delegitimize history, making it necessary to postulate an ideal definitive fulfilment, a radical consummation in which no more contradictions will occur. But we can also dream with a potentially infinitely open history, with a history capable of constantly reinventing itself and of inaugurating a real *novum* in the course of times, in which the eternal and permanent will not be at the end of history, and at the expense of the disappearance of history, but in the *hic et nunc* of history, in the dynamism of history itself.

Humanity must dare to look at history with hope, rather than with fear. We know that we have no patience for eschatology, and that we cannot bear, as the Hegelian spirit, the infinite pain. We need to anticipate salvation in the reality of knowledge, love, and beauty, as contradictory as it may be.

I find it extraordinary to contemplate, all over the world, in countless cities of almost every country, monuments dedicated to the men and women who have contributed to human progress. Mathematicians, physicists, biologists, philosophers, musicians, writers, painters, saints . . . Memorial buildings, statues, busts, stamps, all remind us of their achievements.

Behind this tradition we can see the human will to preserve its collective memory, especially manifested in those individuals who have been capable of leading human civilization towards a higher state of scientific, ethical, and aesthetic development. Ancient cultures erected monuments to their gods and kings; now, humanity erects monuments to the wise people, to the saints, to the creators, to those who have consecrated their lives to the pursuit of knowledge, of ethics, of beauty. The reverence for the wise and the saints edifies a true "devotion" of humanity for itself.

This sentiment of devotion of humanity for itself does not suppress the particular religions, because it does not dare to offer a similar content of transcendence. It rather consists of looking at the past with devotion, with the hope of finding in the works of the wise people and of the saints a teaching that may help us face an always uncertain future. Traditional religions are too attached to the past, but we need to be capable of turning our attention to the future, of going beyond inherited traditions in order to open ourselves to the new challenges of history, making history meaningful to all men and women.

The devotion of humanity for itself cannot be identified with any particular religious tradition, be it Christianity, Judaism, Islam, Buddhism, Hinduism, and any other historical creed. It stays in a strictly human sphere and therefore represents an expression of the legitimate admiration of humanity for itself. As Edward Schillebeeckx said, "belief in God is impossible without belief in man."

The reverence for humanity assumes the idea that, in spite of our numerous and constant mistakes, it has been worth living as human beings integrated within the natural and historical dynamism, and so it was for people like Imhotep, Thales of Miletus, Pythagoras, Buddha, Socrates, Plato, Aristotle, Archimedes, Jesus of Nazareth, St. Augustine, Avicenna, St. Francis of Assisi, Leonardo da Vinci, Copernicus, Michelangelo, St. Teresa of Ávila, Galileo, Newton, Bach, Euler, Kant, Goethe, Beethoven, Marie Curie, Tolstoy, and Einstein, who have ennobled our spirit in the quest for knowledge, love, and beauty.

Remembering these and other great geniuses, seeing their images in the monuments of towns and cities, on postage stamps, and in portraits in museums and libraries, must make us feel proud to belong to the same humankind. This sentiment of fraternity/sorority, visible in the narrow union with the great spirits, is one of our most valuable moral treasures, for nothing can join humanity to such a degree as knowledge, love, and beauty.

Bibliography

Abumalham, Montserrat. *El Islam: De Religión de los Árabes a Religión Universal.* Paradigmas: Biblioteca de las Ciencias de las Religiones 42. Madrid: Trotta, 2007.

Albertz, Rainer. *A History of Israelite Religion in the Old Testament Period.* Vol. 2, *From the Exile to the Maccabees.* Translated by John Bowden. Old Testament Library. Louisville: Westminster John Knox, 1994.

Althusser, Louis. "Remarque sur une catégorie: Procèes sans Sujet ni Fin(s)." In *Réponse á John Lewis*, 91–98. Paris: Maspero 1973.

Aranda Pérez, G., et al. *Literatura judía intertestamentaria.* Introducción al Estudio de la Biblia 9. Estella: Verbo Divino, 2005.

Aristotle. *The Politics.* Translated by E. Barker. Oxford World's Classics. Oxford: Oxford University Press, 2009.

Assmann, Jan. *Tod und Jenseit im Alten Ägypten.* Munich: Beck, 2001.

Augustine. *Enchiridion*, with a new introduction by Thomas Hibbs. Washington DC: Regnery Gateway, 1996.

Ausín, S. Review of *La Croyance des Esséniens en la Vie Future: Immortalité, Résurrection, Vie Éternelle? Histoire d'une Croyance dans le Judaïsme Ancien*, by Émile Puech. *Scripta Theologica* 27 (1995) 1007–12.

Bakhos, Carol. Review of *Resurrection and the Restoration of Israel*, by Jon D. Levenson. *Journal of the American Academy of Religion* 75 (2007) 427.

Barrer, M. Review of *Apocalypticism in the Dead Sea Scrolls*, by J. J. Collins. *Journal for the Study of the Old Testament* 79 (1998) 182–83.

Barthes, Roland. *Mythologies.* Translated by Annette Lavers. New York: Hill & Wang, 1972.

Benjamin, Walter. *Illuminations.* Translated by Harry Zohn. New York: Schocken, 1969.

Berger, Peter, and Thomas Luckmann. *The Social Construction of Reality: A Treatise in the Sociology of Knowledge.* Garden City, NY: Doubleday, 1966.

Bernabé, Alberto, and Ana Isabel Jiménez San Cristóbal. *Instructions for the Netherworld: The Orphic Gold Tablets.* Translated by M. Chase. Religions in the Graeco-Roman World 162. Leiden: Brill, 2008.

Beyerle, Stefan. *Die Gottesvorstellungen in der antik-jüdischen Apokalyptik.* Supplements to the Journal for the Study of Judaism 103. Leiden: Brill, 2005.

Blackburn, Robin, editor. *After the Fall: The Failure of Communism and the Future of Socialism.* London: Verso, 1991.

Blanton, Ward. Review of *Resurrection, Immortality, and Eternal Life in Intertestamental Judaism and Early Christianity*, by G. W. E. Nickelsburg. *Journal for the Study of the New Testament* 30 (2008) 23–24.

Bloch, Ernst. *Atheismus im Christentum: Zur Religion des Exodus und des Reichs.* Gesamtausgabe 14. Frankfurt: Suhrkamp, 1968.

———. *The Principle of Hope*. Translated by Neville Plaice and Paul Knight. 3 vols. Oxford: Blackwell, 1986.
Blumenberg, Hans. *Die Legitimität der Neuzeit*. Frankfurt: Suhrkamp, 1966.
Boethius. *De Consolatione Philosophiae*. Edited by C. Moreschini. Bibliotheca scriptorum Graecorum et Romanorum Teubneriana. Munich: Saur, 2000.
Braaten, Carl. "The Current Controversy in Revelation: Pannenberg and His Critics." *Journal of Religion* 45 (1965) 225–37.
Brooke, George J. Review of *Die Gottesvorstellungen in der antik-jüdischen Apokalyptik*, by Stefan Beyerle. *Journal for the Study of the Old Testament* 30 (2006) 160–61
Bultmann, Rudolf. *Essays Philosophical and Theological*. Library of Philosophy and Theology. New York: Macmillan, 1955.
Byron, J. Review of *The Resurrection*, by Geza Vermes. *Ashland Theological Journal* 40 (2008) 98–100.
Cavallin, Hans Clemens Caesarius. *Life after Death: Paul's Argument for the Resurrection of the Dead in 1 Cor 15*. Coniectanea Biblica. New Testament Series 7. Lund: Gleerup, 1974.
Charlesworth, James H., editor. *The Old Testament Pseudepigrapha*. 2 vols. Garden City, NY: Doubleday, 1983–1985.
Chomsky, Noam. *Hegemony or Survival: America's Quest for Global Dominance*. American Empire Project. New York: Holt, 2004.
———, and Michel Foucault. *The Chomsky-Foucault Debate: On Human Nature*. New York: New Press, 2006.
Clanton, Dan W., Jr. Review of *Resurrection, Immortality, and Eternal Life in Intertestamental Judaism and Early Christianity*, by G. W. E. Nickelsburg. *Journal of Hebrew Scriptures* 8 (2008). Online: http://ejournals.library.ualberta.ca/index.php/jhs/article/view/7263/5971/.
Cohen, Shaye J. D. "Josephus, Jeremiah, and Polybius." *History and Theory* 21 (1982) 366–81.
Cohn, Norman. *Cosmos, Chaos and the World to Come: The Ancient Roots of Apocalyptic Faith*. New Haven: Yale University Press, 1993.
Collins, Adela Yarbro. *Crisis and Catharsis: The Power of the Apocalypse*. Philadelphia: Westminster, 1984.
———. Review of *The Open Heaven: A Study of Apocalyptic in Judaism and Early Christianity*." *Journal of Biblical Literature* 103 (1984) 465–67.
Collins, John J. *The Apocalyptic Imagination: An Introduction to the Jewish Matrix of Christianity*. New York: Crossroad, 1984.
———. *Apocalypticism in the Dead Sea Scrolls*. Literature of the Dead Sea Scrolls. London: Routledge, 1997.
———, and Gregory E. Sterling, editors. *Hellenism in the Land of Israel*. Christianity and Judaism in Antiquity 13. Notre Dame: University of Notre Dame, 2001.
———. "Prophecy, Apocalypse and Eschatology: Reflections on the Proposals of Lester Grabbe." In *Knowing the End from the Beginning: The Prophetic, the Apocalyptic and Their Relationship*, edited by Lester L. Grabbe and Robert D. Haak. 44–52. Journal for the Study of the Pseudepigrapha Supplement Series 46. London: T. & T. Clark, 2003.
———. "Towards the Morphology of a Genre." *Semeia* 14 (1979) 40–46.
Condorcet. *Esquisse d'un Tableau Historique des Progrès de l'Esprit Humain*. Introduction and notes by Monique and François Hincker. Les Classiques du Peuple. Paris: Sociales, 1966.

Coogan, Michael D. *The Old Testament: A Historical and Literary Introduction to the Hebrew Scriptures.* New York: Oxford University Press, 2006.
Díez Macho, Alejandro, editor. *Apócrifos del Antiguo Testamento.* Vol. 4. Madrid: Cristiandad, 1982.
Dilthey, Wilhelm. *Der Aufbau der geschichtlichen Welt in den Geisteswissenschaften.* Theorie. Frankfurt: Suhrkamp, 1970.
———. *Einleitung in die Geisteswissenschaften: Versuch einer Grundlegung für das Studium der Gesellschaft und der Geschichte.* Gesammelte Schriften 1. Stuttgart: Teubner, 1959.
Eckstein, Arthur M. "Josephus and Polybius: A Reconsideration." *Classical Antiquity* 9 (1990) 175–208.
Eddy, Samuel Kennedy. *The King Is Dead: Studies in the Near Eastern Resistance to Hellenism, 334–31 B.C.* Lincoln: University of Nebraska Press, 1961.
Eliade, Mircea. *Le Mythe de l'Éternel Retour: Archétypes et Répétition.* Les Essais 34. Paris: Gallimard, 1949.
Ellacuría, Ignacio, and Jon Sobrino. *Mysterium Liberationis: Fundamental Concepts of Liberation Theology.* Maryknoll, NY: Orbis, 1996.
Endsjø, Dag Øistein. "Immortal Bodies before Christ: Bodily Continuity in Ancient Greece and 1 Corinthians." *Journal for the Study of the New Testament* 30 (2008) 417–36.
Erskine, Andrew. *A Companion to the Hellenistic World.* Blackwell Companions to the Ancient World. Ancient History. Oxford: Blackwell, 2003.
Faber, Richard et al., editors. *Abendländische Eschatologie: ad Jacob Taubes.* Würzburg: Königshausen & Neumann, 2001.
Ferrater Mora, J. *Diccionario de Filosofía.* New ed., rev., aug., and ed. by Josep-María Terricabras. 4 vols. Barcelona: Ariel, 1994.
Feuerbach, Ludwig. *Das Wesen des Christentum.* Berlin: Akademie, 1984.
Fine, Lawrence. *Physician of the Soul, Healer of the Cosmos: Isaac Luria and his Kabbalistic Fellowship.* Stanford Studies in Jewish History and Culture. Stanford: Stanford University Press, 2003.
Foucault, Michel. *Philosophie: Anthologie.* Edited by Arnold I. Davidson and Frédéric Gros. Collection Folio. Essais 443. Paris: Gallimard, 2004.
Fraijó, Manuel. *Dios, el Mal y otros Ensayos.* Colección Estructuras y Procesos. Serie Religión. Madrid: Trotta, 2004.
Freud, Sigmund. *The Future of an Illusion.* Translated and edited by J. Strachey, with a biographical introduction by P. Gay. New York: Norton, 1989.
Gadamer, Hans-Georg. *Wahrheit und Methode: Grundzüge einer philosophischen Hermeneutik.* Tübingen: Mohr, 1960.
García Martínez, Florentino. "The Apocalyptic Interpretation of Ezekiel in the Dead Sea Scrolls." In *Interpreting Translations: Studies on the LXX and Ezekiel in Honour of Johan Lust.* Bibliotheca Ephemeridum theologicarum Lovaniensium 192. Leuven: Leuven University Press, 2005.
———. "Apocalypticism in the Dead Sea Scrolls". In *The Encyclopedia of Apocalypticism.* Vol. 1, *The Origins of Apocalypticism in Judaism and Christianity*, 162–92. Edited by Bernard McGinn et al. 3 vols. New York: Continuum, 1998.
———. Review of *La Croyance des Esséniens en la Vie Future: Immortalité, Résurrection, Vie Éternelle? Histoire d'une Croyance dans le Judaïsme Ancien*, by Émile Puech. *Journal for the Study of Judaism in the Persian, Hellenistic and Roman Period* 25 (1994) 114–18.

Gibellini, Rosino. *La Teología del siglo XX*. Translated by R. Velasco. Colección Presencia Teológica 94. Santander: Sal Terrae, 1998.

Gignilliat, Mark S. Review of *Resurrection and the Restoration of Israel*, by J. D. Levenson. *Horizons in Biblical Theology* 30 (2008) 83–84.

Gnuse, Robert. Review of *Resurrection and the Restoration of Israel*, by J. D. Levenson. *Catholic Biblical Quarterly* 69 (2007) 334–35.

Goethe, Johann Wolfgang von. *Faust: Eine Tragödie*. Edited by Albrecht Schöne, with a commentary by Ralf-Henning Steinmetz. Suhrkamp BasisBibliothek 107. Frankfurt: Suhrkamp, 2009.

Goldstein, Jonathan. "Jewish Acceptance and Rejection of Hellenism." In *Aspects of Judaism in the Graeco-Roman Period*, edited by E. P. Sanders et al, 64–87. Jewish and Christian Self-Definition 2. London: SCM, 1981.

Grabbe, Lester L. and Robert D. Haak. *Knowing the End from the Beginning: The Prophetic, the Apocalyptic and their Relationships*. London: T. & T. Clark International, 2003.

Green, P. *Alexander to Actium: The Historical Evolution of the Hellenistic Age*. Updated ed. Hellenistic Culture and Society 1. Berkeley: University of California Press, 1993.

Greshake, Gisbert. *Auferstehung der Toten: Ein Beitrag zur gegenwärtigen theologischen Discusión über die Zukunft der Geschichte*. Koinonia 10. Essen: Ludgerus, 1969.

Gutiérrez, Gustavo. *The Power of the Poor in History: Selected Writings*. Translated by Robert R. Barr. London: SCM, 1983.

———. *A Theology of Liberation: History, Politics, and Salvation*. Translated by Sister Caridad Inda and John Eagleson. Maryknoll, NY: Orbis, 1973.

Haag, Herbert. *Abschied vom Teufel*. Theologische Meditationen 23. Ensiedeln: Benziger, 1969.

Habermas, Jürgen. *Erkenntnis und Interesse*. Theorie 2. Frankfurt am Main: Suhrkamp, 1968.

———. *Teoría y Praxis*. Translated by S. Mas Torres and C. Moya Espí. Altaya: Barcelona, 1994.

Hagedorn, A. C. Review *Resurrection and the Restoration of Israel*, by J. D. Levenson. *Journal for the Study of the Old Testament* 32 (2008) 170–71.

Hahne, Harry Alan. *The Corruption and Redemption of Creation: Nature in Romans 8.19-22 and Jewish Apocalyptic Literature*. Library of New Testament Studies 336. London: T. & T. Clark, 2006.

Hamilton, Alastair. *The Apocryphal Apocalypse: The Reception of the Second Book of Ezra (4 Ezra) from the Renaissance to the Enlightenment*. Oxford-Warburg Studies. Oxford: Clarendon, 1999.

Han, Jin Hee. *Daniel's Spiel: Apocalyptic Literacy in the Book of Daniel*. Lanham, MD: University Press of America, 2008.

Hanson, Paul D. *The Dawn of Apocalyptic: The Historical and Sociological Roots of Jewish Eschatology*. Philadelphia: Fortress, 1975.

Harrington, Daniel J. Review of *Apocalypticism in the Dead Sea Scrolls*, by John J. Collins. *Theological Studies* 59 (1998) 176–77.

Hegel, G. W. F. *Vorlesungen über die Philosophie der Religion*. Theorie—Werkausgabe 16. Frankfurt: Suhrkamp, 1969.

Heidegger, Martin. *Being and Time*. Translated by John MacQuarrie and Edward Robinson. Oxford: Blackwell, 1973.

———. *Vorträge und Aufsätze*. Gesamtausgabe 7. Frankfurt: Klostermann, 1975.

———. *An Introduction to Metaphysics.* Translated by Ralph Manheim. New Haven: Yale University Press, 1959.

Hengel, Martin. *Judaism and Hellenism.* Translated by John Bowden. 1974. Reprint, Eugene, OR: Wipf & Stock, 2003.

Henze, M. Review of *Die Gottesvorstellungen in der antik-jüdischen Apokalyptik*, by S. Beyerle. *Catholic Biblical Quarterly* 69 (2007) 348–49.

Hesiod. *Works and Days; and Theogony.* Translated by S. Lombardo, with introduction, notes, and glossary by R. Lamberton. Indianapolis: Hackett, 1993.

Hick, John. *The Metaphor of God Incarnate.* London: SCM, 1993.

Hogeterp, Albert L. A. "Resurrection and Biblical Tradition: Pseudo-Ezekiel Reconsidered." *Biblica* 89 (2008) 59–69.

Horkheimer, Max. *Anhelo de Justicia: Teoría Crítica y Religión.* Translated by J. J. Sánchez. Colección Estructuras y Procesos. Madrid: Trotta, 2000.

Hultgard, Anders. "Persian Apocalypticism." In *The Encyclopedia of Apocalypticism.* Vol. 1, *The Origins of Apocalypticism in Judaism and Christianity*, 39–83. New York: Continuum, 1998.

James, E. O. "Prehistoric Religion." In *Religions of the Past*, edited by C. Jouco Bleeker and Geo Widengren, 23–38. Historia Religionum: Handbook for the History of Religions 1. Leiden: Brill, 1969.

Jaspers, Karl, and Rudolf Bultmann. *Myth and Christianity: An Inquiry into the Possibility of Religion without Myth.* New York: Noonday, 1958.

Jonas, Hans. *Der Gottesbegriff nach Auschwitz: Eine jüdische Stimme.* Suhrkamp Taschenbuch 1516. Frankfurt: Suhrkamp, 1987.

Josephus. *Judean Antiquities.* Translated by Louis H. Feldman. Leiden: Brill, 2000.

Kaku, Michio. *Parallel Worlds: A Journey through Creation, Higher Dimensions, and the Future of the Cosmos.* New York: Doubleday, 2005.

Kaminsky, Joel, and Anne Stewart. "God of All the World: Universalism and Developing Monotheism in Isaiah 40–66." *Harvard Theological Review* 99 (2006) 139–63.

Kant, Immanuel. *Kritik der praktischen Vernunft.* Edited by Otfried Höffe. Klassiker Auslegen 26. Berlin: Akademie, 2002.

———. *On History.* Translated by L. W. Beck et al. The Library of Liberal Arts. Indianapolis: Bobbs-Merrill, 1963.

———. *Die Religion innerhalb der Grenzen der blossen Vernunft.* Edited by Bettina Stangneth. Philosophische Bibliothek. Hamburg: Meiner, 2003.

Käsemann, Ernst. "The Beginnings of Christian Theology." In *Apocalypticism*, edited by Robert W. Funk, 17–46. Journal for Theology and the Church 6. New York: Herder & Herder, 1969.

Kellerman, Ulrich. *Auferstanden in den Himmel: 2 Makkabäer 7 und die Auferstehung der Märtyrer.* Stuttgarter Bibelstudien 95. Stuttgart: Katholisches Bibelwerk, 1979.

———. "Überwindung und Todesgeschicks in der alttestamentlichen Frömmigkeit vor und reden dem Auferstehungsglauben." *Zeitschrift für Theologie und Kirche* 73 (1976) 259–82.

King, Karen. *What Is Gnosticism?* Cambridge: Belknap, 2003.

Kloppenborg, John S. *The Formation of Q: Trajectories in Ancient Wisdom Collections.* Studies in Antiquity and Christianity. Philadelphia: Fortress, 1987.

König, Franz. *Zarathustras Jenseitsvorstellungen und das Alte Testament.* Vienna: Herder, 1964.

Koziel, Bernd Elmar. *Apokalyptische Eschatologie als Zentrum der Botschaft Jesu und der frühen Christen? Ein Diskurs zwischen Exegese, Kulturphilosophie und systematischer Theologie über die bleibende Bedeutung einer neuzeitlichen Denklinie.* Bamberger theologische Studien 33. Frankfurt: Lang, 2007.

Küng, Hans. *Islam: Past, Present and Future.* Translated by John Bowden. Oxford: Oneworld, 2007.

Kraus, Th. J. Review of *Die Gottesvorstellungen in der antik-jüdischen Apokalyptik,* by Stefan Beyerle. *Expository Times* 117 (2006) 39.

Kvanvig, Helge S. *The Roots of Apocalyptic: The Mesopotamian Background of the Enoch Figure and of the Son of Man.* Wissenschaftliche Monographien zum Alten und Neuen Testament 61. Neukirchen-Vluyn: Neukirchener, 1988.

Leibniz, Gottfried Wilhelm. *Essais de Théodicée sur la bonté de Dieu, la liberté de l'homme et l'origine du mal.* Bibliothèque philosophique Paris: Aubier, 1962.

Lenzi, Alan. Review *Resurrection and the Restoration of Israel,* by J. D. Levenson. *Journal of Hebrew Scriptures* 8 (2008). Online: http://ejournals.library.ualberta.ca/index.php/jhs/article/view/7258/5966/.

Levenson, Jon D. *Creation and the Persistence of Evil: The Jewish Drama of Divine Omnipotence.* San Francisco: Harper and Row, 1988.

———. *Resurrection and the Restoration of Israel.* New Haven: Yale University Press, 2006.

Löwith, Karl. *Weltgeschichte und Heilsgeschehen: Die theologischen Voraussetzungen der Geschichtsphilosophie.* 2nd ed. Urban-Bücher 2. Stuttgart: Kohlhammer, 1953.

Lubac, Henri de. *Le Drame de l'Humanisme Athée.* 7th ed., rev. and aug. Traditions Chrétiennes 15. Paris: Cerf, 1983.

Lucretius. *De Rerum Natura III,* with an introduction, text, translation, and commentary by P. M. Brown. Warminster, UK: Aris & Phillips, 1997.

Luz, Ulrich. *Matthew: A Commentary.* Translated by J. Crouch. 3 vols. Minneapolis: Fortress Press, 2001–2007.

Madigan, Kevin J., and Jon D. Levenson. *Resurrection: The Power of God for Christians and Jews.* New Haven: Yale University Press, 2008.

Maier, J. Review of *La Croyance des Esséniens en la Vie Future: Immortalité, Résurrection, Vie Éternelle? Histoire d'une Croyance dans le Judaïsme Ancien,* by Émile Puech. *Biblische Zeitschrift* 41 (1997) 308–11.

Mainville, Odette, and Daniel Marguerot, editors. *L'Aprés-mort dans le Monde Ancien et le Nouveau Testament.* Le Monde de la Bible 45. Montreal: Médiaspaul, 2001.

Marques, José O. A. "The Paths of Providence: Voltaire and Rousseau on the Lisbon Earthquake." *Cadernos de História e Filosofia da Ciência.* Series 3 15 (Jan–Jun 2005) 33–57. Online: http://www.unicamp.br/~jmarques/pesq/.

Marx, K. "A Contribution to the Critique of Hegel's Philosophy of Right, Introduction." In *Early Writings,* introduced by L. Colletti, 251 . Translated by R. Livingstone and G. Benton. The Marx Library. New York: Vintage, 1975.

McKay, Heather A. Review of *Apocalypticism in the Dead Sea Scrolls,* by John J. Collins. *Expository Times* 109 (1998) 151.

Meier, John P. *A Marginal Jew: Rethinking the Historical Jesus.* Vol. 1, *The Roots of the Problem and the Person.* Anchor Bible Reference Library. Anchor Yale Reference Library. New York: Doubleday, 1991.

Migne, J.-P. *Patrologiae Cursus Completus.* Series Latina 44. Turnhout: Brepols, 1956

Milik, J. T., editor, with the collaboration of Matthew Black. *The Books of Enoch: Aramaic Fragments of Qumran Cave 4.* Oxford: Clarendon, 1976.

Millar, William R. *Isaiah 24-27 and the Origin of Apocalyptic.* Harvard Semitic Monograph Series 11. Missoula: Scholars, 1976.

Moltmann, Jürgen. *Theologie der Hoffnung: Untersuchungen zu Begründung und zu den Konsequenzen einer christlichen Eschatologie.* Munich: Kaiser, 1964.

Monod, Jacques. *Le Hasard et la Nécessité: Essai sur la Philosophie Naturelle de la Biologie Moderne.* Paris: Seuil, 1970.

Mowinckel, Sigmund. *He That Cometh.* Translated by G. W. Anderson. Oxford: Blackwell, 1956.

Nickelsburg, George W. E. *Jewish Literature between the Bible and the Mishnah: A Historical and Literary Introduction.* Philadelphia: Fortress, 1981.

———. *Resurrection, Immortality, and Eternal Life in Intertestamental Judaism and Early Christianity.* Harvard Theological Studies 56. Cambridge: Harvard University Press, 2006.

———. Review of *Life after Death: Paul's Argument for the Resurrection of the Dead in 1 Cor 15*, by H. C. C. Cavallin. *Journal for the Study of Judaism in the Persian, Hellenistic and Roman Period* 6 (1975) 100–102.

Nietzsche, Friedrich. *The Gay Science.* Translated by Thomas Common. Dover Philosophical Classics. Mineola, NY: Dover, 2006.

———. *Thus Spoke Zarathustra.* Edited by A. del Caro and R. B. Pippin. Translated by A. del Caro. Cambridge Texts in the History of Philosophy. Cambridge: Cambridge University Press, 2006.

Niskanen, Paul. *The Human and the Divine in History: Herodotus and the Book of Daniel.* Journal for the Study of the Old Testament Supplement Series 396. London: T. & T. Clark, 2004.

Oates, Whitney J., editor. *Basic Writings of St. Augustine.* 2 vols. New York: Random House, 1948.

Oegema, Gerbern S. Review of *Die Gottesvorstellungen in der antik-jüdischen Apokalyptik*, by Stefan Beyerle. *Journal for the Study of Judaism in the Persian, Hellenistic and Roman Period* 37 (2006) 414–16.

Pannenberg, Wolfhart. *Anthropologie in theologischer Perspektive.* Göttingen: Vandenhoeck & Ruprecht, 1983.

———. *Beiträge zur systematischen Theologie.* 3 vols. Göttingen: Vandenhoek & Ruprecht, 1999–2000.

———. *Gottesgedanke und menschliche Freiheit.* Göttingen: Vandenhoeck & Ruprecht, 1972.

———. *Grundfragen systematischer Theologie: Gesammelte Aufsätze.* Göttingen: Vandenhoeck & Ruprecht, 1967–1980.

———. "Heilsgeschehen und Geschichte." *Kerygma und Dogma* 5 (1959) 259–88.

———. *Metaphysik und Gottesgedanke.* Kleine Vandenhoeck-Reihe 1532. Göttingen: Vandenhoeck & Ruprecht, 1988.

———. *Systematic Theology.* Translated by Geoffrey W. Bromiley. 3 vols. Grand Rapids: Eerdmans, 1991–1998.

———. *Theologie und Reich Gottes.* Gütersloh: Mohn, 1971.

———, et al. *Offenbarung als Geschichte.* Kerygma & Dogma Beiheft 1. Göttingen: Vandenhoek & Ruprecht, 1961.

Pelikan, Jaroslav. *Jesus through the Centuries: His Place in the History of Culture.* New Haven: Yale University Press, 1985.

Plato. *Phaedo.* Translated by B. Jowett. New York: Scribner, 1871.

Polybius. *The Histories*. Translated by W. R. Paton. Revised by F. W. Walbank and C. Habicht. 2 vols. Loeb Classical Library 128, 137. Cambridge: Harvard University Press, 2010.
Pope, Alexander. *An Essay on Man*. Edited by Maynard Mack. New Haven: Yale University Press, 1950.
Prigogine, Ilya, and Isabelle Stengers. *La Nouvelle Alliance: Métamorphose de la Science*. Bibliothèque des Sciences Humaines. Paris: Gallimard, 1979.
———. *Order out of Chaos: Man's New Dialogue with Nature*. Toronto: Bantam, 1984.
Primavesi, Anne. *From Apocalypse to Genesis: Ecology, Feminism and Christianity*. Minneapolis: Fortress, 1991.
Puech, Émile. *La Croyance des Esséniens en la Vie Future: Immortalité, Résurrection, Vie Éternelle? Histoire d'une Croyance dans le Judaïsme Ancien*. 2 vols. Etudes Bibliques, new series, 20–21. Paris: Gabalda, 1993.
Quainton, Malcolm. *Ronsard's Ordered Chaos: Visions of Flux and Stability in the Poetry of Pierre de Ronsard*. Manchester: Manchester University Press, 1980.
Rad, Gerhard von. *Theologie des Alten Testaments*. 2 vols. Einführung in die evangelische Theologie 1. Munich: Kaiser, 1965.
Raphael, Simcha Paull. *Jewish Views of the Afterlife*. North Vale, NJ: Aronson, 1994.
Ratzinger, Joseph, and Jürgen Habermas. *Dialectics of Secularization: On Reason and Religion*. Translated by Brian McNeil. San Francisco: Ignatius, 2006.
Reale, Giovanni, and Dario Antiseri. *Il Pensiero Occidentale dalle Origini ad Oggi: Storia delle Idee Filosofiche e Scientifiche*. 3 vols. Brescia: La Scuola, 1985.
Ricoeur, Paul. "Tâches de l'Educateur politique." In *Lectures*, Vol. 1, *Autour du politique*, 239–55. La Couleur des idées. Paris: Seuil, 1991.
Román Lopez, Maria Teresa. *Un Viaje al Corazón del Budismo*. Madrid: Alianza, 2007.
Rousseau, J.-J. *Œuvres Complètes*. Edited by Bernard Gagnebin and Marcel Raymond. 5 vols. Paris: Gallimard, 1959–1995.
Rowland, C. *The Open Heaven: A Study of Apocalyptic in Judaism and Early Christianity*. New York: Crossroad, 1982.
Russell, D. S. *Divine Disclosure: An Introduction to Jewish Apocalyptic*. London: SCM, 1992.
———. *The Method and Message of Jewish Apocalyptic, 200 BC–AD 100*. The Old Testament Library. Philadelphia: Westminster, 1964.
Sacchi, P. *L'Apocalittica Giudaica e la sua Storia*. Biblioteca di Cultura Religiosa. Brescia: Paideia, 1990.
———. *Historia del Judaísmo en la Época del II Templo*. Madrid: Trotta, 2004.
———. Review of *La Croyance des Esséniens en la Vie Future: Immortalité, Résurrection, Vie Éternelle? Histoire d'une Croyance dans le Judaïsme Ancien*, by Émile Puech. *Biblica* 76 (1995) 439–42.
Santoso, Agus. *Die Apokalyptik als jüdische Denkbewegung: Eine literarkritische Untersuchung zum Buch Daniel*. Marburg: Tectum, 2007.
Saramago, J. "Quantos Haitis?" Online: http://caderno.josesaramago.org/2010/02/08/quantos-haitis/.
Schaper, Joachim. *Eschatology in the Greek Psalter*. Wissenschaftliche Untersuchungen zum Neuen Testament 2/76. Tübingen: Mohr/Siebeck, 1995.
Schelling, F. W. J. *Werke*. Stuttgart: Frommann-Holzboog, 1976.
Schillebeeckx, Edward. *Gott die Zukunft des Menschen*. Mainz: Grünewald, 1969.
Schleiermacher, Friedrich. *On Religion: Speeches to Its Cultural Despisers*. Translated and edited by R. Crouter. Cambridge Texts in the History of Philosophy. Cambridge: Cambridge University Press, 1996.

Schnackenburg, Rudolf. *God's Rule and Kingdom*. Translated by J. Murray. Montreal: Palm, 1963.

Schneider, G. Review of *Life after Death: Paul's Argument for the Resurrection of the Dead in 1 Cor 15*, by H. C. C. Callavin. *Biblische Zeitschrift* 22 (1978) 136–37.

Scholem, Gershom. *Die jüdische Mystik in ihren Hauptsströmungen*. Frankfurt: Metzner, 1957.

Schutte, P. J. W. Review of *Resurrection, Immortality, and Eternal Life in Intertestamental Judaism and Early Christianity*, by G. W. E. Nickelsburg. *Hervormde teologiese studies* 64 (2008) 1075–89.

Schweitzer, Albert. *Von Reimarus zu Wrede: eine Geschichte der Leben-Jesu-Forschung*. Tübingen: Mohr/Siebeck, 1906.

Scott, Clive. *The Riches of Rhyme: Studies in French Verse*. Oxford: Clarendon, 1988.

Segal, Robert A., editor. *Structuralism in Myth: Lévi-Strauss, Barthes, Dumézil, and Propp*. Theories of Myth 6. New York: Garland, 1996.

Sen, Amartya. *Development as Freedom*. New York: Knopf, 1999.

Setzer, Claudia. *Resurrection of the Body in Early Judaism and Early Christianity: Doctrine, Community, and Self-Definition*. Boston: Brill Academic, 2004.

Sevenster, J. N. Review of *Life after Death: Paul's Argument for the Resurrection of the Dead in 1 Cor 15*, by H. C. C. Callavin. *Nederlands theologisch tijdschrift* 29 (1975) 180–82.

Sicre, J. L, translator. *Introducción al Antiguo Testamento*, by Otto Eissfeldt. Estella: Verbo Divino, 2000.

Singer, Peter. "The God of Suffering?" *The Ethics of Life*. Project Syndicate: A World of Ideas blog. Online: http://www.project-syndicate.org/commentary/singer36/English/.

Smith, Mark S., and Elizabeth Bloch-Smith. Review of *Beatific Afterlife in Ancient Israel and in the Ancient Near East*, by K. Spronk. *Journal of the American Oriental Society* 108 (1988) 277–84.

Smith, John D. *Mahābhārata: An Abridged Translation*. London: Penguin, 2009.

Sobrino, Jon. *Jesus the Liberator: A Historical-Theological Reading of Jesus of Nazareth*. Translated by P. Burns and F. McDonagh. Maryknoll, NY: Orbis, 1993.

Sölle, Dorothee. *Die Hinreise: Texte und Überlegungen*. 2nd ed. Stuttgart: Kreuz, 1976.

Spronk, Klaas. *Beatific Afterlife in Ancient Israel and in the Ancient Near East*. Alter Orient und Altes Testament 219. Neukirchener: Neukirchen-Vluyn, 1986.

Stendahl, Krister, editor. *Immortality and Resurrection*. New York: Macmillan, 1965.

Taubes, Jacob. *Abendländische Eschatologie*. Beiträge zur Soziologie und Sozialphilosophie 3. Bern: Francke, 1947.

———. *Die politische Theologie des Paulus*. Edited by Aleida Assmann and Jan Assmann. Munich: Fink, 1993.

Theissen, Gerd. *The First Followers of Jesus: A Sociological Analysis of the Earliest Christianity*. Translated by John Bowden. London: SCM, 1978.

Thomas Aquinas. *Summa Theologica*. 60 vols. New York: Blackfriars, 1964.

Tiemeyer, Lena-Sofia. Review *Resurrection and the Restoration of Israel*, by J. D. Levenson. *Expository Times* 118 (2007) 408–9.

Tomasino, Anthony J. "Oracles of Insurrection: The Prophetic Catalyst of the Great Revolt." *Journal of Jewish Studies* 59 (2008) 86–111.

Torres Queiruga, Andrés. *Repensar la Revelación: La Revelación Divina en la Realización Humana*. Madrid: Trotta, 2008.

Unamuno, Miguel de. *Del Sentimiento Trágico de la Vida.* Austral 4. Madrid: Espasa-Calpe, 1967.
Vaux, Roland de. *Les Institutions de l'Ancien Testament.* Vol. 1, *Le nomadisme et ses survivances. Institutions familiales. Institutions civiles.* Paris: Cerf, 1958.
VanderKam, James C. *Enoch and the Growth of an Apocalyptic Tradition.* Catholic Biblical quarterly Monograph Series 16. Washington DC: Catholic Biblical Association of America, 1984.

———. Review of *La Croyance des Esséniens en la Vie Future: Immortalité, Résurrection, Vie Éternelle? Histoire d'une Croyance dans le Judaïsme Ancien,* by Émile Puech. *Journal of Biblical Literature* 114 (1995) 320–22.

Vermes, Geza. *The Resurrection.* New York: Doubleday, 2008.
Vital, Hayyim ben Yosef, I. *The Tree of Life: Chayyim Vital's Introduction to the Kabbalah of Isaac Luria; the Palace of Adam Kadmon.* Translation and with an Introduction by D. Wilder Menzi and Z. Padeh. Northvale NJ: Aronson, 1999.
Voltaire. *Candide.* Edited and annotated by F. Deloffre. Paris: Folio. Classique 3889. Gallimard, 2003.

———. *Questions sur l'Encyclopédie.* In *Les Oeuvres Complètes de Voltaire,* vol. 38. Geneva: Institut et Musée Voltaire, 1968.

Wallerstein, Immanuel. *The Modern World-System.* Studies in Social Discontinuity. New York: Academic, 1974.
Weber, Max. *Ancient Judaism.* Translated by H. H. Gerth and D. Martindale. Glencoe, IL: Free Press, 1952.
Weiss, K. Review of *Life after Death: Paul's Argument for the Resurrection of the Dead in 1 Cor 15,* by H. C. C. Cavallin. *Theologische Literaturzeitung* 100 (1975) 907–8.
Whitley, J. B. Review of *Resurrection, Immortality, and Eternal Life in Intertestamental Judaism and Early Christianity,* by G. W. E. Nickelsburg. *Horizons in Biblical Theology* 30 (2008) 89–90.
Whittaker, Thomas. *Schopenhauer.* Philosophies Ancient and Modern. London: Constable, 1909.
Wilford, John Noble. "Found: An Ancient Monument to the Soul." *New York Times,* November 17, 2008. Online: http://www.nytimes.com/2008/11/18/science/18soul.html?_r=4&8dpc/.
Woschitz, Karl Matthäus. *Parabiblica: Studien zur jüdischen Literatur in der hellenistisch-römischen Epoche.* Theologie, Forschung und Wissenschaft 16. Vienna: Lit, 2005.

Index of Names

Adorno, T., 15
Alcimus, 88
Alexander Balas, 88
Alexander the Great, 58, 76, 77, 79, 98, 131
Althusser, L., 45
Álvarez Mendizábal, J., 187
Antiochus III, 84, 85
Antiochus IV, 78, 81, 82, 84–88, 93, 107, 109, 115, 127, 136, 144–46, 148, 156, 167, 169, 176, 179, 180
Archimedes, 214
Aristotle, 2, 36, 37, 74, 79, 214
Assmann, A., 110
Assmann, J., 110
Ausín, S., 159
Averroes, 37
Avicenna, 37, 214

Bach, J. S., 214
Bakhos, C., 170
Bakunin, M., 51
Báñez, D., 31
Barth, C., 159
Barth, K., 9, 19, 25, 199
Barthes, R., 150
Bayle, P., 3, 12
Beaufret, J., 48
Beckett, S., 5
Beethoven, L., van 214
Benedict XVI, 72
Benjamin, W., 49, 211

Beyerle, 104, 109, 113, 114, 173–75, 178, 180
Blanton, W., 143
Bloch, E., x 45, 49, 50–57, 73, 135, 201
Blumenberg, H., 46
Bobbio, N., 205
Boethius, 43
Böhme, J., 17
Bonhoeffer, D., 210
Bossuet, J.-B., 12, 20, 46, 57
Bretschneider, K. G., 43
Buda, 214
Bultmann, R., 8, 19, 47, 68, 71, 73, 128, 150, 188, 198, 199
Burckhardt, J., 45
Byrennios, P., 189
Byron, J., 154

Cabet, É., 51
Calvin, 9
Campanella, T., 51
Camus, A., 4, 25
Cavallin, H. C. C., 148, 149, 151–54, 161, 162, 175, 176, 179
Charles, R. H., 98, 131
Chomsky, N., 62, 65
Clanton, D. W., 143
Clement of Alexandria, 30
Cleopatra, 84
Collingwood, R. G., 128
Collins, A. Y., 110

Collins, J. J., 95, 96, 97, 104, 105, 115, 147, 151, 168, 171–73, 177, 178
Comte, A., 4, 46
Condorcet, 45, 46, 57, 58
Cook, S. L., 106
Copernicus, N., 214
Cuckson, D., 202
Cullmann, O., 197
Curie, M., 214
Cusanus, N., 23
Cyrus, 134
Cyrus the Great, 131

D'Souza, D., 5
Darwin, C., 23, 62
Dawkins, R., 56
De Carvalho e Melo, José de, 10
De Lubac, H., 4
Demetrius I, 88
Dennett, D., 56
Derrida, J., 15
Descartes, R., 58, 142
Dilthey, W., 67, 68
Dodd, C. H., 197
Domitian, 125
Dostoyevski, F., 4, 25
Duns Scotus, 38

Einstein, A., 74, 214
Eliade, M., 119
Ellacuría, I., 195, 201
Engels, F., 139, 204
Epicurus, 16
Euler, L., 214

Feuerbach, L., 4, 10, 14, 32, 53, 55, 56, 201, 202, 209
Fichte, J. G., 51, 206
Fiore, Joachim of, 46, 51
Foucault, M., 15, 65
Fourier, C., 51
Fraijó, M., 6
Freire, P., 206
Freud, S., 4, 30, 49, 50, 53, 140, 209

Gadamer, H.-G., 188, 203
Galileo, G., 30, 74, 214
García Martínez, F., 93, 159
Gignilliat, M., 166
Gnuse, R., 166
Goethe, J. W. von, 37, 54, 214
Goldstein, J., 81, 82
Grabbe, L. L., 106
Gramsci, A., xi
Gutiérrez, G., 203, 205

Haag, H., 7
Habermas, J., xi, 18, 42, 54, 58, 61, 65, 74, 205
Haeckel, E., 23
Hagedorn, A. C., 166
Hahne, H. A., 118
Hanson, P., 95, 107
Harnack, A. von, 72, 196
Harris, S., 56
Hegel, G. W. F., 7, 14, 18, 20, 42, 45, 46, 48, 54, 61–67, 69, 70, 71, 73, 140, 153, 200, 208
Heidegger, M., x, 5, 15, 18, 21, 45–49, 52, 57, 63, 67, 68, 73, 74, 137, 138, 150, 199, 202
Hengel, M., 76, 77, 80–82, 90, 91, 115, 126, 130, 135
Herodotus, 131
Hesiod, 133
Hick, J., 71
Hillel, rabbi, 193
Hobsbawm, E., 205
Horace, 59
Horkheimer, M., 14, 54, 211
Hultgard, A., 132, 134, 135
Hyrcanus, 85

Imhotep, 214
Irenaeus, 209

Jason, 81, 85, 86
Jesus of Nazareth, ix, x, 29, 34, 35, 48, 69, 70–73, 184–89, 191, 192, 194–202, 214

Index of Names

Jonas, H., 15–17
Jonathan (Maccabeus), 88
Joseph the Tobiad, 85
Josephus Flavius, 84, 148
Judas (Maccabeus), 88

Kaminsky, J., 121
Kant, I., 9, 11, 22, 33, 45, 49, 59–61, 69, 73, 102, 139, 193, 196, 214
Käsemann, E., ix
Kellermann, U., 175, 176
König, F., 134
Kvanving, H. S., 107

Lactantius, 16
Laplace, 22
Lawrence, R., 95
Leibniz, G. W., 3–5, 11, 12, 21, 28, 32, 36–38, 40, 46, 74
Lenzi, A. C., 166
Leonardo da Vinci, 60, 214
Lessing, G. E., 67
Levenson, J. D., 166–70, 177
Louis XIV, 57
Löwith, K., 45
Lücke, F., 95
Lucretius, 52
Luria, I., 17, 18
Luther, 9, 20, 29, 188
Luz, U., 185, 187, 189, 193

Magen, Y., 92–94
Maier, J., 159
Malagrida, G., 11
Marx, K., 4, 14, 18, 45, 48, 55, 73, 139, 201, 204, 205, 209
Mattatiah (Maccabeus), 87, 88
Meier, J. P., 188
Menelaus, 86, 88
Meyer, R., 84
Michelangelo, 214
Miller, G., 154
Molina, L. de, 31
Moltmann, J., 56, 198, 201–3
Monod, J., 22, 62

Mowinckel, S., 105, 149

Napoleón, 22
Nebuchadnezzar II, 87, 91
Newton, I., 28, 214
Nickelsburg, G. W. E., 99, 143, 144, 146–48, 151, 153, 154, 156, 161, 171, 175, 176, 179, 178
Nietzsche, F., 4, 9, 32, 51, 140,€ 183
Niskanen, P., 129

Onias II, 84, 85
Onias III, 85, 86, 87
Onias IV, 87
Origen of Alexandria, 133
Otto, R., 208
Owen, R., 51

Pannenberg, W., 19, 20, 23–29, 32, 33, 35–37, 39–43, 45, 64, 66–73, 96, 114, 115, 117, 128, 198, 199, 200, 201, 209
Pelagius, 9
Peleg, Y., 92, 93, 94
Pelikan, J., 188
Philo of Alexandria, 148, 151, 152, 155
Plato, 51, 69, 79, 141, 214
Plutarch, 132
Polybius, 84, 88
Pombal, marquis of, 10
Pope, A., 11, 12
Prigogine, I., 41
Proudhon, P.-J., 46, 51
Ptolemy V., 84
Puech, É., 94, 147, 151, 155, 159–64, 176
Pythagoras, 214

Rahner, K., 208
Raphael, S. P., 164–66, 177
Ratzinger, J., 42
Rendtorff, R., 19
Rendtorff, T., 19
Ricoeur, P., 183

Index of Names

Ritschl, A., 196
Rivkin, E., 102
Rousseau, J. J., 11–15, 59
Rowland, C., 96, 97
Russell, D. S., 97, 98, 106, 119, 120, 135

Sacchi, P., 83, 86, 87, 94, 98, 159
Saint-Simon, count of, 51
Santoso, A., 108
Saramago, J., 10
Sartre, J.-P., 32
Schaper, J., 181
Schelling, F. W. J., 17, 18
Schillebeeckx, 184, 214
Schleiermacher, F., 196, 208
Schnackenburg, R., 206
Schopenhauer, A., 141
Schumpeter, J., 66
Schutte, P. J. W., 143
Schweitzer, A., 188, 196
Seleucus IV, 85, 88
Sellin, E., 156
Sen, A., 3
Simon (Maccabeus), 88
Simon II, 85
Singer, P., 5
Smith, C., 202
Sobrino, J., 197, 200–204
Sócrates, 61, 214
Sölle, D., 140
Spinoza, B. de, 17, 38
Spronk, K., 155–59, 177
St. Augustine, 6–9, 12, 13, 20, 29, 32, 46, 51, 57, 141, 196, 214
St. Bonaventure, 38
St. Francis of Assisi, 214
St. Gregory of Nyssa, 32
St. Jerome, 9
St. Maximilian Kolbe, 137
St. Paul, 21, 29, 34, 96, 118
St. Teresa of Ávila, 214
St. Thomas Aquinas, 6, 7, 12, 22, 36, 38

St. Thomas More, 51
Stendhal, K., ix, 153
Stewart, A., 121
Stirner, M., 51
Suárez, F., 38

Taubes, J., ix, 110
Teilhard de Chardin, P., 200
Thales, 214
Theissen, G., 191
Theopompus, 132
Tiemeyer, L. S., 166
Titus, 87
Tolstoy, L., 192, 197, 214
Tomasino, A. J., 129
Torres Queiruga, A., 71, 200
Turgot, A.-R.-J., 46

Unamuno, M. de, 139

Vanderkam, J. C., 136, 159
Vermes, G., 154, 155, 175, 176
Voltaire, 1, 4, 11, 12, 14, 36, 46
Von Rad, G., 96

Wallace, A. R., 23
Weber, M., 179
Weiss, J., 191, 196
Whitley, J. B., 143
Wilckens, U., 19
Woschitz, K. M., 124

Yashua, 85

www.ingramcontent.com/pod-product-compliance
Lightning Source LLC
Chambersburg PA
CBHW051639230426
43669CB00013B/2364